The N&P Aspects of Life series seeks to develop awareness and understanding across the diversity of interests associated with people's lives, from the serious responsibilities that we face through to the aspirations we develop.

As we seek more from our lives we face a balance between what we would like to do and what we need to do. The Aspects of Life publications endeavour to help people realise a better quality of life, providing creative, stimulating and sometimes amusing insights into life's differing circumstances and opportunities.

Hautes Cuisines is designed to contribute to the pleasure of skiing and mountain walking by providing a unique Guide for readers who want to find good food and drink in an enjoyable atmosphere after the rigours of healthy exercise in the Alps.

HAUTES CUISINES
A SKIER'S GUIDE TO LUNCH ON THE MOUNTAINS

by
Mike Aalders and David Hall

N&P
ASPECTS OF
LIFE
SERIES

N&P Publishing

Provincial House

Bradford

West Yorkshire BD1 1NL

Hautes Cuisines
Edited by Mike Aalders and David Hall

Cover design and illustration by Sandy Molloy
Line drawings by Yvonne Davies

The contents of this book are believed to be correct at the time of printing. Nonetheless, the publisher can accept no responsibility for errors or omissions or changes in the details given.

Published 1992

Text copyright © 1992 N&P Publishing
Illustrations © copyright N&P Publishing

N&P Publishing, Provincial House,
Bradford, West Yorkshire BD1 1NL

ISBN 1-897634-00-5

Originated and printed by
Pindar Graphics plc,
Thornburgh Road,
Eastfield, Scarborough
YO11 3UY

Contents

Foreword by the Editors	6
Wine, Man, Mountains by Joseph Berkmann	7
The High Mountain Gourmet by Ian McNaught-Davis	9
My Perfect Hut by Mike Molloy	11
Food for Thought by Richard Shepherd	13
Inspectors	14
Resorts Listed Alphabetically	15
Glossary, English: French/Italian/German	174
French Glossary	175
Italian Glossary	181
German Glossary	188
Ski Club Information	197

LETTER FROM THE EDITORS

'Hautes Cuisines' was born of a love affair, the passions involved in this conception being skiing on the one hand and food and drink upon the other. The great joys of skiing are compounded by the presence on many ski slopes throughout Europe of restaurants and cafes where any refreshment from morning coffee to an impressive dinner can be consumed in attractive surroundings complemented by stunning views. Admiration for the sheer variety of those establishments and the hard work and skill that alone make them viable, prompted us to produce this guide.

Given our starting point of food and drink plus skiing, we have avoided for the most part any restaurant that is not sited on or near a piste. Exceptions have been made where a paucity of choice compels the discriminating to head for the valley floor. Readers will note, too, that there are gaps. The explanation is simple: if we did not like it, we left it out. Very few self-service restaurants have made the grade and in our judgment are unlikely ever to do so. You may disagree with our selection. If you do, write to us. Additional informed views will be welcomed and we look forward to adding your name to our list of inspectors in future editions.

We have also included a marking system, the five snowflakes of excellence. Based on a combination of ambience, views and quality of food and drink, they run from one for ordinary to five for superb. There is only one five snowflake award and, having read it, you will understand why.

Compiling 'Hautes Cuisines' gave us a lot of pleasure and we are extremely grateful to the Ski Club of Great Britain for their help and the contributions of our other inspectors whose names appear in the list on page 14. We hope you enjoy reading it and find the recommendations valuable when settling those vital questions of where to go for the next pit stop or lunch.

Mike Aalders   David Hall

JOSEPH BERKMANN was born with skis on in the Austrian Tyrol. Unfortunately both were left skis, so that he kept on breaking legs until it affected his already awkward walk. Twelve years later he moved to London to open his first restaurant - and broke a leg. Having thus defeated the jinx blamed on his skis, he returned to take up his passion and hasn't stopped since. Thanks to a generous intake of daily wine (and fortified by the minerals contained in red wine) he neither has broken, nor will break a bone ever again.

WINE, MAN, MOUNTAINS
by
JOSEPH BERKMANN

In winter, mountain air can be as dry as air in the Sahara. Inexperienced skiers then melt in their space-suits and the loss of liquid can be prodigious. I remember walking up the slopes of La Saulire in Meribel with a friend, years ago, and arriving at the top drenched, ordering a double 'alcool blanc', or what my Tyrolean forebears call 'Schnapps', and no sooner had we drunk it than my friend fell to the floor, lying there as stiff as a board. As good luck would have it, there was a doctor in the house who at once forced a spoonful of salt between his lips and, after a few minutes, the 'stiff' recovered. Henceforth, I knew why Mexicans take salt with tequila; also to start on the spirits after dinner only, compensated by the fact that you can drink rather a lot at height without the usual hangover in the morning.

The ideal drink in the mountains is light white wine, the first glass mixed with Perrier. Inexpensive country wines are easily the most enjoyable, like Apremont or Seyssel from the French Savoie and the Jura, or their Swiss cousin Fendant or the Austrian Gruner Veltliner. Another favourite is Muscadet of the last vintage. All these wines have in common a fairly high natural acidity, low alcohol content and no residual sugar; refreshing and totally harmless until such time as puritan green politicians introduce breathalysers on ski slopes.

With a proper meal, Chardonnay comes into its own: not the heavy and often blowsy New World variety, but its much more elegant European version. There are one or two good Chardonnays made in the Savoie, and several delicious ones from the Italian Friuli and the Veneto, the vineyards around Gorizia to the north of Trieste. My own favourite, however, is Saint Veran, an up-market white from the region of Macon, which is not too heavy, perfectly balanced and usually at an accessible price.

Champagne, strangely enough, is not a great mountain wine. At 2000 metres the relative pressure in the bottle is much increased and the wine's fizziness becomes exaggerated. Too heavy and alcoholic to be a thirst quencher, it also disappoints with the less subtle flavours of Alpine food.

Red wine at high altitude is much more difficult. Tannic wines taste inky and even the slightest oxidation shows at once. Clarets are, therefore, disappointing, while fresh and fruity wines where acidity replaces the tannin, triumph. A good Beaujolais-Villages, Chiroubles or Morgon becomes the ideal wine, although the biggest surprise comes with wines made from Pinot Noir: its fruit and acidity find a harmony I should love to find in my wines in London!

One of the most memorable bottles drunk off the piste at the excellent restaurant l'Etoile des Neiges in St. Martin de Belleville, was a very simple, fresh young Pinot from the Savoie. It was perfection with the local ham, fresh bread and lunch on a sunny terrace in March. Pinot Noir produces just as delicious wines in the South Tyrol (or Alto Adige as the Italians insist on calling it), in Alsace, but above all in Burgundy. Drink a bottle of young Côte de Beaune by the sea, whether in England or the South of France, and you will feel that you have been short changed. In the mountains it is a revelation. I have always known that the best spot on earth to uncork a great Burgundy was in the Ardennes, or the French/Swiss Jura. I have only just recently added Courchevel to that list.

One word that crops up all through this evaluation is 'young'. Old, or what we might call mature, wines do not like height. The reduction in oxygen magnifies even the slightest oxidation in wine. No point, therfore, in lashing out on 'great' bottles of wine; a simple Beaujolais would most likely massacre them.

IAN McNAUGHT-DAVIS is president of the British Mountaineering Council. He has presented live television programmes on mountain climbing including the Old Man of Hoy, The Matterhorn and The Eiffel Tower, also many programmes on Computers (Micro Live) and Inventions. He is Chief Executive of Comshare International, a Worldwide Corporate Software Company. He has skied for over forty years in Asia, the Alps, America and the Arctic without improving significantly.

THE HIGH MOUNTAIN GOURMET
by
IAN McNAUGHT-DAVIS

From Zermatt the Gornergrat railway carries tourists and winter skiers high on a ridge where they can admire the view of some of the highest mountains in Europe or enjoy some pleasantly mild skiing. If they get off the train at Rotenboden, they can walk on the path that leads to Monte Rosa. It ends at a glacier deeply scarred by crevasses that deter all but the most determined walkers or skiers from making a crossing, and, by looking carefully at the foot of the mountain, it is possible to make out the Swiss Alpine Club hut where the climbing starts.

It was the first mountain hut where I spent any time. Then known as the Betemps hut, it was run by Alexander Graven, a retired guide of some distinction. Age and too many days spent dragging clients up high mountains had cast him into the unenviable position of hut warden, prising mountaineers out of bed at 2.00am to climb the highest peak in Switzerland. Breakfast consisted of hot water and, on occasional days, some stale bread. I lived there for several weeks over a couple of summers, climbing on skis to just below the summit of Monte Rosa to dig a hole in the ice for glaciological research.

Graven grumpily dished out the hot water and played his only record over and over again on an ancient wind-up gramophone. Gradually, the crackly, mournful Italian soprano drove everyone to complain. Graven pretended to be deaf and waved a soup ladle around his head like a mad conductor. Then just as we had all abandoned any hope of stopping the dreadful row, he would turn and face us, take off the offending record and shout "Finita la musica, cominciere la festa". Then the food arrived: thin soup, stale bread and maybe some sausages, unless you had brought up your own steak, which he gleefully converted into a small, burnt wooden plank. For years I thought all mountain restaurants were like that.

I have always hated self-service restaurants. In fact, they cannot be called restaurants, with the line to pick up a greasy tray, the usual formula food that seems to have been made in an automated factory far away, goulash that even the poorest Hungarian would turn away from, the ever-present steak and pommes frites that only the acrid wine makes eatable, and a level of hospitality that makes Graven's seem warm and friendly by comparison. Does anyone ever taste the food before it is flopped on the plate?

But the unique saving grace of self-service cafeterias is that they are cheap and quick. In fact, they are usually so rapid that it is possible to get in, have something to eat, and get out again without either tasting the vileness of the food or noticing the depressingly drab surroundings. All this is ideal for the over-keen piste bashers who prefer to spend their cash on the latest in skiwear, boots and skis in the vain hope that these will make him or her a better skier. It is a false god. The only thing that makes a good skier is good food, wine and company; all the rest is as sapping to the inner spirit as Captain's night at a third rate golf club.

Zermatt is, of course, largely run by the old Valais families, the Biners, Aufdenblattens, Perrens, Julens and the Taugwalders. They have guided parties up peaks in the area even before Edward Whymper's party fell from the Matterhorn to their doom over a hundred years ago, and they are still guiding them today, climbing, skiing, walking, and running huts and restaurants. The mountain restaurant that possesses just about all the ideal qualities that one dreams about far from the mountains is at Findeln, and is run by the Julen family. It has a perfect location near, but not too close to, the bottom of a ski lift, avoiding the huge crowds at the top and is set in a high village that is still a farming community in the summer. It is run enthusiastically by the family who care about every detail, and, if the mood takes him, the patron may even sing for you. The food is home cooking of a robust and high standard and the waitresses are all beautiful. Both in summer and in winter, it commands the best views of the Matterhorn, probably the most photographed mountain in the world.

Well, I suppose the answer is something completely different. How about being able to reserve a table in a pretty restaurant at the top of a mountain where some delightful skiing takes you down perfect snow through birch and pine trees, where you are welcomed by young men in dinner jackets with a chilled glass of Chassagne Montrachet at a price you can afford (maybe it was a mistake!), and are offered fresh green lipped New Zealand mussels and Buffalo burgers at three times the price of the restaurants in the valley? Delicious food that is so expensive you are not tempted to eat too much of it and top quality wines that are cheap enough to drink to excess, seems an ideal formula for convivial enjoyment, so it seems a crime that the place often appears full of aged, teetotal feminist vegetarians. It could only happen at Gwyn's High Alpine restaurant in Snowmass, Colorado: a near ideal place, pity about the company.

But for sheer boisterous enjoyment, there is nothing quite like a good hut in Austria. Full of enthusiastic eaters and drinkers, they are a million kilometres from the depressing crowds in the French mountain cafeterias, glumly munching their saucisson bought the previous week in a Paris supermarket. A good plate of rösti and a couple of fried eggs with a litre or two of Weissen beer, stimulates the digestive juices and encourages everyone to join in the jollity, although I am still puzzled about whether or not the leather-clad group on the big table in the corner were really shouting "Ski Heil" as our Austrian friends insisted. It sounded curiously like "Sieg Heil", but after all it was Christmas and we gave them the benefit of the doubt.

MIKE MOLLOY *was editor of the Daily Mirror for ten years and then Editor-in-Chief of the Mirror Group Newspapers until the publication of his best selling novel "The Century" in 1990. His most recent book "Sweet Sixteen" is about to be filmed for television. He has been an enthusiastic skier for 10 years and remains an absolute beginner.*

MY PERFECT HUT
by
MIKE MOLLOY

Funny business; skiing. When I took it up ten years ago I thought it would come naturally, like smoking; or eating Chinese food with chopsticks. I was wrong. My wife and daughters did not seem troubled; but somehow the knack evaded me. Don't misunderstand me, I can get down a black run - if the conditions are right - perfect weather and hard in the tracks of an old Ski Maestro who knows the mountain like a rat knows its favourite sewer.

Of course, old Ski Maestros tend to be expensive accessories these days. So I usually ski alone; cruising down the blues, humming a selection of Bing Crosby numbers, while the rest of my family hurtle down another part of the mountain, fearlessly emulating The Ride of The Valkyeries.

Good luck to them! My stately progress gives me plenty of time to think and a question I sometimes ponder is: what are the necessary constituents if you wish to create the Perfect Hut? First, I define what they should not be; and size is important here. Anything larger than a London bus is out of the question.

Snow-bound motorway cafes are particularly repellent. You know the sort of place: where you have to point to gigantic illuminated photographs of various dishes that all look as though they were manufactured by Mickey Mouse in the Magic Kingdom - and taste as if the main ingredients are putty, plastic and polystyrene.

In such establishments - by some mysterious law of the mountains - there are always fifty sneering Frenchmen at the head of the queue and the food is invariably luke-warm by the time you have trudged to your debris-ladened table.

The Perfect Hut should not be too ethnic. There is no joy in stopping at some cluttered hovel where they only speak some strange, guttural patois and the sullen waitress hands you a menu scrawled with incomprehensible hieroglyphics; then stands sighing impatiently while you attempt to mime: 'bring me a beer and a plate of chips'.

'So what am I looking for? The approach is important: The Perfect Hut should be located at the foot of a wide, gentle slope. Just below the confluence of black, red and blue runs that mingle in a thick pine forest. Thus any inadequacies of ability shall be concealed from the dazzling beauties seated on the terrace, who watch your arrival, and judge your personality and character from the price of your sunglasses rather than the skill with which you negotiate a steep mogul field. (I mean no sexism here, ladies. The dazzling beauties I mention will, of course, include a sprinkling of those types who people the Kelvin Cline (Calvin Klein, or is this a subtle dig at the 'Sun'?) advertisements - men who look as if their patchy tans are achieved by dabbing boot polish on their faces)

Actually, the purpose of the terrace is to keep these types on the outside. I mean sprawlers; sun-worshippers and National Ski Teams. They are best left in the open air - to wind-dry like sausages. I am an 'Inside Person'; so here are my specifications for the interior. Seasoned wood, with a staircase leading to a wide gallery. The general style and ambience somewhat similar to the hunting lodge in 'The Prisoner of Zenda'. There must be a stone fire place, wide enough to roast an oxen - in fact, now I come to think of it, there always should be an oxen roasting.

The proprietor - clad in lederhosen and smoking a pipe the size and shape of a cuckoo clock - will greet one at the door. He, and his entire staff, should speak English, but they must have quaint accents. The host and his wife must look like the Austrian refugees in 'Casablanca'. You remember the chubby, loveable old couple: "Which watch is it, mein liebling?" The waitresses - of which there will be many - will base their costumes and conversational style on Ann Blyth, as she performed in 'The Student Prince'.

There should also be a few characters from the local village: inglenook men, with faces like pickled walnuts, who can tell you tales of the days before the skiers came - when they had to exist on a diet of toasted cheese and pine needles throughout the endless winters of perfect snow.

The beer should be good enough to make you sing - in fact, singing shall be obligatory. There will be song sheets printed on the back of the menus. Good old-fashioned knee-slapping, rib-nudging numbers. None of your Costa Brava, sing-along-with-the-Beatles stuff; this is Sigmund Romberg country.

By now you will have gathered that my concept of 'The Perfect Hut' is heavily influenced by Hollywood's interpretation of Alpine Ruritania - at least as far as the staff and decor is concerned. As for the food, regulation ski-fodder will suffice: robust soups; rösti, bratwurst, spaghetti, oeufs and frites, the usual sort of thing; but with the addition of one particular item on which I insist: the British Bacon Sandwich. If only I could have laid my hands upon such a delicacy over the years, my skiing would have improved beyond the wildest shores of imagination.

RICHARD SHEPHERD *was the chef behind Langan's Brasserie: now he is the man up-front. Chef, bon viveur and raconteur, he is only thankful that he cooks better than he skis, otherwise he wouldn't be contributing here.*

FOOD FOR THOUGHT
by
RICHARD SHEPHERD

Without using too much imagination, it is not difficult to assume that, provided one has good and reliable suppliers, qualified and professional staff, a controlled booking system and reasonable prices, a restaurant should have a pretty good chance of succeeding. But, as we all know this is not always the case, and many restaurants fail. We have all heard the complaints: food cold, service slow, too expensive, no atmosphere and, I am sure, plenty of others. And that is on terra firma.

So, therefore, what happens when we move half-way up a mountain to ski resort restaurants? How difficult is it for them to get supplies up the mountain? To serve hot food when temperatures are well below freezing? Not knowing whether one or one hundred people will arrive because there is a blizzard outside? The effect that altitude has on cooking times? Everybody wants to enter, order, eat and leave, not necessarily as swiftly as possible, but with everything flowing as it should and feel that they have received value for money. How can this be achieved? With difficulty, I can assure you!

If I was to make one criticism, it would be that a lot of restaurants try to be too comprehensive. I have always been a believer, and I know it is taking it to extremes, that if you do one dish superbly well you will always have a clientele, and sometimes not enough thought is given to this.

Although attitudes are getting better, it never ceases to amaze me that, while skiers (and I am one) are prepared to pay large sums of money for travel, accommodation, skis, outfits and ski passes, they "economise" on the essentials of life: food and drink.

Staff motivation and job satisfaction are extremely difficult as they break their backs for four to five months solid, and then everyone goes with the snow.

In the restaurant business the problems are rarely caused by the constants. It is the variables that wreak havoc, and the weather is the greatest variable of all. And we, the customers, just take it all for granted.

HAUTES CUISINES INSPECTORS

We are grateful to all our inspectors for their hours of selfless endeavour and sacrificed digestions and livers. We are especially grateful to the Ski Club of Great Britain for their help and support and to Bladon Lines for the reports submitted by many of their reps. What you read in 'Hautes Cuisines' comes to you courtesy of the following people:

Evie Aalders, Mike Aalders, Tim Casey, Peter Cooper, Sarah David, Graham Elliott, Michael Foley, Susie Fortune, Olivia Gordon, Tony Gover, Jo Grant, Christopher Griffin, David Hall, Julia Hawke, Adrian Hodges, Peter Hooper, Louisa John, Lucinda Kent, Lisa King, Phil Lord, Lisa Matthews, Christopher Milburn, Kate Molloy, Sue Newall, David O' Brien, Dinny Ravet, David Ross, Alan Owens, Alison Owens, Christine Shepherd, Angie Smeaton, Denis Steinmann, Richard Wallace, Bernard Wiehahn, Ed Wolkey, Paul Youden

HAUTES CUISINES

ALPE D' HUEZ
1850m. - Top Station 3330m.
FRANCE

Alpe d' Huez is a post World War II, purpose-built resort that is consequently somewhat short on traditional charms, but has many compensating advantages: a sunny setting, a large ski area, good slopes for all grades and fine scenery being among them.

In addition to demanding black runs for the proficient, there is also excellent off piste skiing and more than 200 kilometres of pisted skiing in total. If that proves insufficient, there is a helicopter link to Les Deux Alpes.

Hotels, boarding houses, chalets and appartments are plentiful and night life can be vigorous. We have had few reports about good mountain restaurants, so more information will be welcomed.

To reach Alpe d' Huez, fly to Lyons or Geneva. Linked resorts are Auris-en-Oisans, Villard-Reculas, Vaujany and Oz Station.

CHEZ PASSOND
aka AUBERGE DE L' ALPETTE

❄❄

Skiing down from Alpe d' Huez towards Vaujany, turn left at the mid stage of the cable car towards Oz. Just before you get to the bottom of the drag, hiding on the left is a charming stone-built building with a small wooden terrace. Near an old cow shed, Passond and his wife built their restaurant. They are of old farming stock and the father still walks up in summer to pasture his cows. He is horrified by the new structure.

Passond, bearded, intelligent and mayor of Oz (as opposed to Wizard), is a traditional host. His wife cooks most of the food, but Passond makes the gorgeously garlicky gratin dauphinois, and the Tomme in the summer from the milk of his own animals.

The food is simple, the selection small and the prices reasonable. He used to get flustered when too many people came because he likes to serve them all well.

One memorable afternoon, our inspector and two friends went in for a quick late lunch. One had rabbit and polenta; one had cold meats and one cheese. Another customer gave wine to go with the cheese and then everybody had to have more cheese. Then Passond offered marc and gnepi, fait maison. They just had time to ski down the path to Oz and catch the last bubble back to Alpe d' Huez. A wonderful afternoon.

Chez Passond is simple, small and clean and the pisteurs and lift attendants eat there.

LA BERGERIE DU VILLARD
VILLARD-RECULAS

❄❄

There are very few antique shops on the piste, particularly ones that

15

HAUTES CUISINES

have a log-fed open fire and are willing to serve you lunch, dinner or just a drink, but La Bergerie is one of them. The stock consists of various cow bells of all shapes and sizes, oil lamps, straw hats, wicker baskets and implements for getting boy scouts out of horses' hooves. The stock in trade is catering for the hungry and thirsty.

M. and Mme. Barlerin have been here for 22 years, during which time they have collected not just what hangs on the walls but a faithful following of customers who return every year to the fare of this quaint old cow barn.

The menu runs from a simple croûte to what the Barlerins refer to as a festival meal, although for the latter it would be wise to telephone in advance. Tel: 76.80.36.83. The rest of the menu offers the traditional and local with fondues and raclettes taking their usual starring roles.

The wines are strongly local, and none the worse for it. If only England could produce them and sell them at the same price.

The service is quick for those in a hurry, but unpressed for those who wish to linger. On sunny days the views from the terrace are spellbinding.

The loo is good for a cow barn, but there is only one, so remember to knock first.

Ski here on the Villard red run, which, although it is red, is fairly easy. The more adventurous take the Forêt black down and take an extra cold beer before lunch. After lunch the Souveraine lift pulls you back up to the Petit Prince and thence down into Alpe d' Huez via greens, blues or reds.

LA FORÊT DE MARONNE

❈❈

Whether you cruise down on the Farcis blue run, or test your skills on the Fuma black run, you would be wise to bring a good appetite: a wholesome lunch awaits you.

Although of fairly recent construction, this restaurant has become a firm favourite with the many skiers who have discovered the delights of this surprisingly large ski area, the Massif des Grandes Rousses, which offers a variety of skiing that some of its larger, and better known, relations must envy. There are 126 marked runs and as much off piste as the average skier can contend with. Finding an appetite, therefore, should not be a problem.

Like most mountain restaurants, the cuisine is strongly local, but here it is served with more imagination than usual. The house salad is served with the locally cured ham, fromage blanc and chives. The escalope de veau comes with a mountain of wild mushrooms. The list is not long, although it offers a choice of three menus du jour at 95 francs, 120 francs and 145 francs. Each is well thought out and an example of the excellent value that eating in France can provide. The wine list is also quite short, but long on value with the Savoie Pinot Noir at 68 francs.

The restaurant is cheered by the log fire that burns in one corner and, because the room is not over large, seating about 50 people, everyone benefits from the warmth it provides.

Outside, the sun terrace looks out across the Romanche valley at the whipped cream peaks which rise above the tree line. Sun chairs provide the well lunched with an alternative pace of digestion while the

HAUTES CUISINES

keener walk back up to the Chatelard lift to rejoin the action.

LE TETRAS
AURIS EN OISANS

❋❋

Le Tetras is a pizzeria. If this sounds an unpromising start for serious lunchers, do not be deterred. Many French eat here daily, such is the quality of the pizzas and the various dishes of the day, most of which contain the local Reblochon cheese in some form. The owners of Le Tetras pay particular attention to the care of their Reblochon: they buy them young and nurture them in the basement of the restaurant until they are ripe and creamy for their customers.

The proprietors are friends who have known each other from school days. One acts as chef, the other as waiter and host, from which you will rightly infer the restaurant is small and booking is thus essential. Tel:76.80.11.67. A tiny terrace has been tacked on the back. Despite the limited numbers and staff, the service is prompt and friendly. The wine list is a good one.

To join this select band, take the Sarenne run and then up and over to the bottom of Auris.

SUPER SIGNAL

❋❋

"Descente aux Flambeaux" promises the card at this delightful restaurant. Well, a word of advice. Torchlight descents are best watched from the village. Skiing for most of us is a test in itself. Skiing in the dark while balancing a flaming wax torch from which small fire balls drop onto your ski suit (new, of course), is best left to Australian pyromaniacs and people six feet four inches tall called Jean-Claude, who do it backwards on one ski and still look bored.

So, let us assume it is daylight and you have come here to the Super Signal for lunch. What are you going to have? Well, you could start with an excellent homemade quiche for 22 francs and, because you are feeling hungry, follow it with a saucisson chaud aux choux gratin at 68 francs. A couple of glasses of local wine will wash everything down perfectly, and you will be restored and refuelled for about 100 francs. The really hungry might have started with the excellent goulash soup and still have room for the caillettes gratin; and even have left enough space for a tarte au choix. Whatever you choose here, you will not be disappointed, or asked to pay too much.

The interior of this popular hut has the same savoyarde flavour as the cooking. Hand-painted Alpine flowers adorn the beams and the tables and the wood panelling on the stone-clad walls confirms the cosiness generated by the friendly wood-burning stove.

Outside, the sun reflects off the Massif des Ecrins and the Grandes Rousses, and sun bathers toy with a cold drink for hours upon end. The well positioned wind breaks make sure their rest is not disturbed.

Pierre Teyssier has been here for nigh on four years and does his best to ensure all his customers get value and enjoyment. It is an easy ski here on the Signal piste and walkers stroll here from the village and really earn their lunch in the process.

HAUTES CUISINES

PARADISE ON SNOW
ALPENPLACE

❊❊❊❊❊

Blink and blink again. Yes, trusty Alphonse is running towards you; the outline of the hut dwarfs him as he emerges from its shadow. The sun glints on his white gloves as he takes your ski poles and presses your bindings, releasing you from your skis.

Leaving Alphonse to clean and park your skis, you walk across the hot air ducts, hand your hat and gloves to Maria to be dried, and seat yourself in the plush leather armchair in front of the blazing log fire. Maria presses the house cocktail of champagne and fresh strawberries into your hand and leaves you for a few moments of contemplation before bringing you the menu. Meanwhile, the young lad has removed your boots and presented you with a pair of sheep skin-lined slippers with a coat of arms embroidered upon them.

Your fellow lunchers, the few that are here, discuss the ski down, the fresh powder fields you have glided through leaving your own fresh tracks uncrossed by others, and, even more, the wall of delight you will descend after lunch.

The menu is all you would expect: Beluga caviar by the spoonful, served with a glass of iced pepper vodka, followed by a sizzling filet de boeuf, cooked over a vine wood fire. The vegetables are all al dente and as fresh as garden produce can be. A hearty burgundy, the Reserve du Patron 1978, washes this feast down.

Pausing before your light dessert of fragrant lemon ice, your eyes glance across the paintings which line the walls: an early, blue period Picasso, a small, but pleasing, Chagall, and, somewhat out of context, a sunburnt Van Gogh surmounting the chimney breast.

Your dessert despatched, coffee consumed and the magical house digestif that immediately goes to your knees, swallowed, you rise to take your leave. Awaiting you in the garderobe, your boots, hat and gloves all dried and warmed, bring a gentle glow as you put them on. Outside, Alphonse has your skis lined up and you tip him as you step into them; a decent tip because, after all, lunch has cost approximately the equivalent of ten English pounds.

You ski away refreshed, renewed, rewarded. If you know this hut, then please write to the editors and tell them where it is.

HAUTES CUISINES

ARGENTIERE
**1250m. - Top Station 3800m.
FRANCE**

Overshadowed by its neighbour, Chamonix, Argentière is an old village of a certain charm. These days it is a mecca for the serious skier. It lies at the foot of the Grands Montets, is linked by lift and bus to Chamonix and supplies a quieter alternative to the big town bustle of Chamonix. Contiguity provides most of the advantages of Chamonix such as good scenery, a large ski area and plentiful off-piste skiing. It is, however, quite low with the disadvantages that this can create. A car is useful for getting about both in the valley and for visiting other resorts in the area.

LE CHALET-REFUGE DE LOGNON

❄❄

Mountain people are of a certain kind. They have a closeness to nature and its elements. Their creed is to know and love the mountains in their summertime glory and their wintertime challenges. Marc Bonin is one such. If you feel you are of the same sympathy, albeit for only one or two weeks a year, then this solid, granite built chalet is your haven.

At 2033 metres, it is reached from the Grand Montets. Set alone and apart from the bustle of the Middlestation, it stands proud in a secret world among the ice blue-green of the Argentière Glacier which pleases the eye and the soul majestically.

The turn-of-the-century chalet sleeps 20 people in either double bedrooms or rooms for three or four people. There are loos inside and jugs and basins for washing for those who stay the night. For passing trade, there are outside facilities.

Evening entertainment is home made in the form of lengthy 'mountain experience' discussions in the wood-clad salon, or a game of backgammon or cards with other visitors.

Marc Bonin will be pleasant and informative company and, coming from the local village of Servoz, he will cook local dishes for you. His speciality is a dish called Farcement, a stew of potatoes, bacon and eau de vie soaked plums and raisins cooked for four hours in a special saucepan set in a bain marie. This he cooks for weekend visitors.

There is, also, a filling croûte au fromage, served with a sauce, the ingredients of which are a secret kept by M. Bonin. The food is wholesome, regional, peasant fare at very low cost.

The house wine is 25 francs for a half pichet and a room for the night is 70 francs. Half board is 140 francs and full board 200 francs. One surprising addition to the wine list is champagne and, at 180 francs a bottle, is the cheapest we have found in the Alps.

Marc Bonin has only recently taken over the chalet and it will be interesting to see what he makes of it in future years. He has started off enthusiastically, decorating the walls with photographs he has taken of small mountain animals and flowers together with pictures of fellow climbers on the summit of Mont Blanc.

All mountain lovers should toast M. Bonin in his new endeavour and visit him to guarantee his future in the Chalet Refuge de Lognon. For reservations tel: 50.54.05.45.

HAUTES CUISINES

LE RESTAURANT LE CHAVANNE

❋❋

A two minute walk avoiding skiers (or as long as it takes to ski a two minute walk avoiding walkers) from the cable car's middle station La Croix de Lognan, beside the Bochard chair lift, sits Le Restaurant Le Chavanne. It is conveniently situated at the end of two black runs which lead from Aiguille des Grands Montets at 3300 metres where there is a snack bar with spectacular views. But for gastronomes a snack falls far short of a good meal. Anyway, a black run behind a skier makes for better digestion after lunch.

In the restaurant, tables are linen covered with pressed, fan-shaped napkins adorning each place setting. There are limited views from the windows, which are small. The views from the terrace, also seating about 80 people are, naturally, less restricted.

Niblets are served with aperitifs, brought to the table by a waitress uniformed in local dress. The pretty waitresses speak excellent menu English, should translation be required, but do not put this skill to more demanding test. They will recommend, justifiably so, the chef's specialities and list in depth the ingredients as well as the method of cooking.

The 'Savoyarde tartifilette', a local speciality, consists of potatoes, bacon and onion in a creamy, Reblochon sauce. The dish comes steaming to the table in an oval, orange, fireproof casserole. It is filling and tasty, ideal for carbohydrate lovers. It costs 65 francs and is served with a salad.

Cold starters include two sorts of foie gras: goose at 80 francs and duck at 75 francs. The hot starters include an excellent fish soup, a mountain bouillabaise and, although far from Marseilles, it tasted good.

Locally caught trout and salmon make an appearance in the fish section. There are, of course, the usual steaks in various sizes and sauces. The French favourite, duck, is also on the menu, served in a green pepper sauce at 90 francs. Recall, when ordering this dish, that the French definition of 'pink' does not suit all palates and sensitivities.

A children's menu (adults' ideas of what children eat anywhere, anytime) consists of hamburgers and chips at 55 francs.

In general the prices are good and the choice of wine is well suited both to menu and pocket.

PLAN JORAN RESTAURANT

❋❋❋

Plan Joran is situated at 1920 metres at the bottom of the Route de Liaison, an easy run which starts at the cable car station, La Croix de Lognan.

One cannot imagine the vastness of the place from the approach at the front of the restaurant, the entrance being deceptive. The main door opens onto a bar to the left with tables seating approximately 50 people. Beyond this, through swing doors, there is a huge restaurant with a high vaulted ceiling. A mammoth, wooden structure built six years ago in larchwood from the surrounding forests, the main room seats 260 people in a self-service area offering an extensive and varied menu at reasonable prices. Although the room has immense

HAUTES CUISINES

volume, the pine benches and tables are positioned for comfort and intimacy, with lower cross beams and rafters diminishing the sense of height. Very large picture windows invite diners and larch trees to stare contentedly at each other. In the centre of the room is a huge, open fireplace of baronial proportions. The chimney, which required a helicopter to place it in position, reaches up through the full height of the room and out into the sky. The modern, efficient bar, all gleaming chrome coffee machines and white crockery, is on the opposite side of the chimney breast. Set aside, hidden from this arena by trellises, is a restaurant for the lazy and more discerning with time on their hands. In this separate section you will not be worried about balancing food on a slippery tray, struggling in boots not made for walking while trying to find a space at a table. Concealed from the eyes of the envious, cossetted with table cloths and personal service, 40 people can eat in comfort the food prepared by chef Phillipe Suze, whose diploma is proudly displayed on the wall, promising the ordered calm of an acclaimed Parisian restaurant. The long haute cuisine menu can compete with no hesitation. Fish, shell fish, foie gras and ragouts, salads and cheeses together with desserts that delight, are all created to the highest standards by Phillipe Suze.

The wine list is all one might expect with prices ranging from 70 francs for a good Beaujolais to a not unreasonable 190 francs for a Grand Cru Château Marzelle 1983.

And just when you think you have exhausted the possiblities of Plan Joran, you will find another floor of equal size in the basement for those who bring their own, hors sac or picnic. No need to fumble furtively in the ruck-sack, bring it all out, set it out for all to see and order your beverages from the bar. You are welcome. There are 120 places for picnickers and a further 100 on the terrace where you can mingle with the self service lunchers enjoying the food, the sun and the view.

HAUTES CUISINES

AROSA
1775m. - Top Station 2650m.
SWITZERLAND.

It is very hilly in Arosa. The resort is built on a steep slope with most of the accommodation set on the main road that climbs through the middle of the town. The view is excellent back down the Schanfigg Valley.

The pistes are in two main areas: the Oversee and the Inner-Arosa. Links by lift are good and there is fine skiing for most grades of skier, although some claim that for advanced skiers what is on offer is too tame. Ski touring is possible to resorts such as Klosters and Davos (qv). Cross country skiers are well catered for as are walkers.

Not as popular with British skiers as some other Swiss resorts, Arosa nonetheless offers an attractive combination of skiing with non-skiing pastimes such as skating, curling and sleigh rides. Night life is lively, too. The nearest airport is Zürich and the road up has more bends than you can count.

HOTEL ALPENBLICK

❄❄

The treeline in Europe is aproximately 2000 metres. Above that, one enters the lunar landscape, the undulating white, which seems to lack any meaning without the depth, perspective and feeling of life that trees bring. On the Hörnli side of Arosa, there is one tree. It stands proudly, defiantly at 1950 metres. It stands on the terrace of the Alpenblick Hotel. Which came first is unknown, but it would be nice to think that they started out together in 1911 when the first hut on this spot was built.

If you are skiing down here from Hörnli, watch which way you go, the restaurant sits on a small ledge under a knoll of snow, and is easily missed. When the sun shines, the terrace attracts people all day: the early powder hounds as well as the last-down-the-mountain, must-have-a-schnapps-on-the-way, brigade.

Inside, there are three homely stüblis, slightly folksy but with a personality that many mountain places lack. The Moro family, who have been here for 12 years, treat it as a home; and it shows. The menu breaks no new ground. Here, all is homemade and the portions are generous. A ravioli is 13 Swiss francs and green noodles al pesto are the same. Also listed are Schnitzels, liver and steak, both with sauces and without. On the terrace is a chicken grill, which the hurried pick at before a rapid return to the slopes.

There are two stars shining out of the wine list, a Fleurie and a good St. Emilion 1986, both of which refresh the palate (after a diet of Dôle it can be necessary). Walkers get here on one of the many well-marked walking paths that crisscross the region.

GSPAN

❄❄

For those skiing down from Hörnli or Plattenhorn, there are several stops on the way whether you are calling it a day or taking the bubbles back up. A good one is Gspan, especially for lunch.

There is a little grill stübli at one end of the terrace where the cooking is done over a wood fire, and

HAUTES CUISINES

the aromas will not only excite your taste buds but everybody else's as well. There is an excellent choice of chops, steaks and cutlets and the wood smoke flavour brings an extra dimension to sunshine eating in the snow. The terrace has a barbecue as well. The restaurant at the other end of the terrace offers more conventional fare with Schnitzels, spaghetti, salads and soups.

The prices here are average for the area. A meal for two, including wine, should work out at 20 to 30 francs.

The Gspan is well marked on the route down to the Hörnli express.

HÖRNLI HÜTTE

❆❆

The ride up in the Hörnli bubbles provides a relaxing way to view this big pudding-basin of snow that provides so much pleasure to skiers of all grades. The rest on the way up should give you enough energy to climb the remaining 100 metres or so to the Hörnli Hütte, the pinnacle of skiing on this side of the valley. The Arosa Ski Club was founded in 1903, and not long afterwards they founded a hut on this spot and there has been one here ever since.

The brow-dampening pull up is rewarded by the party atmosphere that thrives all over Arosa. Live music starts ski boots tapping, and the more energetic dancing. The less energetic lie on the sunbeds around the ice bar and the hungry grab the menu, which, like most in this area, is good value.

The speciality is Hörnli mit Gehacktem, a special sort of macaroni with bacon for 13 Swiss francs. The hole filled is bigger than the one it leaves in your pocket.

Inside, the walls are lined with old photographs that trace the history of skiing in this area and the development of the hut itself. The panoramic view brings walkers here and fills an afternoon with dreams as they try to count the surrounding peaks before taking the bubble back down to Arosa.

SKI HÜTTE CARMENNA

❆❆❆❆

In the world of famous huts, the Carmenna is a legend. The walk up from Arosa is not inconsiderable and yet many people do it every day, and not just for the exercise.

The menu has 126 items on it of which 85 are for drinking and the remainder is lunch. The most famous item is the Kotelet vom Grill. You remember that old saying 'I could eat a horse', well this is the horse. In fact, it is a pork chop of Brobdignagian proportions, served with a vast heap of either rösti or a wonderful potato salad and an ice cream scoop of herb butter. Finish it if you can. Our inspector first visited the Carmenna more than ten years ago. He arrived with a party of 15, all hungry, all thirsty and all determined to order first. When Fritz the waiter appeared, mispronounced orders in English rained down on his head, interspersed with questions seeking

HAUTES CUISINES

to identify different items on the menu. Fritz remained impassive, not writing anything down, just waiting for the noise to stop and when it had, he turned tail and disappeared. The party was dismayed. A few moments later, a table started to approach. It was clearly a trick of the light because it was heaped with food, drink, wines and beers. It stopped by the party's table and a little head appeared. It was Fritz, who proceeded to serve everyone exactly what they had finally ordered.

The magic works best when the sun shines, but even on a cold day the trivia-clad, candelit stüblis inside have something special. Some people come to Arosa just to visit the Carmenna but nobody who comes to Arosa misses it.

Ski down from the Sesselbahn Bänkli or walk up from the village. To make a truly showy entrance, paraglide in.

PS If you finished your cutlet with the potato salad, then perhaps an hour or two on one of the comfortable double day-beds is what you need. Seven Swiss francs for half a day. Prices here are remarkable value.

PPS Occasionally, instead of a digestif, the brave take a drop on the bungee rope which hangs from a crane set up beside the restaurant.

TSCHUGGEN HÜTTE

❄❄

The Tschuggen Hütte has changed over the years. The wood, too old for outside, has been replaced and used inside. But change as it has, it has not forgotten why it is there. It sprawls across the snow, its deck chairs intermingling with tables. Children build snow castles with empty yogurt cartons while the older and wiser relax, particularly after the business of lunch.

Most Alpine restaurants of this size have become self-service depots. But not here. The blue-and-red-smocked waiters and waitresses cheerfully rush hither and thither. The menu offers a good range of hot and cold dishes and the daily Tageskarte always adds five or six more. A big bowl of Gulaschsuppe is eight Swiss francs and a big sausage in onion sauce with rösti is 11 francs.

The dessert list provides rewarding temptations. The homemade Apfelkuchen (something like an apple quiche) is delicious for five francs. The wines start at 14 francs for half a litre and, unusually, champagne is served by the glass, brut or rosé.

The Tschuggen is one of those huts you go back to without remembering exactly why, but you do go back. A few hundred metres below the top of the Tschuggen chair, it is easily found.

RESTAURANT WEISSHORN-SATTEL

❄❄

If what they said sounded like "we are going to the Weisshorn, saddle up", you have not fallen asleep and woken in the wild west. No, they meant "We are going to meet at the Sattel Hütte", which sits on the saddle between the Weisshorn and the Bruggerhorn.

The present hut was built about 30 years ago, and is another example of how the good burghers of Arosa are keeping self-service away. In many other resorts, the temptation

HAUTES CUISINES

to cut cost and 'service' as many skiers as possible would be irresistible. The friendly terrace attracts the bronzed and the soon to be, while the fairer-skinned sit around inside waiting for the next person to say, "Oh look, there's a real saddle on the rafters".

If you come for lunch you will not be disappointed. If you can, get a table in the Klub Stübli with its stained glass windows depicting magic moments in the long life of the Arosa winter sports club. The big, blue enamel stove is good for cold fingers, bottoms, gloves and hats.

The menu is predictable but the Tagestellers change daily. Lunch with wine should be about 20 Swiss francs. Children under 11 get fed up for 7.50 francs. Live music frequently raises the tempo.

Deck chairs, of the London park variety, take the strain and the ski back down offers a pleasing cruise all the way to the village.

If you just pop in for a coffee, try the Saltkafi mit Rahmlikör. It does more for the knees than a day in ski school and it only costs six francs.

Get there by either the Bruggherhorn chairs or the Weisshorn cable.

HAUTES CUISINES

AVORIAZ
1800m. - Top Station 2280m.
FRANCE

Like many purpose-built French villages, Avoriaz offers well organised skiing, good shopping and general facilities to compensate for the lack of any vestige of traditional architecture or charm. If you like tower blocks of flats, then Avoriaz will thrill you; the Prince of Wales would probably blow it up.

Movement around the resort is aided by a ban on motor cars, the need for which is greatly diminished anyway by the closeness of the lifts to the centre.

There are four ski areas, les Hauts Forts, the Plateau Les Lindarets, Cubore-Licherett and Pas de Chavenette all interconnected. For long stay and really determined skiers a pass is sold which covers the Portes du Soleil area, providing access to 13 resorts in France and Switzerland. There is skiing to suit all capabilities.

Avoriaz is about one hour's drive from Geneva with bus links between the two. Linked resorts include Champéry (qv), Chatel, Champoussin, Les Crosets, Morgins and other stations of the Portes du Soleil.

CHEZ DENIS
PLAINE DRANSE

❋❋❋

On the day our inspectors arrived it was snowing hard and they ventured in and out of the two adjacent self-service restaurants at Plaine Dranse. Chez Denis, an establishment that pampers with table service, was pointed out by a helpful lady in one of the self-services.

Chez Denis is a long, low building covered in wooden shingles, which the proprietor, Denis David Rogeat, has converted from a cow shed. A large, florid man with a broad smile, he was asked by the inspectors, who surveyed an empty room with trepidation, if they had indeed arrived at a restaurant. "Yes," he replied. "Where then, are your customers?" they inquired. "Out to lunch!" he riposted.

Denis started his restaurant on New Year's Day, 1992. It was, thus, only ten weeks old and, because it was not as yet sign posted, it was merely another building in the little hameau of Plaine Dranse.

The dining room is big and spread around a large, cast-iron stove, ideal for drying hats or gloves. The decor has an impromptu air to it and will, no doubt, improve with age, but its simple honesty is in keeping with the Denis menu.

His potée savoyarde is a country dish of cabbage, bacon, potatoes, sausages and chunks of ham. His speciality is bertoud, a dish of melted cheese and white wine into which you dip home grown potatoes. He makes the cheese himself. He has in effect created a menu which represents what a mountain farmer would need to sustain him in his constant struggle with nature.

The prices are cheap for the mountain. The bertoud was 40 francs and a litre of red wine cost the same. For 20 francs one could have started with the soupe paysanne but few would have room for both soup and bertoud.

What Denis has done bucks the local trend to self-service. So make the effort and visit it, you will remember it and next year Denis will sign post it. A little hard to find, it sits just above the two Rocharsons chairs.

HAUTES CUISINES

LES MARMOTTES
LES LYNDARETS

❄❄❄

Weathered timbers outside, mellow timbers inside, and set amongst a forest of pines from which no doubt it was constructed, Les Marmottes is an unusual combination of restaurant and self-service. No long, stainless steel bar here on which to slide the tray. Nor is there a display of tiring lettuce and curling sandwiches. No, here, having perused the menu, one enters the kitchen and demands of M. Lanvers he cook before your very eyes, the lunch of your choice.

The choice is made from the plats du jour: three courses for about 70 francs, or one of the omelettes for which Les Marmottes is justifiably renowned. There is always a bonne soupe to warm the bones on a cold day and at 20 francs it is very good value.

The local Gamay is 55 francs, the pleasantly petillant Apremont is 60 francs or there is the usual Côtes du Rhône at 50 francs. A goat, mounted on the wall, keeps a watchful eye and a kindly old cast-iron stove, set in the stone fireplace, warms the room.

Les Marmottes is situated just below the top of the telecabine Ardents, a must for the eggcentrics. The loo here must be good for there is always a queue for it.

LE VERARD

❄❄❄

Sitting proudly near the end of the World Cup run, Le Verard has hidden beneath its traditional stone-covered roof, a hearth of warmth and welcome. Named after a floral member of the Gentian family, it has sat on this spot since 1887 but only serving as a restaurant for the past 20 years.

The low-ceilinged, pine clad interior seats only 38 and is candlelit. A large fireplace dominates one corner and the aroma of home cooking greets one as welcomingly as le patron Tommy Kusar and his wife Geneviève.

The menu economises on kitchen staff. Le patron cooks here. It also economises on the alphabet. Its brevity discourages indecision. Soupe de paysanne comes in an earthenware bowl full of vegetables, a big slice of local cheese, a basket of bread and a smile for 35 francs. The sandwich jambon is 25 francs and the assiette de montagne, a plate of local meats, sausages and cheeses, is 75 francs. That is the menu.

The wine list is simpler still. They have red and white at 65 francs a bottle.

If he likes you, Tommy will produce his guest book signed by the famous and famished who have supped and skied on. Do not miss it. There are very few of its like in this modernised mountainscape.

HAUTES CUISINES

BORMIO
1225m. - Top Station 3010m.
ITALY

The small town of Bormio is located in a bowl at the foot of the Stelvio Pass, which separates Italian speaking Italy from German speaking Italy. This sunny and sheltered situation was the venue for the 1985 World Alpine Championships. The old village centre with its cobbled streets has a tempting selection of high quality shops, restaurants, cafes and open air markets.

There is an old Roman thermal bath in a cave outside the town and modern spa facilities for those seeking a cure for something or a little pampering for its own sake. Bagni Vecchi Terme has facilities to bathe in water from the thermal springs, either singly or communally in the new pool or the old pool that is carved out of the rock of the mountain.

The skiing area is quite limited in scope and more likely to appeal to intermediate rather than advanced skiers.

There are ten restaurants in all on the mountainside. There are three we particularly recommend but our inspectors' favourite is La Rocca, which demands a visit. In addition there is Ristorante Taula which is a gastronomic and romantic evening delight in the heart of Bormio.

The nearest international airport is Milan.

BAITA DE MARIO
❄❄

Based at the Ciuk ski station, thereby guaranteeing access for non-skiers as well as skiers (the latter, if so minded, can ski down the blue Ermellini run or the red Stelvio or La Rocca runs), the Ristorante Albergo Baita de Mario is owned by the Zappa family, looks rather like an old hunting lodge and serves good, basic Italian food consisting largely of polenta, pasta and standard favourites such as carpaccio.

The restaurant is in every sense traditional and comfortable. There are no old oak beams or burning fires, but the atmosphere for all that is considered to be redolent of an Italian family Sunday lunch. The large and small tables can be arranged to accommodate about 200 people.

There is a large sun deck but food is served inside, with drinks only available outside.

Prices were par for the local piste but there was a 3000 lire cover charge and the wine list was wholly Italian.

Service was a trifle slow, possibly augmenting the Sunday lunch impression. Rooms are bookable for those who would like to base themselves away from the main village. Tel:901424

LAGHETTI
❄

This restaurant, reported our inspector, had stuck in his mind and had irritated him ever since he visited it. The dining room, he maintains, is nothing special, maybe even a little drab, but it would not require much to alter that. The major appeal of the Laghetti, on a side of the mountain not over-endowed with fine establishments, is the view from the loo, quite the best he has seen from any loo anywhere. If, therefore, you need to spend a penny while parting with

HAUTES CUISINES

the lire, then this is the place to go.
In these circumstances, it is something of a bonus that Pierluigi Bracchio serves some very pleasant food, including good homemade soups, pasta and excellent apple strudel.

The restaurant only seats about 50 people, so when it is busy you may, weather permitting, have to find a table outside. You will not enjoy a marvellous view as the terrace faces up the mountain in order to catch the sun, but you will have a very agreeable lunch.

Laghetti is to be found about half way up and to the left of the Nicoletta drag lift and access is gained either by a walk up from the Bormio 2000 cable car or by skiing down the red run, Stella Alpina, from the Laghetti chair.

LA ROCCA

❄❄❄

La Rocca is considered by many to be the best restaurant on the mountain in Bormio. Sited at the La Rocca station, it provides skiers who want an exciting lunchtime prelude with a black approach down the Valbella piste. Anyone desiring a gentler approach to gastronomy can sweep down the red, Praimont, or the blue, Raccordo Rocca.

The restaurant consists of an old, low, attractive building of blackened wood, which houses a self-service area together with a bar, to which has been added a modern extension containing a proper, table service restaurant with seats for about 50.

As you enter there is a nose-warming smell of burning wood produced by the two stoves, one in each main room. The staff are smiling, friendly and efficient.

The food is good value even after accepting the 3000 lire cover charge. A pizza adds 5000 lire to the bill, the house wines 5000 for half a litre or 8000 for a whole one. Particularly recommended was the bresaola with fragrant oil and lemon, 10000 lire, followed by an outstanding grilled steak for 16000 lire. There is, for those who still have room, a wide range of desserts. The menus are in English and there is no piped music. This is a remarkable treat. The more normal local combinations are no English menus and no music, or English menus with intrusive music.

The only downside to this restaurant is that the terrace, being angled up the slopes to catch the sun, deprives its tenants of a great view. Non importa. It is a great place for lunch.

TAULA

❄❄❄

After a hard day's ski and with an empty stomach because you were skiing on the wrong side of the mountain, it is nice to know there is something very special waiting for you in the heart of Bormio at dinner time. Taula's restaurant is very special. It is sited in a stone-vaulted

HAUTES CUISINES

barn dating from the 17th century and only serves dishes from the local Valtellina region. The restaurant consists of a series of beautiful rooms arranged on different levels, embellished with fine stone work.

The food is of comparable quality. A selection of locally cured meats, 14000 lire, and venison steak in a pink pepper sauce, 19000 lire, are particularly recommended.

Lucio and Clara Zulian also restrict themselves in what they call their ristorante tipico, to local Valtellina wines. Make sure you ask to try their special dessert wine.

Found at Via Dante 6, but closed on Tuesdays, Taula makes an ideal place for a little apres ski romance. To book tel:904771

HAUTES CUISINES

BRUCK
700m. - Top Station 3025m.
KITZSTEIN AUSTRIA

Close to Kaprun and Zell-am-See, Bruck is a lesser known village doubling as both a summer and winter resort. Like Kaprun, it provides glacier skiing on the Kitzteinhorn and the amenities of the nearby lake. In the summer tennis, golf and hiking tempt the energetic.

In the winter the skiing around Bruck itself is not very extensive but the Kitzteinhorn together with the closeness of Kaprun and Zell am See offer a wide choice to skiers.

The nearest international airport is Salzburg but more frequent flights are to be found in Munich.

GASTOF HOLLERN

❄

Situated by the nursery slopes and the departure point for langlaufers, the Gastof Hollern is popular throughout the day being especially favoured in the evenings for apres-ski drinks, when its well stocked bar is a general gathering point for the resort.

A big traditional building, it has one big restaurant and two small cosy stüblis. In all it can comfortably seat 150 people and frequently needs to, although the lively ("full of fun" said our reporter) waitresses always seem to serve everyone promptly.

For the area the prices are reasonable and the wide ranging à la carte menu offers vegetarian dishes for non-carnivores.

Outside sun chairs give the semi-recumbent the chance to stare happily at wonderfuld views of the Grossglockner mountains.

HAUTES CUISINES

CERVINIA
2050m. - Top Station 3490m.
ITALY

High, wide and handsome, Cervinia has long been one of Italy's top resorts. Sitting below the less well known, and some say less attractive, side of the Matterhorn, it offers attractive and sunny skiing that flatters most visitors. Long runs are readily available down to Zermatt or from the top of Plateau Rosa down to the sleepy little village of Valtournenche.

The resort is high, 2050 metres, and the top station is at 3490 metres. Snow conditions, therefore, tend to be better than many parts of Italy these past few seasons, despite Cervinia's delightfully sunny situation. The village is quite large, reflecting the development associated with Cervinia's status as one of the earliest skiing centres to be exploited in Italy. It is not particularly pretty but has a definite charm.

There is a very large ski area although there are complaints about the lack of really demanding runs.

Our inspectors have submitted few reports of piste-side restaurants in Cervinia, many preferring to eat in the village, so more information would be appreciated.

The nearest airport is either Turin or Milan.

IGLOO PUB

❄

Somehow the word pub is an absolute, although there are an infinite variety in Britain. Those that are found in foreign climes always manage to be the same place: designed by someone who believes that everyone from Great Britain wears tartan and likes to be surrounded by prints of beefeaters and, what is more, drinks chilled beer. It is hard to decide whether these pale imitations of the real thing are a vain attempt at flattery or, instead, describe the breadth of the cultural gap initiated by the English Channel.

Anyway, for those who cannot live without British beer, the Igloo Pub is here to provide. "It's a nice place", someone was heard to comment, and, indeed, it is a fair comment. For friendly snack service, the Igloo has it, and, sitting as it does on a mountain that is seriously undernourished, it deserves six out of ten for trying. There is always a good fire burning, score one. The cooking is homemade, score two. The prices are good value, score three. If you like British beer at altitude, score four. The views from the large terrace are wonderful, score five. And for those afficionados of a good loo in the 'English' style, it is here, score six.

This is a friendly place that gives good hamburgers and, on occasions, organises evening parties which culminate in a torch light descent, some say a jolly descent idea.

The Igloo sits on the Ventina run, which glides wonderfully down from the Plateau Rosa and eventually ends at the main cable car station which pumps you back up into the system.

LINO'S

❄❄

Cervinia is a flattering resort. Its wide open pistes flatter everyone's skiing, particularly for those con-

HAUTES CUISINES

cerned with bella figura; for those concerned with transforming their complexion from pale to French polished, the sunshine record excels; and for those British who enjoy travel, snow and an occasional plate of spaghetti and all at a price that leaves change for the duty frees on the way home, this is definitely the place to go.

Say, upon waking one morning, one felt like bacon, eggs, toast, marmalalade and a pot of tea while watching Sky News and catching up on the latest football news or disaster of the week, then one would head for Lino's. If, later in the day, one decided to ski back to the resort for a good Italian lunch with a hearty bottle of Barolo, then one might well head for Lino's again. And if, in the evening, one felt like playing for high steaks at low prices, then once again one could head for Lino's. And if, having finished that steak, a good cheap drink seemed appropriate, and it was between 9.30pm and 10.30pm, then one would stay in exactly the same spot for Lino's happy hour.

Lino Perron has been here for 35 years and his little, almost Tyrolean style, restaurant has learned to cope with, and provide for, almost anything. The restaurant is beside the ice rink, so take our advice and slip in and try it.

HAUTES CUISINES

CHAMONIX
1040m. - Top station 3790m.
FRANCE

Chamonix lies at the foot of Mont Blanc, the highest mountain in Europe. It offers exciting skiing and the best of climbing in the summer. Around these two activities a large and sprawling town has grown up, with a mixture of tall, modern buildings and old-style architecture. Chamonix became famous in 1786 with the first ascent of Mont Blanc. Subsequently, it was host to the first Winter Olympic Games in 1924. It is a busy, noisy town with many restaurants, bars, crêperies and pizzerias. There is also a cinema, casino, jazz club and discotheques.

The valley incorporates Les Houches, Le Brévent, Argentière, La Flégère and Le Tour, areas all linked by bus and, with the exception of Les Houches, the fare is included in the Mont Blanc area ski pass. Passes of five days or more allow one day in Courmayeur. The booklet given with the ski pass and entitled Chamski, has piste maps of all the resorts in the valley.

Chamonix is, of course, famous for the 20 kilometre run (a drop of 2770 metres) of the Vallée Blanche. Take the cable car to the Aiguille du Midi, 3840 metres, a thrilling experience in itself and, after standing in wonderment at the view, you can stand in wonderment at the first stages of the run down. A perilous, precipitous ridge has first to be negotiated without skis, but happily with the aid of a rope to cling to. When the terrain plateaus, you can put your skis back on and enjoy sight-skiing the formation of seracs and crevasses, the glaciers and superb views of the Mont Blanc range. For the non-skier, a trip to the Aiguille du Midi should not be missed. A continuation of the cable car goes to Courmayeur on the Italian side of the mountain.

LA FLEGERE

La Flégère is less awesome than Brévent, being mostly tough blue and tough red runs. There is only one run to the valley and that is difficult and often closed. It lies on the north side of the valley and is a sunny area with good, medium-grade skiing. There is only one access lift, so it becomes rather crowded during the peak season.

BREVENT

Brévent was the original skiing centre at Chamonix. It has links to other areas in Chamonix, but it is basically one good piste.

RESTAURANT '3842'

❄❄❄❄

Lunch at 3842 metres at the summit of l'Aiguille du Midi. Halfway up the cable car from Chamonix the restaurant looks like a castle in the sky. From the top it looks a very basic stone structure dating from 1955. It houses a souvenir and self-service bar where one can buy key rings, cuddly toys, cow bells, coffee and sandwiches and the plat du jour at 49 francs.

There is, however, one jewel: the Restaurant 3842, pretty and petite with painted panels on the dresser and similar panels on the walls depicting local scenes. The windows are small, mean considering the sensational view. It seats 35 people and is open from the beginning of March to the end of November.

M. Morot, the director, states that 3842 is the highest gastronomic

HAUTES CUISINES

restaurant in the world. Difficult to argue, really. There are three, four-course menus, at 130 francs, 160 francs and the menu gastronomique at 240 francs; local dishes of cheese or meat fondues are 89 francs and 95 francs. Raclette is offered at 110 francs. Fresh produce is brought up daily fom the valley.

The wine list is adequate, if uninspiring, with a local Aprement (a Savoyard white wine) at 67 francs. The local Gamay Rouge at 66 francs and a selection of Loire, Bordeaux and Burgundy may owe more to altitude than the patron's attitude. The 3842 is costly, but this really is 'haute cuisine'.

Non-skiers can take a day trip from Chamonix going through the Aiguille du Midi, crossing the Glacier du Géant with the Helbronner gondola, down to Courmayeur in Italy and return to Chamonix by bus (from March/April to September). For skiers there is the famous Vallée Blanche route which will furnish an unforgettable experience. Or you can simply go and enjoy lunch at the highest gastronomic restaurant in the world. Reservations tel: 50 55.82.23.

RESTAURANT LE PANORAMIC
SUMMIT OF BREVENT

❄❄❄

Mountains are full of surprises, some to delight and some to discourage. Well, the Restaurant Panoramic is a surprise, but neither of those described previously. The interior would be more at home somewhere else, but where? The rag-rolled walls, pink and blue table cloths, pastel grey ceiling and black plastic designer-chairs, are not what one would expect at the top of a mountain.

The menu is also somewhat unexpected. There are local specialities, like Pella des Aravis, a dish of potato, onions and bacon, covered with the valley Reblochon cheese and popped under the grill, fondue savoyarde aux cêpes, and the inevitable croûte. The unexpected comes in the form of the three 'menus', starting at 115 francs for three courses and rising to 200 francs for the menu gastronomique offering a choice of foie gras, smoked salmon or ris de veaux aux cêpes. For a main course there is a choice of escalope de saumon or the magret de canard aux myrtilles. Then follows the assiette de fromage, a salade de saison and the 'chariot of desserts'. The wine list is adequate and the best value on it is a Côtes du Rhône (cellier des Dauphins) at 48 francs a bottle.

On a clear day, the terrace provides truly spectacular views of the Mont Blanc range and the valley below. Indeed, being situated at the top of the Brévent cable car, it is a restaurant with more of an appeal to sightseers than to skiers. The little bar which is adjacent to the restaurant will make the skier feel more at home. Two good value menus, one at 60 francs and the other at 72 francs, offer good choices of simple food; and on a day when one is about to tackle the long black run from Brévent down to Plan Praz, or even all the way down to Chamonix, then a heart starter at the top may be in order. On sunny days it would be advisabe to reserve a table on the terrace. Tel:50.53.44.11. The loos are clean and worth a visit.

HAUTES CUISINES

REFUGE DES COSMIQUES
VALLEE BLANCHE

❄❄❄

Rarely does a copper-bottomed recommendation come copper-plated, but here it does. The Refuge des Cosmiques was rebuilt and reopened on 21 June 1991. It replaces the old research centre which was burned down. This glittering edifice greets skiers about one third of the way down the famous and beautiful Vallée Blanche run from the Aiguille du Midi, just below the summit of Mont Blanc.

The interior is strangely modern in this glacial landscape. It has brightly coloured curtains and crisp, white tables, but for those who have embarked on this ski tour adventure, it is a glimpse of comfort in an otherwise barren, but spectacular, landscape.

Those who want to make more than just a lunch stop can stay the night in the dormitory, where 210 francs covers the cost of the bed and a hearty dinner of savoyarde potée (a substantial local stew), and breakfast in the morning. Wine is extra and starts at about 66 francs a bottle from the small, but adequate, wine list.

The total run is about 24 kilometres, with the real excitement at the top. It is approached either by the old, hair-raising triple cable car from Courmayeur, or from the Aiguille du Midi cable up from Chamonix. This route involves a careful step down on the steep snow bridge, which provides a heart-thumping start.

The valley is full of crevasses and the sensible take a guide. Some of the thrill is diminished on a clear day by the sheer number of skiers who form an unending queue all the way down.

The Refuge des Cosmiques is a rewarding stop, particularly if the weather changes. They get their supplies by helicopter and the same journey can be taken by those who want this extraordinary experience without the need to learn to ski.

At weekends it pays to 'phone in advance and reserve, particularly if one intends to stay the night. For most it is a unique experience. Call Mme. Janine Monterrain on 50.54.40.16

HAUTES CUISINES

CHAMPERY
1050m. - Top Station 2280m.
SWITZERLAND

Champéry lies close to the French border and is easily reached from Geneva. It is also set in the Portes du Soleil area, which may help explain why a small and rather quiet Alpine village has developed a sports centre (good for skating, curling and other icy sports) and a 125 person cable car. The village looks across to the intimidating Dents du Midi.

There is a wide range of skiing and the possibility of ski trips across to France. The nursery slopes are high up at Planachaux involving trips up in the cable car.

Night life is not in the lively league but the charm of the old village has great appeal.

Linked resorts include Avoriaz (qv), Les Crosets, Morgins (qv) and other Portes du Soleil stations.

LE CHAUDRON

❄❄

This big built Swiss chalet promises little from the exterior, except perhaps a rest for tiring limbs. The steel plated front door is somehow more reminiscent of the rougher areas of inner cities than the clean air of the Swiss Alps.

Inside there is a large bar and a comfortable restaurant. Below stairs (and rightly so in our mind) is a self- service restaurant.

The menu in the main restaurant is standard mountain fare at average mountain prices. The wine list reminds you that you are in Switzerland both by price and choice. Ernest Vieux and his family, who own and run Le Chaudron have an interesting point of view about sustenance.

There is a breakfast menu which offers bread, butter, cheese and jam plus tea, chocolate, ovaltine or coffee for 7 Swiss francs. So far so good, but as an option one can take teawine or grog, or tearum or vin chaud.(Well when in Switzerland.). Ham and eggs appear on the lunch menu along with a crop of croûtes and an average of omelettes. Somewhat short on atmosphere but sunny days on the terrace change one's view.

RESTAURANT COQUOZ
PLANACHAUX

❄❄❄❄

Squatting in the snow a two minute ski down from the top of the Champéry cable car (or a five minute walk), Le Coquoz epitomises all that is best about traditional Swiss chalets: wood outside, good inside. This is quite a popular restaurant and its terrace on a sunny day is crammed and noisy.

Like all the best restaurants, this is a family enterprise and, with a name like Gex-Collet-Coquoz, they bring three times the normal energy and enthusiasm. First, is the welcome and the warmth supplied by the family and the large circular fireplace set in the middle of the restaurant. The large, suspended circular chimney is decorated with

HAUTES CUISINES

reliefs of marmottes, deer, foxes and is signed by the artist a M. Casanova (a man who obviously loved his work).

Secondly, is the menu which does much to change the usual pace of mountain offerings. It has a good choice of hot and cold dishes, both simple and gourmet. There is also a vegetarian menu and two children's menus.

The restaurant was built in 1952 and claims to be the first mountain restaurant in the Portes du Soleil. It is open all year with the exception of May and November when the family sets about collecting the wild mushrooms (bolets, cêpes, chanterelles, morilles and others) that are so much a feature of their cuisine.

Their third enthusiasm is the wine list, possibly the most extensive and carefully planned one is ever likely to find in the Valais. There are 33 different varieties of grape in the Valais and on this list of over 120 different wines one can find them all, from the single rarities like the Humagne Blanche to the five-variety blends like the Fin Bec Mer. In order to encourage taste and trial, and to give their customers the opportunity to understand the different wines, they offer little snacks with an appropriate glass of wine: mouthfuls of sausage and locally cured bacon with a ballon of pinot noir, or some mountain cheese with a glass of the curiously named Lafnetscha. Many different wines of quality are available by the glass. Desserts are homemade ice cream or patisserie prepared with locally picked apricots, plums and cherries. The prices are not the cheapest but nor are they unreasonable. Downstairs, there is a self-service restaurant. Outside, the terrace provides a view of the Dents Blanches and the Col du Bretolet, one of the main migration routes for non-skiing birds flying to Africa to avoid a winter in the Alps. Deck chairs are provided for sunbathers.

LE TOUPIN

❋❋

Josephine is English and her husband Stephane is from Champéry. They have owned and run Le Toupin for 14 years and all that time they have resisted the temptation to greet the invading hordes by becoming a self-service restaurant. Long may they continue to do so.

Stephane and his father converted L'Echereuse from an old farm and even Heidi would feel quite at home here. The food is traditional and simple. There is a daily menu for about 15 Swiss francs and occasional specialities like a salade dent-de-lion (dandelion salad), which is delicious and full of the iron one needs for one's legs. There are good soups, steaks, fondues, assiette valaisanne (dried meats and mountain cheese), spaghetti or sandwiches which start at only five francs.

Jospehine is friendly and chatty and will proudly tell about her life in the mountains and the challenges of running a restaurant at altitude. Some of the disasters that are commonplace would have most of us running for cover.

Outside, the sunny terrace provides enchanting views across to Les Dents du Midi.

The restaurant is situated at the bottom of both the Ripaille button and the new four-seat Pauvre-Couche chair lift, both of which climb towards the border with France, useful for those looking to visit Avoriaz and other parts of the Portes du Soleil.

HAUTES CUISINES

CHAMPOUSSIN
1580m. - Top Station 2300m.
SWITZERLAND

Slightly larger than its near neighbour of Les Crosets, the village has local charm and the development has been done sympathetically. It is mainly apartments, but there are a few hotels one of which boasts a disco. The views from the village are of the Dents du Midi and are quite spectacular.

The skiing from the village is quite adequate, for those who seek more, the Portes du Soleil offer all they need.

Linked resorts are Champery (qv), Les Crosets, Morgins (qv), Chatel, Avoriaz (qv), (Portes du Soleil).

The nearest airport is Geneva.

CHEZ GABY

❄❄❄

There are three ways to get to Chez Gaby. In this instance, with the help of a constant companion and guide, we took the telecabine up from Les Crosets to the Ponte de Mosselle, from there we followed a goat track across the mountains, little used by skiers and even less so by sensible goats. After half an hour of struggling along this oft disappearing route, lacking the sense of balance of the average mountain goat, we turned off. We then skied across grass, rocks and emergent bushes until a mirage of a hut, with a Valais flag flying, came into view. Encouraged by one's guide, an uphill assault on this oasis was attempted. Climbing up the last few yards and clambering out of one's skis, the name, Refuge de Relais, peeling off the side of the hut, could be seen. An old menu in a glass case promised refreshment, a lunch, a drink and a rest.

Our efforts were viewed with some amusement by the occupiers, who explained rather brusquely that it was no longer a restaurant and offered no help as we silently climbed back into our skis. Their laughter could be heard as we skied off, encouraging the rage and despair within us. After another tortuous half hour we came to a tarmac road, took off our skis and walked the mile back to Les Crosets. Once there, we started again, this time taking the Ponte de l'Au chair to the Ponte de l'Au and thence by an easy, agreeable ski down to Champoussin, where, at the top of the Champeys drag lift we found Chez Gaby.

This route has the disadvantage of wasting two hours, wearing out skis and putting human relationships to the test.

Was it worth it? What happened then? Well, Chez Gaby is just what one needs at the end of such an adventure, all you would ask to restore the mind and the body, and repair a somewhat worn relationship. Housed in a converted bergerie (cow shed), Chez Gaby has all the warmth that Nansen would have prayed for on reaching the Pole, Inside, the old stone walls and low wooden ceiling envelope you and the multiplicity of artefacts that adorn the walls distract you from the menu. Gaby, for that is the name of the patron, opened the

HAUTES CUISINES

restaurant in 1976 and it has become the local's favourite. The menu offers such specialities as a pierrades (strips of beef cooked on a hot stone in the middle of your table), or the fondue de tomate, prepared with local cheese and tomatoes, and served with potatoes to dip in, instead of the usual pieces of bread.

There is a salade d'alpage, consisting of green salad with chanterelles, jambon cru, saucisson, fromage, walnuts and cumin and at 13.50 francs, it is plate to remember. Every day there are two plats du jour and all the desserts are homemade. Gaby heads his brigade of five in the kitchen and produces one of the widest menus we have found in this area.

Outside the terrace provides the inevitable wonderful views and the waitresses, dressed in local Valais red smocks, provide friendly and efficient service.

The wines are all local as is much of the clientele.

Prices are average for the mountain although the specialities are not cheap. Those with less adventure and energy get there by the short walk up from Champoussin. The route you take to get there is open to choice but Chez Gaby is a must.

HAUTES CUISINES

LA CLUSAZ
1100m. - Top Station 2490m.
FRANCE

Less than an hour's drive from Geneva lies one of the oldest ski resorts in the French Alps. An old village with 35 hotels and pensions, which together with the chalets and apartments offer over 18000 beds, La Clusaz has only recently come to the attention of the packaged tour industry.

The skiing, whilst not as extensive as some of its near neighbours like Megève (qv), is considerably more interesting and challenging. During the season La Clusaz is a mecca for the young and so is commensurately lively. The apres ski offers the usual distractions with the addition of floodlit cross country tracks, joy rides on snow cats, floodlit ice skating and even the opportunity to visit one of the many surrounding farm houses where Reblochon cheese is made. On Mondays new arrivals are fêted in the square with free mulled wine and some local entertainment.

The skiing covers five distinct areas all of which are linked by the lift system and from four of which it is possible to ski back to the village.

RESTAURANT LE BERCAIL

✤✤✤

They are meticulous builders and carpenters in the Alps. Six years ago, this restaurant was restored using the timber from the orginal building which had been run up in 1756. And the result? A fine, traditional-looking chalet that has obviously been constructed from nicely matured pine.

It is quite small, Le Bercail. Inside, the central fireplace dominates the dining room, which, apart from people, it shares with an elderly grandfather clock and a mechanical piano. Baskets and sprigs of dried flowers hang from the rafters. These various artefacts will not, however, succeed in distracting you from the smell of fennel on the sea bream that is cooking over the log fire. Alternatively, you may watch your medaillon of sole being grilled.

The patronne of Le Bercail is Yolande Zarzour who, with her chef Jean-Noel Baffert, insists that everything is absolutely fresh. It is for this reason that not all the dishes on the menu are always available. It is a sacrifice well worth making for outstanding food. The choice, in any case, is extremely wide. On offer are savoyarde specialities, or, in the evenings, something Vietnamese, or Chinese, North African, Spanish or even Italian. There are fondues available, too. Among the desserts, the speciality is coupe Bercail: ice cream with chestnut cream, and chantilly with something savoyarde from a special bottle.

If seeking a light lunch, the savoyarde salad (salad leaves with Beaufort cheese, bacon and garlic croûtons) is recommended as one of the best in the Alps and only 48 francs.

Le Bercail is an easy ski down from the Cret du Merle. Alternatively, you can return in the evening (but, please, book), by driving up to the Cret du Merle and then being chauffeured the rest of the way in the restaurant's snow cat.
Tel:50.02.43.75.

HAUTES CUISINES

CHEZ FONFON

❄❄❄

Lovers of ail in the sky will appreciate the garlic ridden menu of Chez Fonfon. Ski down an easy green from the top of the Beauregard, olfactory senses twitching, and 100 metres from the Croix Fry chair lift is Chez Fonfon. Inside this popular, family restaurant you may start your lunch with sizzling snails in garlic butter for 100 francs, progress to the rabbit in garlic and mustard with rice or polenta, and finish with the house speciality, coupe Fonfon. This last, ice cream dish, does not contain garlic. One feels that somehow, somewhere, they lacked the true courage of their convictions; although it has to be admitted, that this confection of nougat ice cream, covered in caramel and heaped with chantilly cream, is seriously delicious even if it does lack the vital alliaceous vegetable.

Chez Fonfon is small and frequently packed, which says much for the quality of the food and the moderation of the prices (a plat du jour at 50 francs, for example).

Michelle, the owner, majors on ice cream in the desserts. Apart from the aforementioned coupe Fonfon, there is a myrtille melba, a very reasonable raspberry melba for 26 francs, or the vacherin maison, which consists of meringue, strawberry and vanilla ice cream with chantilly cream as well. After all that, with your palate pounded into submission, you will be relieved to learn that Fonfon is surrounded by easy runs.

LE PRESSOIRE

❄

A pressoire, as the French speakers among you will have spotted instantly, is the place where the grapes are crushed during wine making. This, broadly alcoholic, reference is reflected in the restaurant's offerings to customers. Food is mostly croque monsieurs or pizza, albeit fresh from the oven. On the other hand, there is a remarkable range of cocktails, mostly about 40 francs, with regulars such as Irish coffee and black velvets vieing for space on the list with 'zombies', 'belly-ups' and 'paradise'.

The wine list itself is not remarkable, so the vinous would be advised, for once, to turn their attention to thirst-quenching beer, of which 110 varieties are available. The conventionally minded can stick to a vieux temps blonde (gentlemen have always preferred them), while the adventurous can punt 90 francs on a bottle of framboise fondroyante. Most nationalities are represented (beers as well as customers), and bière pression is on tap, too.

The clientele, while mixed, has a large component of locals, who can watch, when drinking their raspberry beers, the latest Saloman/K2 videos on any of the three television sets in the room.

If, after all of that, you want a chaser to your 'paradise', pizza or even your 'zombie', then try a delicious chocolat Viennois for 17 francs or a chocolat Kirsch for 20 francs. Float back to your chalet or hotel.

HAUTES CUISINES

LE VIEUX CHALET

❄❄❄

A lot of nouvelle cuisine for a vieux chalet, M. and Mme. Faber's restuarant is, with Le Bercail, one of the two gastronomic piste markers in La Clusaz. Perhaps a little more sophisticated than Le Bercail, perhaps a touch less cosy, who can say, but they are both places you should visit before leaving the resort.

The Fabers have a large following that arrives from Geneva to sit in the little rooms that make up the dining area, to finger the red table cloths and admire the matching curtains. In this mountain setting, they can enjoy good fish and seafood, such as the foie gras homard at 110 francs or the salade d' homard foie gras at 140 francs, or toy with salmon or rouget.

Three menus gastronomiques are priced at 90, 180 and 250 francs for three courses. They include salades paysannes, gribelette de pied de porc, eggs en cocotte, mignons de veau, good cheeses and desserts. Children have their own menu at 45 francs. It is more imaginative than the usual hamburgers, and includes soup or sausage, grilled ham or fish garni, followed by dessert.

The desserts are a delight: mousse orange, coulis exotique, parfait aux pistaches or nougat glace au lait d'amandes, compete for attention.

The wine list matches the quality of the food.

As well as being a fine restaurant, Le Vieux Chalet is M. and Mme. Faber's home, which they converted from an old savoyarde farmhouse. Bedrooms are available for those who like to sleep close to a good kitchen. Le Vieux Chalet is to be found half way down the Cret du Merle at the top of the Patinoire cabin from La Clusaz. Tel: 50.02.41.53.

HAUTES CUISINES

CORTINA D'AMPEZZO
1220m. - Top Station 2930m.
ITALY

Like many a ravishing beauty, Cortina is misunderstood, accused of being frivolous and flighty and, good heavens, not really serious about the business of skiing. Many people are thus tempted to avoid this undeniably expensive town. In so doing, they deprive themselves of fine skiing and some of the most spectacular views and pistes available anywhere.

The skiing is widely scattered (Passo Falzarego, for example, is 16 kilometres from the centre) but the compensating advantages are a great variety of snow conditions and the ability to move on if there are queues. On an average holiday it would be very difficult to get bored. In addition, recent investment, in new chair lifts for example, has countered objections from those who believe that facilities have been neglected. And all the time you are surrounded by the ragged, tattered grandeur of the Dolomites, so different from the smoother contours of the Alps.

Dotted around the pistes are many outstanding bars and restaurants. Inspectors in the 1991-1992 season visited around 25 and failed to cover them all, so more reports, please.

BAITA PIE TOFANA

❊❊

Baita Pie Tofana is a skiing destination or resting place on the way down from Pomedes (2340) to the edge of Cortina, or a parking place for those who wish to ascend the Rumerlo-Duca d'Aosta lift system. However one travels to or from Baita Pie Tofana, one cannot help noticing the air of a traditional travellers' hostelry.

The atmosphere is loud and unpretentious, jovial and relaxed. No one is in a hurry, including the staff.

A fairly large deck is full to the brim with benches and tables, set out as if for a mediaeval banquet or a German beer festival. The Baita is set in a natural bowl which catches the afternoon sun wonderfully: one has a choice of sitting with one's back to the sun, looking at the splendid log cabin style building, or facing the sun and wooded slopes over the extensive car park in the foreground.

Inside the setting is quite beautiful. Of special note are two small areas off the main dining room: one provides a secluded alcove for perhaps ten diners, the other a table edging an open grill and 'hanging' chimney hood of iron.

A handwritten menu is, perhaps, then a surprise in quite such an elaborate setting. The variety of cold and hot dishes did not lack however, and of particular note was the Roast Beef All'Inglese.

Baita Pie Tofana caters for some 80 people. On the day of the visit it was just recovering from a full Sunday lunchtime session. This area of Cortina's extensive slopes has much to attract on an off-piste afternoon but the restaurant succeeds in attracting its share of attention and clientele.

EL CAMINETO

❊❊❊❊

A touch grand is El Camineto. The waiters, splendid in white jackets at lunchtime, are the first indication as

HAUTES CUISINES

you approach the large, elegant building, off the Falzarego road at Gilardon, just by the Pie Tofana chair lift. In the evenings, the absence of anything so common as a menu or the mention of anything so vulgar as a price, are secondary indicators that this is no ordinary establishment.

The dining rooms, there are two, contrive a combination of the traditional (wooden floors, curved wooden ceiling like the deck of a ship), with a hint of luxury (sheepskins thrown over benches and lots of exotic pot plants) that is undeniably appealing. The two main restaurants seat around 40 people each, with a further 50 people accommodated outside.

The inspection took place in the evening, when tables are bookable, tel: 0436.868424. The maitre d' offers one a drink and then talks about the dishes available that evening and recommends wines to accompany them. The approach is seductive and orders are rapidly made. However, long before you reach anything you have actually asked for, a proud chef offers little appetisers to tease the taste buds. First, there appeared a fish pâté on a square of polenta, accompanied by two deep fried pieces of bread, sandwiching parma ham and cheese. Delicious.

The next arrival were tiny pizzas, glorious dough topped with ham and mozzarella cheese seasoned with oregano, that filled a spot nicely in one's rapidly overloading digestive system. After that, the first courses requested, turned up. But just when you thought everything was operating normally . . .

On offer had been either boiled or grilled shrimps. One inspector opted for grilled shrimps, the other for a grilled steak. "Just to offer a taste", there appeared boiled shrimps on a bed of spaghetti, accompanied by strips of zuchini. It has to be conceded that the shrimps were superb. Fresh, beautifully cooked and redolent of the Mediterranean, they were magnificent. After that, there appeared the grilled shrimps on a bed of salad and a fillet steak wrapped in bacon.

With this modest supper, there was drunk a fine Italian cabernet sauvignon. The only solecism in the entire evening occured when, a second bottle having been ordered (all that food had to be washed down, somehow), the waiter poured the new wine, untasted, into the wine in the existing glasses.

The maitre d' then reappeared and offered puddings, cheese and other delicacies. At this point, our inspectors waved a white flag and conceded surrender. The combinations of protein and carbohydrate had defeated even their determined professional enthusiasm.

The bill when it arrived, was, for the type of restaurant at that altitude, 1560 metres, of eye watering dimensions, the equivalent of £100 for two people.

El Camineto, then, is good. But you have been warned.

CAPANNA TONDI

❄❄❄

Intrepid inspectors battled against gale winds and stinging snow to sample the fare at Capanna Tondi, a wood and stone chalet skilfully positioned to attract the high altitude skier seeking shelter from the natural processes of attrition.

Set at 2362 metres, the hut, on a fine day, enjoys panoramic views across a number of Dolomite valleys. A large open deck provides a

HAUTES CUISINES

level platform on which to relax and view the results of geological stress. But, be warned, the deck is literally 'open' at one end, and although the drop is not precipitous, it might be calamitous.

Safely inside, one has a choice between formal set tables in one room or casual pine 'kitchen' tables in the other. The menu is the same in both, as indeed are the casually turned-out staff.

The food, however, is far from casual, and actually rather exciting. The warmth of a nutritious pasta e fagioli soon permeated even those parts of the inspector's anatomy normally cut off from circulation by ski boots. Equally as tasty and perhaps even more filling was a 'thick' dish of gnocchi with spinach. Both dishes were reasonably priced, and with some light liquid refreshment the bill was extremely satisfactory considering the height and the distance ingredients would have had to travel.

In winter these ingredients would take a similar route to skiers - a single chair lift (Rio Gere-Pian de Ra Bigontina) across a delightful valley stream from the road side at Rio Gere in the Passo Tre Croci, a redrun ski down to a twin-set of chairs (Girilada) followed by a long haul up to Tondi.

The standards of decor, furniture and cleanliness were high.

RIFUGIO AVERAU

❈❈❈❈

Perched precariously on a limestone ledge with 360 degree views of the Dolomites, Rifugio Averau sits at the edge of the top of the world.
Reached by two slow single chair lifts from Cinque Torri and a short 20 metre climb, the view is one of the most wonderful from any restaurant anywhere, with the mountains rolling away for mile upon tens of miles.

A large deck can seat about 50 people, although this is likely to be a breezy, chilling experience. Inside is a complete contrast. A big tiled stove is fitted with a wooden seat so that new arrivals can warm their backs while waiting for one of the ten or so tables. This is likely to be necessary. On the day of inspection, the slightly smoky interior was packed with mostly Italian skiers rattling away like parrots.

The food is well worth any short wait. The long wide pasta strips of papardelle were exquisitely fresh as were the funghi that accompanied them. The gnocchi carote were also outstanding. Roast beef was finely flavoured, if fractionally tough, while lamb cutlets were tender. 'T' bone steaks were observed to be enormous. Hungry skiers note. Spinach salads were crisp, with rich virgin olive oil and proper, freshly grated parmigiano. The house wine, served in ceramic jugs, is young, fruity and rounded.

The house puddings are cakes. One portion for two people is recommended. The wine cake sampled was slightly dry but the icing was excellent. The grappa that followed grabbed one powerfully by the throat.

For ten years Sandro Siorpoes has presided over one of Italy's most popular and successful mountain restaurants. The fact that there is from time to time no water supply in the loo is a small price to pay.

To be shut in by the weather at Rifugio Averau would be a considerable pleasure and a risk any visitor to Cortina is encouraged to take.

HAUTES CUISINES

RIFUGIO BERGHAUS POMEDES

❄❄

Leave the car at Pie Tofana, take a double chair to Duca d'Aosta, then a single chair up to Pomedes, ski 50 metres and you have arrived at the Rifugio Berghaus Pomedes.

Some 2300 metres above sea level, built in 1956 of stone and wood, this is a handsome and well positioned restaurant deserving of custom. Inside, the furniture and settings are reminiscent of a doll's house, all meticulously set tables and fancily carved chairs.

The menu is wide and varied, both hot and cold. The lasagne al forno was the best our inspector had tasted. Crêpes, advertised on the menu as omelettes, were also a tasty choice. Wines were listed from different regions right across Italy.

Sunday lunch in mid March was comfortably full including a fire side contingent of the local polizia. The presence of police or military is usually a sign of quality and value and certainly a guarantee of a lack of chianti louts.

Service was friendly and efficient and the waitress spoke highly, in fluent English, of the restaurant proprietor, Luigi Ghedina, a former ski instructor generally known as Bibi.

Rifugio Berghaus Pomedes is one of the more sophisticated eating houses to be found at such high altitude. It is well worth the visit.

RIFUGIO DUCA D'AOSTA

❄❄

There is a gastronomic line in Cortina. From the top of Pomedes, through Duca d'Aosta, encompassing Pie Tofana and on down to El Camineto, hungry skiers have the chance to breakfast, pit stop, lunch and dine, all on the same piste. This is not to suggest that the other, highly commended, restaurants in Cortina are not worthy. It merely highlights the quantity of fine establishments there are.

Duca d'Aosta enjoys a number of distinctions. First, it has been owned by Paulo Lancedelli since 1938, which must constitute some sort of record. Secondly, it provides an English translation of its Italian menu. This is by no means unique, but for an undiscriminating English palate (of which, regrettably, there are a number) the translation of polenta as 'mush' has a certain irresistible logic.

The menu is slightly more basic than the more highly sited Pomedes, consisting mostly of omelettes and polenta, with few meat dishes. The prices are correspondingly lower. The house dish is polenta, mushrooms, cheese and sausage, enough fuel to see anyone through a blizzard. There are 12

HAUTES CUISINES

wines available. Three desserts, chocolate cake, strudel and jam tart are offered.

The restaurant is wood panelled, attractively carved, wood floored and divided into two rooms (each providing seats for about 30 people), with the tables and benches arranged in booth style. The staff are friendly and often multi-lingual. If you want to stay in the same ski area all day, Duca d'Aosta is a handy, additional inducement.

RIFUGIO LAGAZUOI

❄❄

A short, if steep, walk up from the top of the cable car from the Passo Flazarego, the Rifugio Lagazuoi is available to skiers and non-skiers, although the latter are advised to make their return by the same route rather than by the red run down the piste.

Set at 2750 metres, the restaurant has what is known in the guide book trade as commanding views of the Dolomites. Cortina is a fine town in a spectacular setting and the higher huts profit accordingly.

The restaurant itself, fronted by a big wooden deck, is simple and cheerful: tile and plank floors with big windows (bright even on a day of cloud and snow) with tables set with coloured cloths. Total internal capacity is about 80 people.

The restaurant contains a long bar (meals, nonetheless are served by waiters) which also sells post cards and souvenirs. An interesting historical note about fighting in the area between Austrians and Italians in the first World War is available in several languages free of charge.

A spotlessly clean kitchen is just visible behind the bar.

Menus are printed in German and Italian and major on such regional specialities as gnocchi, polenta and pasta. The wine list deals exclusively in Italian wines but is, nonetheless, long and varied.

Prices are average for the area, nobody ever accused Cortina of doing anything on the cheap, and the Rifugio provides a high point to a day's skiing in more than one sense.

RISTORANTE RIO GERE

❄❄

Ristorante Rio Gere is in a wonderful position to capture passing trade, whether on skis, on foot or in a car.

Situated some 6 kilometres from Cortina, on the Passo Tre Croci road, this modern chalet style restaurant and bar is placed in the middle of two facing ski areas, Son Forca and Tondi.

Chair lifts take skiers up on either side of the road, and the restaurant's large deck looks over a sizeable car park area.

A clean, tidy pine furnished interior is complemented by old agricultural instruments wall mounted in an attempt to give a 'rustic' air to the establishment. The tiled stove is authentic, and warming whether one has just skied or driven through a blizzard.

Visitors can choose from a self-service bar or a sit-down dining area. The menu is a tribute to the versatility of Italian food, plenty of pasta and polenta for those in a hurry to test their skills on the pistes, but also an appetising selection of more thoughtful dishes requiring quality, time and indeed some digestion.

Particularly noteworthy, were the

HAUTES CUISINES

succulent looking grilled vegetable starter and the extensive looking cheese platter offered for dessert. Either could be accompanied by the red and white wine on draught - draught wine not a common sight in mountain huts so availability here perhaps a symptom of the Rio Gere's roadside position.

Although quiet on the day of our visit, there is no doubt that the Rio Gere's accessible position would help make it a most popular venue for large numbers.

HAUTES CUISINES

COURCHEVEL
1300m. - Top Station 3200m.
FRANCE

"The largest ski area in the world." Or as they say in the Trois Vallées, "le plus grand domaine skiable du monde". Of the four resorts which make up this area Courchevel is undeniably the smartest, although itself split into four resorts, 1850, the main station, 1650, 1550 and 1300, the delightful old village of Le Praz, which was the site for the 1992 Olympic ski jump.

Investment in ski lifts is continuous and the area offers everything from the well groomed, gentle beginners' pistes to the couloirs of courage that hang above La Saulire.

The resort has a good snow record and yet there is an abundance of snow making machines to guarantee skiers a ride back to the village.

The area is extremely well served by hotels at all levels and some of the best restaurants to be found in the Alps. The young at heart will find the night life plentiful.

The nearest airports are Geneva, Lyon or Chambéry, although Courchevel has its own Altiport much used by Les Parisiens and those with a lot of money.

Linked resorts are Méribel (qv), Val Thorens (qv) and Les Menuires.

ALTITUDE 21

❋❋

At all airports, the buildings that surround them are subject to height control and Altitude 21 is no exception. Protruding slightly from the snow, this pastel pink building offers little architectural promise from the outside.

Inside, it is a different story. Once again, the Mediterranean flavour that seems to pervade Courchevel is to be found: a sloping stuccoed roof supported by scrubbed pine rafters, a slate floor with, in one corner, natural boulders erupting through it. The moods change as you ramble through the different areas. At the front, continuous glass windows let the light and dramatic scenery in. At the back, cushioned banquettes surround bleached wooden tables for longer, more conversational lunches. In a room right at the back, tables are set out pullman style, and in one corner there is a blanket-covered single bunk, usually empty. Pictures of mountain flowers hang irregularly around the white plastered walls.

The menu is a combination of traditional theatre with a little variety thrown in. There are four starters, assiettes of crudités, jambon cru, jambon blanc or terrine, and then anything you like as long as it is a char grilled chop or steak or a selection from one of their two pizzas.

Forgive their single-mindedness. The steaks are grilled to your order before your very eyes and the pizzas are prepared and baked 'au feu du bois' by a flour-covered chef while you watch and wait.

For those who do not eat pizza on the principle that you should never eat anything bigger than your head, there is a daily plat du jour and a lasagne, or, for the asbestos fingered, corn on the cob from the charcoal grill.

An average meal here would be 100 francs including wine.

On a clear day the sunchairs outside are full of browning faces looking up towards 'Le Suisse', the steep black run down from Vizelles, and, perhaps, dreaming that they are one of those chaps who appear from nowhere, wedelling past you with

HAUTES CUISINES

their Dallas shoulders leaving a turbulent wind in your face.
Altitude 21 is easily found above the Altiport by skiers, walkers or pilots.

LE BELAIR

❊❊❊

Frank Lloyd Wright would have approved. Le Belair is all simplicity, light and conviction of construction. No rustic pretence here. Le Corbusier would have called it an eating machine, but for the hundreds of skiers who come here every day, Le Belair is a delightful experience.

This ranch-style chalet has a great, open fire place, and outside, three terraces that step down before it into the snow. Designed by les frères Gormier, it was built by them too, beam by beam, bolt by bolt and, during the 18 years it has stood, it appears to have ignored the ravages of the weather and looks as fresh today as it did then.

There is always a queue of people trying to claim a table. "Did you book?" "Of course." "Did you?" The staff are never less than helpful, a smile is never far away and, almost miraculously, nobody is disappointed.

Christophe Gormier, the son of a frère, works here with his uncle George, the frère of a frère. Both have been ski instructors and both understand that skiers want to eat well and fast and get back to the slopes.

For this reason they keep the menu simple but varied, and not the usual mountain fare. Their salade montagnarde is a good starter of lentils, onion and bacon. Or if that fails to start you, try the salade Belair, a generous portion of crisp lettuce, walnuts, cheese and dressings. This excellent salade is also served with the plat du jour, always filling and served with a choice of frites or pommes gratinées (have the gratinées) for 105 francs. This is not the cheapest restaurant on the mountain but it is hard to argue with the value that Christophe and Uncle George provide. Two good courses with wine should cost about 130 francs. Wines start at 55 francs a bottle for the reserve du patron.

The service is fast and friendly, but not hurried.

The Belair sits conveniently at the top of the Ariondaz bubbles up from 1650 and is, therefore, popular with skier and non-skier alike. So if you think steak tartare with all the trimmings for 95 francs is a raw deal, you could be right. Try it and see.

LA BERGERIE

❊❊

Some afficionados claim this restaurant has gone off since it changed hands last year, but one could not mention Courchevel without mentioning La Bergerie.

Beautifully situated on the right of the Bellecôte piste, it has for years been the meeting place of the good, the great and those who merely thought they were. Probably the oldest building in Courchevel, its charming interior is propped up by sawn pine logs, carefully pinioned together. Outside, those whose ski suits cover swim suits, lie on red mattressed sun chairs and soak up gossip and sun.

The menu has changed little since the change of hands. It still offers a wide selection at not unreasonable

51

HAUTES CUISINES

prices. There is even a children's menu. A favourite for lunch is the crozet savoyarde, a regional speciality of pasta, cream, cheese and bacon, not unlike a carbonara, its Italian cousin.

The wine list does not offer any bargains but is drinkable from about 90 francs. Lunch for two, including wine, should cost about 200 francs a head.

On a recent visit, the service lacked lustre and the old welcome was missing. Perhaps the afficionados are right.

LE BISTRO DU PRAZ

❋❋❋❋

Charlie Renaudie has been serving hungry skiers for years at this well known savoyarde hideaway. His moustachioed smile is as well known as his hospitality.

If you have taken the roller coaster black, Jockeys, or the equally testing, Jean Blanc, you will arrive with an appetite. One glance at the menu may convince you that another run may be necessary before lunch, together with a quick check on your wallet or your credit cards.

The menu here is typical of the South West of France, where gourmands and gourmets combine to meet the challenge of the substantial local cuisine. Start, perhaps, with the foie gras de ma façon, possibly accompanied by the vintage sauterne that is sold by the glass. If a simple foie gras is not enough, there are ten further variations on this indulgent theme.

The menu continues with scant regard for diet, cholesterol or any other contemporary concern. Cassolette de coquilles or cassoulet à la landaise, soupe de moules or the glorieuse de mouton, vie for attention and gastronomic attack. Portion control is not heard of here.

The menu goes on and on. If your heart desires it, Charlie can probably provide it. Even the heavy leather menu cover gives a clue about what is to come. A page of desserts with names such as profiteroles géantes ensures the message sinks in.

As you sit in contemplative mood after your lunch, admire the decor: burnished wood contrasts with meringue white walls and 'objets amusants' surround you. A cacophony of local French, overwhelmed by English voices, fills the room. Someone called Binky is always at a nearby table, his penetrating voice recording his morning triumphs.

You will have chosen your wine from an extensive list that spans the spectrum from modest house wine at 60 francs a pichet, to Bordeaux and Burgundies to brood over.

You are supped and satisfied. Le patron will now deliver his coup de grâce. A small glass appears, a strange unlabelled bottle, and Charlie offers, 'on the house' a shot of local anaesthetic, which elegantly precedes the bill.

Lunch for two is an elastic affair. Hungry you will not be and cheap it will not be. Nor, perhaps, should it, for a good time Charlie will provide.

After lunch, the télécabines are a short stagger across the road and then it is back up into the snow for a slower, post prandial piste. Some leave their skis, perhaps for ever, and take a taxi home. For reservations tel: 79.08.41.33

HAUTES CUISINES

LE BOUC BLANC

❅❅

This cedar built, newly opened chalet restaurant, makes a welcome addition to this part of the Trois Vallées. Good is always good to find. Good, and cheap, is even better. Perhaps, in an effort to create trade, the Bouc Blanc is offering stylish restauration (wonderful word) at almost self-service prices.

There is a large, boarded sun deck peering out down to La Tania and the closely wooded slopes that sweep up to Méribel. Inside, on two floors, there are bright, charming dining rooms with open fires, smelling fragrantly of pine. The lower rooms show the work of local artists whose work is for sale. The head of a magnificent, white-bearded goat, mounted as a trophy on the wall, views the works disapprovingly. Upstairs, the high, gabled ceiling and big windows make the most of the mountain air and scenery.

The menu offers a good list of starters at between 40 and 50 francs. Steaks come at 100 francs, although the house speciality, the tarte savoyarde, a local quiche of tomatoes, eggs, cheese, cream and milk, is only 45 francs. The plat du jour of three courses for 105 francs is excellent value.

The wines are very keenly priced. The house red and white are 45 francs a bottle and there is a sprinkling of wines from other French regions. A champagne, Arragone '92, is, at 220 francs, the cheapest on the mountain.

Although not yet as chic a meeting place as some of its older compeititors, Le Bouc B' will, undoubtedly, carve its place with the "Where shall we meet for lunch?" crowd that epitomises Courchevel.

It is situated half way down the wonderful black Jockeys and the red Bouc Blanc and sits at the top of the relatively new La Tania bubble lift.

CHALET DE PIERRES

❅❅❅❅

Chic by chic with Courchevel 1850, just up on the Verdon Piste, Chalet de Pierres was built six years ago with little regard for cost. This large, barn-like chalet, sits on great stones that exude confidence and continuity. The wide, planked terrace, always clear of snow, has comfortable sun chairs where the smart set sit, trying to remember if they have the right sunglasses on.

Inside, the space has been used lavishly: a cheerful coin du feu beckons, while stuccoed walls soar up to the pine gabled roof. Tapestries and sporting trophies decorate the walls and a great stag, with ten-pointed antlers, has a distinctly superior look. But, for all its chic, the Chalet de Pierres is a welcoming hostellerie. The menu welcomes you in English, German, Italian, Spanish and Japanese - oh, and French, just for that international flavour. As always, when a menu is translated, there are dishes with names that amuse. The filets de harengs have become kippers, the pied de porc à la sauce vinaigrette has become foot pork with French dressing, and the omelette forestière has become a forestry omelette (presumably, made with at least tree eggs).

For all this frippery, the food is excellent. The chef, Marcel Nutin, heads an experienced brigade of six sous chefs and two pâtisserie chefs, and is justifiably proud of their skills.

HAUTES CUISINES

Chic, indeed, cheerful, indeed, but cheap was never mentioned. The starters on the menu leap from the terrine de poisson at 55 francs, to an indulgent foie gras et son verre de sauterne at 190 francs. There are always two plats du jours at 125 francs, or poulet de Bresse, filets of beef and fresh fish at 160 francs. If appetite and patience last out (service can be a little slow in high season), there is an excellent list of desserts, light on the stomach although heavy on the pocket.

The wine list reads like a Sotheby's auction catalogue, with rarities and collectors' items rubbing shoulders with more modest offerings. 1850 francs, coincidental surely, will bring you a Chateau Cheval Blanc 1978, and wonderful it will be. For an almost cheap 70 francs, one gets a Moulin de Lagrezette 1989, a vin de cahors. Even the ordinary is not ordinary here: the Lagrazette is produced by the managing director of Cartier.

Under the caring patronage of Yvette Saxe, the Chalet de Pierres is destined to continue to make its mark in Courchevel, bringing an unaccustomed elegance to the ski-booted, bobble hat brigade, who daily rub shoulders with the moon-booted, fur coat brigade.

LE SOUCOUPE

❄❄❄

There is something rather South of France about Soucoupe. Perhaps it is the broad terrace, or the panoramic bow window, or the interior filled with green vines, cacti and other exotic plants. But, then, there is much of the mountain here, too: a big log fire, for example, surrounded by three-legged stools that are better to look at than sit on. Fortunately, there are equally rustic, but more comfortable, rush-seated chairs surrounding thick-topped, wooden tables with legs of silver birch that seem to be growing still.

This confusion of identity does nothing to diminish the eternal popularity of what is the oldest restaurant on the mountain. Started in 1950 as no more than a shack with a tall, iron smoke stack, it was claimed by its then owner, M. Bonvet, to be where self-service was invented. While one may have an opinion about bringing self-service to a world of ever-diminishing values (remember when some smiling person last filled your petrol tank for you), one has nothing but thanks to him for bringing Soucoupe to the mountain.

Although still a self-service, its noisy kitchens bring a home made feel with a sense of personality, usually lacking in the land of the stainless steel rail.

There are good plats du jour, a steaming home made soup, only 27 francs, good main courses like rôti de veau or boeuf bourguignon, and if you like sausage and chips, this is the place.

The wines are excellent value and are a reminder that we do not yet get the best out of the Common Market. The cuvée du restaurant is 36 francs a litre and the Fiole du patron is 38 francs a litre.

The prices here are claimed to be the cheapest in the resort and the evidence suggests that this is true. The current owners, Mlle Brunet and Mlle Fejoz, say they have customers who have returned every year since 1950. This is not surprising, for they have turned this 'first' self-service into a first class value-for-money lunch on the mountain.

HAUTES CUISINES

LE VERDON

❄❄❄

Like its next door neighbour, the Arc en Ciel, Le Verdon is done no favours by being squeezed in between the aircraft hangar architecture of the Verdon bubbles, the Saulire cable car and the Vizelles cabins. It is the cross roads of Courchevel and, like most cross roads, is a busy meeting place.

It is rather more charming on the inside than one expects. There is a long wooden, oval bar where vin chaud flows. Posters, Dutch Delft tile plaques, skins, bells, swords, copper pots and plates line the walls. For 30 years M. Bochot has been greeting and providing eating - a smile for the first and a practised hand for the second. His speciality is potée, a conglomeration of bacon, ham, garlic sausage, smoked cabbage and more sausage, cooked together with fresh vegetables and served steaming hot. And at 50 francs, it makes a great lunch. His steaks come thick and fast and, unless you mention it, they come very rare. At 50 to 60 francs, they come very reasonably, too.

The cuvée maison is 36 francs a bottle and a quick glass of red at the bar is ten francs.

The lingua franca here is English, and M. Bochot proudly claims that he serves 100 English for every three French. Perhaps all the French are outside working on their tans in the sunloungers provided.

HAUTES CUISINES

COURMAYEUR
1230m. - Top Station 3450m.
ITALY

Courmayeur hangs on the Italian side of Mont Blanc at the end of the Aosta Valley, and is reached by road from France through the Mont Blanc Tunnel. Sounding more French than Italian, it is very much in Italy when you try the pasta; for, although the French are undoubtedly good cooks, there can be no argument with the fact that the Italians know their pastas.

Popular with Italians and French, it is also a favourite of the British. The heart of the village is a maze of mediaeval cobbled streets and alleyways concealing small, hideaway restaurants and bars. The main street has a variety of shops selling everything from homemade pasta to the latest fashions from Milan; it has typical Italian cafés and bars and smart restaurants, too. It is a stylish and charming village, a pleasure to stroll around during the day or at après ski time. Cars are kept to a minimum. It is one of the most attractive Italian resorts.

The skiing allows beginners and intermediates to feel comfortable in a small, but picturesque, resort. For those who have progressed to challenges, there is the 12 kilometre of off piste run from the top of the four-stage cable car at Cresta d'Arp, 2755 metres, to Dolonne; alternatively, you can take the Helbronner Gondola from Entrèves, which links with Chamonix and the famous and testing 20 kilometres of the Vallée Blanche. A bus will return you to Courmayeur. There are also good cross-country and touring facilities.

At night time there are discotheques for the young, and more sedate entertainment in the hotels and restaurants.

The nearest international airport is Geneva.

RISTORANTE LA GROLLA
VAL VENY

❄❄❄❄

For most of us, skiing down the 'competitzione' would be an end in itself. This long, black, unpisted, steep, bumpy ride through the forest is something that the strong-limbed, lithe and light-weight slide down easily and the rest of us get down eventually. In a storm, any port is welcome, particularly when the storm is inside your ski suit and the steam is appearing through the zip. But any port is not what awaits you. La Grolla is a pine-built oasis that, once you have cleared your goggles, will beckon you to enter. It is low of ceiling, walled in pine, full of clocks and photographs, features old farm implements, worn wooden tables and big, old cast-iron radiators. Take off your jacket, loosen your boots and spend an hour or two.

Upstairs, in the restaurant proper, the walls are lined with interest: glass cases containing old pocket watches and skiing trophies. A stuffed marmot smiles at the local history. Iron-legged men with granite faces that have built this place as a climbing Mecca, stare down as you sit elegantly in this smart mountain restaurant.

The dynasty that has created La Grolla is the famiglia Truchet and the current incumbent is Ephrem. His brother carries on the valley's other great tradition: he is a mountain guide.

When you have soaked up the interest and the history, you may find time for the menu, and time it will need. Many restaurants at valley

HAUTES CUISINES

level, in town centres and beside markets, do not offer the variety of La Grolla, which is abundant with rissottos, raviolis, pastas, polentas, consommés, crêpes, carpaccio and coppettas; and those are just the starters. The list of secondi piatti is too extensive to do justice here, but it is Italian rather than just local.

The prices reflect the quality, although they should not break any bank. The average for starters is about 10000 lire, and main courses range from 15000 to 20000 lire. The wines are from 12000 lire to 20000 lire. Some afficionados lunch here every day, but, for the more modest, at least once on a trip to Courmayeur.

The less intrepid may find their way here down the gentle blue run, Corisa Dzeleuna, or the red Gigante run down from the top of the Peindeint chair.

A sunny terrace with valley views completes the enjoyment. Try not to miss it.

RIFUGIO MAISON VIELLE

❄❄❄

Although most mountain architecture is similar, as though the wind tunnel of necessity has guided the builder's trowel, every region seems to create its own traditions, its own stamp of individuality.

The Maison Vielle is a good example of individuality. Outside the defiant granite promises protection, a random assembly of shapes and sizes offers intrigue and inside black beams and white walls offer cosy comfort. A big enamel stove provides the warmth, both wood and peat burning. It creates a cocktail of aromas.

Giaccomo came here from Florence nine years ago and brought an extra ingredient to the traditional Val d' Aostana hospitality: a Tuscan's love of cooking. Here the spaghetti is homemade and comes with every sauce your stomach desires: carbonara, alla matriciana, al pesto, bolognese, vongole. Pizzas perfecti! Despite the problems of getting the dough to rise at this altitude, Giaccomo promises that his chef has the magic to make it rise as high as the kitchen ceiling will allow.

The only written menu available is in Japanese, otherwise Giaccomo will explain to you in French, English or Italian what is good today. Steaks, stinco, spaghetti, pizza, his natural charm could make a vegetarian order a veal cutlet. The twinkle in his eye is reflected in the mood, the music and the memories you will take away with you. Ten thousand lire will fill you with spaghetti washed down with a quarter litre of robust red wine, while 15 000 lire will bring the stinco con polenta (a succulent knuckle of pork with mashed maize). Whatever you choose, you will not leave hungry.

Outside, the sunchairs stare up at the Aiguille Noir, and 3000 lire can rent you an afternoon of dreams. But be warned, start a conversation with il patronne and lunch will turn into dinner.

Find the Maison Vielle at the top of the chair lift that bears its name.

RIFUGIO MONTE BIANCO

❄❄

Rifugios are, as the name suggests, refuges on the mountain, tradition-

57

HAUTES CUISINES

ally for climbers, but these days also for skiers. The Cai Uget has its roots amongst the boots of the climbing fraternity and the walls of its monastic refectory are covered with historic photographs of the intrepid conquering gravity.

There is an air of quiet reassurance about the regularly arranged long tables with their gingham check table cloths and the discreet politeness of the service. Perched on a ledge between the Zerotta and Peindeint chairs, it is easily found and approached.

The menu has grown to meet the appetites of those who earn them on the mountains: there are ten different polenta dishes, pasta dishes, local cured and cooked sausages and minestrone brimming with vegetables, and cheeses to finish. The prices are average for the mountain with minestrone at 5000 lire and the piping hot polenta with sausages for 9000 lire. The wine list is surprisingly long with local Val d' Aosta wines at 5500 lire per litre and for a celebratory 20000 lire there is a rounded Barolo from 1982.

An occasional virtuoso performance on an accoustic guitar raises the temperature and lowers the chatter.

Outside, a pleasant terrace has more long tables and a view up the mountains and down the valley.

RISTORANTE ZEROTTA

❊❊❊

Sitting at the bottom of the Zerotta chair, amongst the pines of Val Veny, is the Ristorante Zerotta. Built in the 1960s, but in the traditional style, Zerotta offers a good morning pit stop or an equally agreeable lunch time.

The bar and dining room are divided by a huge, red ceramic stove with a built-in black ceramic seat. On cold days it is covered with hats, gloves, scarves and people, and is almost worth a visit on its own. They keep a good, traditional kitchen, and the sign outside which promises 'cucina tipica' does not lie. Antipasti, soups, polenta, and pasta, are followed by grills, roasts and their very good carbonata al vino bianco, or the locally caught trout.

Olivier has owned and run Zerotta for four years, and his mother for 20 years before him. Continuity does not always mean quality, but when it does, the partnership between a satisfied customer and a satisfied restaurateur is surely sublime.

HAUTES CUISINES

CRANS MONTANA
1500m. - Top Station 3000m.
SWITZERLAND

So it went with Buda and Pest and then it hit Crans and Montana: urban sprawl makes single units of them all. Like Budapest, Crans Montana boasts a beautiful setting, but substitutes the valley of the Rhône for that of the Danube. Unlike Budapest, which has some wonderful architecture, Crans Montana's setting and views distract attention from a rather less than lovely town.

There are three main ski areas, Les Violettes-Plaine Morte, offering high slopes and some good off piste opportunities; Aminona-Potit Bonvin, which is a short journey away from Montana; and the Cry d' Err-Bella Lui. Between them they off a large ski area and a wide variety of skiing. The sunny setting of the resort can, however, in these milder seasons, create problems of poor snow conditions.

Smart shops, active night life and good hotels add up to a formula which many people find hard to resist.

Fly into Geneva and take the road for two hours or train to Sierre. For the British, it is one of the easier resorts to reach.

MERBE

❄❄❄

The Merbe is open in the evenings as well as at lunch time and, when there is enough snow, anyone sufficiently skilled or sufficiently foolhardy to wield a burning length of wood along with, or even instead of, their poles, may take part in a torch light descent from the restaurant to the village. If for you discretion is the better part of valour, or you incline to the notion that a torch light descent can only be properly appreciated as a whole and from a distance, then you may additionally comfort yourself with the observation that the Merbe is the sort of establishment which no sensible person hurries to leave.

A restaurant typique, all logs and red shutters, darkly wooded interior and broad sunny terrace, the Merbe can accommodate 150 people on its two floors, although our inspector commented that the upstairs can become smoky and make one feel isolated from the buzz of action below. The menu is as typique as its context: fondues, tortellini, croûte aux quatre champignons and lots of tarts. The quality is excellent and the wines mostly Dôles and Fendants. Prices are comparable with other mountain restaurants in the area.

The Merbe has been owned for the last 12 years by M. Spenger and he and his staff are quick and friendly about their business, although, quite properly, a special welcome is extended to local and regular customers.

The views from the south-facing terrace take in Crans Montana below and the Matterhorn and Mont Blanc far away and above.

The Merbe lies on a path off the Cry d' Err to Grand Signal piste by the middle station of the Crans-Cry d' Err bubbles. It is an easy blue run and the spot is accessible for walkers, too. Given all these attractions it can become very crowded so booking in high season is recommended. Tel:41.22.92.

HAUTES CUISINES

RESTAURANT PLUMACHIT
❄❄

Mme. Yvonne Rose Masserey owns the Plumachit where she commands the kitchen to great effect. The restaurant was built by the family in 1958 and has steadily moved with the times, electricity being installed in the late 1980s. A simple, unpretentious place, it enjoys what an inspector, no stranger to mountains, called the best views she had ever seen. The Rose Masserey family chose their site well.

So customers might enjoy this natural advantage, the restaurant was designed with big windows, making the interior bright and attractive. Only 60 of them can be fitted inside, but on bright days the drift is to the terrace where twice that number can be seated.

The menu provides all the Swiss specialities and to a very high standard. Soups, steaks and sausages, omelettes and lasagne sit alongside raclettes, croûtes, assiette valaisanne and viande séchée. The big open fire is used in the evenings for the preparation of raclette. Prices are comparable with the Merbe (qv).

Local wines, Dôle, Fendant and Johannisberg abound on the wine list and Tuborg, Heineken and Cardinal feature in the beers. The Plumachit is on an easy red run and cross country track below the Plumachit chair lift. But be warned, the drag lift from the restaurant back up to the chair is claimed to be the slowest in Europe.

HAUTES CUISINES

DAVOS
1560m. - Top station 2850m.
SWITZERLAND

With ninety runs providing 180 miles of skiing catering for beginners, intermediates and enthusiastic experts, Davos has been described as the Magic Mountain of skiing. There are five main ski areas, unfortunately linked by bus rather than lift and piste, but each of them offers considerable variety.

The town itself offers little in the way of Alpine charm, but compensates with a variety of distractions: a cinema with English films, swimming pools, ice skating, squash courts, a toboggan run, curling, bowling, a riding school and even sleigh rides. There are many restaurants offering a multinational range from pizza to Peking duck, and a bountiful selection of bars, many with live music and dancing.

Accommodation varies from the grand hotel (there are over 100 hotels in all), to chalets and apartments to suit all tastes and pockets.

The mountain lifts are excellent although one or two of them have more antique charm than efficiency, notably the Strelabahn, which connects the top of Schatzalpbahn with Strelagrat. A car could make all the difference to really enjoying the variety of skiing and ski areas, for although there are ski buses they are not as regular as one would wish. Davos, of course, connects with Klosters (qv) and even all the way down the valley to Kublis, which provides one of the longest runs in the Alps, some 14 kilometres.

The nearest airport is Zürich and the transfer time is approximately two hours.

CHALET GUEGGEL

There is a travelling troubadour sitting at the bar, with John Lennon dark glasses, black hat and floor-length raincoat; he looks like an early Dylan and sounds like he enjoys himself. He is Irish, his name is Peter Purcell, and he strolls from hut to hut, from mountain to mountain and resort to resort, playing, chatting, drinking and hustling along in a tough old world. He has been doing it since 1982 and the whole of Europe is his bar stool.

The bar he is sitting at is log-lined to match the hut beside it, and the stools are covered in sheepskin. At the other side of the terrace, another 'world's largest frying pan' dispenses Mah Meh, a Tai dish of noodles, chicken, vegetables, soy sauce and something that sets fire to your tonsils on the way down.

The Wadtländer Risotto Wurst brings a new dimension to good rissoto. This one comes with that parmesan flavour, stretching strings between plate and mouth, with leeks cooked in a cream sauce lining the middle, and thick slices of mountain sausage to crown it. Both the Mah Meh and the risotto are about 14 Swiss francs.

The young team who run this place will be different next season because only one of the partners will be staying on. It is leased from the owner. When the sun shines, they do well. When it is cold and snowing, the tiny interior hardly offers enough space to pay the electricity bill. The formula that has been created is youthful and attractive, like the Jatzhütte next door, so try it.

Ski down from Jacobshorn; it is at the bottom of the Verbindungsbahn. Smart walkers, who do not like

HAUTES CUISINES

walking, take the cable up to Jacobshorn and the little Verb cable down to the terrace.

GASTHAUS ALPENROSE
DAVOS-PISCHA

❋❋❋❋

The Pischa ski area is up a quiet valley on the way from Davos to the Flüelapass. There is the big cable car and three drag lifts. None of the runs is very demanding, although there is the black Hofji run which comes down to quite a nice self-service hut at the bottom, but our favourite restaurant here is the Gasthaus Alpenrose. You can ski down to it on the Unterer Talli black run and either find a seat inside on a cold day (make sure you get close to the big, brown ceramic stove) or on a sunny day stay out on the terrace.

This is a real travellers' refuge, built of stone with yellow stuccoed walls and local decorations surrounding the windows as was the fashion in this part of the world 150 years ago, and still is today. The menu offers good variety at markedly good prices. A kleiner pot au feu for nine Swiss francs makes a pleasant change from soup and the house fondue at 19 francs per person is hard for even the hardiest appetites to consume entirely; but do try, after all the croûte at the bottom is the best bit.

The wine list gives Burgundy, Bordeaux and Tuscany a chance and has one or two choice vintages. To ski to the door, the Unterer Talli takes a twisting route through the trees, not everyone's cup of skiing, but sitting as it does on the road 100 metre or so from the cable car, access is not a problem.

GASTHAUS ZUM
DAVOS-TSCHUGGEN

❋❋❋❋

If you think the blue mountains are the preserve of Virginia, then early on a sunny morning take the Pischa cable up to the top and set out on the marked, but unpisted and uncontrolled, run down to Tschuggen. The run provides all that most skiers would ask. Even third week skiers could manage it with a guide. At the end of a morning of slow skiing and looking at the blue of the mountains change from bright to white, you will arrive at Tschuggen. Loosen your boots, for this could be a lingering lunch.

A Gasthaus has occupied this spot since 1748, and every hundred years or so they rebuild it to the same design. Inside, low panelled, wooden ceilings immediately set the mood and a few 'grüss Gotts' later you have to decide whether to eat in the restaurant or the little fondue Stübli, where the smell of the cheese has penetrated the wooden walls to provide a hypnotic atmosphere.

HAUTES CUISINES

The menu is, as you would expect, mountain food for mountain travellers. Dried this, cured that, here a cheese, there a cheese and everywhere a spag bog, but all the hot dishes are homemade and cooked to order. There is even a children's menu. Should lunch run into tea and day into evening, there is a very good menu for dinner with an excellent wine list; and should evening run into night, you can stay here in great comfort for as little as 45 Swiss francs a night.

If you do not want a great ski to get here, take a taxi up this hidden valley and enjoy it just the same. There is a little church opposite that adds a distinct toy town feel to this hidden hamlet. Tel:081.46.14.82.

JATZHÜTTE
❃❃

If you are mentally between the ages of 18 and 35, like funky music, outdoor eating from outdoor kitchens, and are prepared to squeeze between a Graubünden beauty and her ski instructor beau, then this is the place for you. Anyone who has been in the army or even to a boy scout camp, will recognise the kitchen equipment, except that is, for the world's largest frying pans which play a major supporting role in this daily carnival in the snow.

One pan has the kind of rösti you could make if you started with a field of potatoes and the other contains enough macaroni for it to rival the trans-Siberian pipeline should anyone ever join it end-to-end. There are huge würsts, serious sausages and charcoal-grilled chickens.

Another stall offers good portions of raclette for six Swiss francs a plate. Wash it down with the Mexican beer.

There are big comfortable lounging beds in the VIP corner, where the young and lithe display the sort of courage normally reserved for the beach in Majorca. This does not represent elegance in any form, but if you have ever seen any of those American frat house movies, then this is your chance to star in one.

Ski or snow board down here from the top of the Jacobshorn cable car. You can even walk it, but remember the walk back is uphill.

SCHATZALP RESTAURANT
❃❃❃❃

It is now safe for the English to return to this delightful restaurant. The Swiss have entirely forgiven, although it is suspected they have not entirely forgotten, the occasion some years ago when an English company (which must remain nameless) rented this larch-logged hostelry for a celebration dinner at the end of their conference.

A more delightful place would be hard to find. Evening light brings the mountains into sharp relief, with views across the valley to the wooded slopes of the Jacobshorn. It is a time for cocktails on the intimate terrace, the smell of pine rising and the lights of Davos below twinkling to the sound of a piano tinkling.

Dinner on this infamous occasion was well chosen from the wide ranging menu, with choices of hot and cold starters, fish, homemade pasta, steaks and cutlets. The wine was from the Valais, where more grape varieties are grown than in any comparable area in the world. Dinner proceeded well. The staff, as always, were polite, smiling and

HAUTES CUISINES

efficient. The pianist contrived to fix a smile as he played popular melodies - well popular with some, that is. How it happened, no one is quite sure. Who exactly was responsible is a well kept secret, but the assembled diners needed no further encouragement, no additional signal. As the first piece of strudel hit the pianist on that part of his head long deserted by hair, the whole room took up the cudgels and the strudel, and in minutes had redecorated this fine, white-walled room, two waitresses and the now-fleeing pianist.

Dinner, including cocktails and wine, came to about 50 Swiss francs a head. With damages, reparation and medical expenses for the pianist, it rose to about 500 francs a head. Still relatively good value by some standards.

After a lunch or dinner here, it is possible to return to the village on the sledge run. Many people, skiers and non-skiers both, take the ageing Schatzalpbahn up from the village, lunch or dine, and slide gently down again.

Children, of course, love it and there is a Kinderteller featuring those all-time favourites, the Max and Moritz, the Pinnochio, the Onkel Dagobert, and the Fix and the Foxi, which, it seems, is a plate of pommes frites with cowboy sauce. How could any child resist?

This restaurant has stood on this spot since 1894. It was rebuilt in 1974 and redecorated in 1981. Long may it continue.

SKIHAUS ALTE SCHWENDI
❋❋❋

If you want to feel how it was on the mountains before skiers skied and sledgers slid, when the sound of the wood choppers axe and the moo of the milk cow were the only intrusions, then step inside this living museum. Nothing has changed here in a century. Beautiful antique lamps, lit by oil, light the dim and cosy interior. The wooden floor leans this way and that, and the tables and benches follow suit. Old muskets and flintlocks hang ready on the walls - passing deer watch out.

Outside, sun seekers sit and shade seekers take a table under the eaves of the old barn. Peep inside the barn and you find another living museum, with sides of Bündnerfleisch hanging from the rafters amidst a confusion of old farm implements.

After absorbing this little time capsule, order from the short but adequate menu. Try the Käseschnitte mit Ei for 13 Swiss francs or the Bratwurst mit Rösti for the same price. The hut belongs to A. Wehrli-Flutsch, that is to say the A.W.F., and his apparent contempt for the new is the best protection for the old; long may he continue.

Conversation with the staff here will not only test your Swiss-Deutsch but also your knowledge of local dialects. In this seriously Swiss hut, bring the jokes with you. The hut is just below the Conterser Schwendi on the Klosters/Kublis run, and the choice can be a difficult one. So, today the Alte and tomorrow is another day.

RESTAURANT SPINA
❋❋

If it ain't broke, don't fix it and if it still works, don't throw it away. For all we know that is what the sign in the loo said, for it is certainly the motto of this famous lean-to on the

HAUTES CUISINES

red run, number four, down from the Rinerhorn to Glaris. It is hard to decide whether the farmhouse leans on the cow-filled barn, or vice versa. Probably there is a Swiss compromise involved and one props up the other. That is certainly the case with the menu.

Everything on offer is made or cured on the premises. The stable to table concept has never been more simply refined than here. There are cold meats and cheese and two hot soups, the Bündner Gerstensuppe and, of course, a good Gulaschsuppe. Bündner, by the way means from Graubünden, the region that encompasses Davos; so Bündnerfleisch is the meat from Graubünden.

What you get may be limited, but it is as good of its kind as you will find anywhere. The wine list comes on a piece of cornflake packet, two inches by six inches, and is carefully written in blue ball point. In the little Stübli there is a white ceramic stove big enough to drive the QEII, a juke box of indeterminate age and a cash register that still works on denarii with the head of Caesar on one side.

The farming family that owns and runs this restaurant live here. Their kitchen is also the restaurant kitchen and the whole place has the honesty and simplicity that any farmer would want and his farm can deliver.

RESTAURANT STRELA ALP

❊❊❊

If next Christmas the postman brings you a large package marked Swiss Chalet Kit, This Way Up, and, upon opening the box, fingers all atremble. you accidentally tear the instructions, do not worry. Catch the next flight to Zürich. Drive to Davos, take the old two-man bubble up to Strelapass and ski down the easy run to the Strela Alp Restaurant. This is the model upon which your kit has been based.

Leave your skis, walk past the sun-seekers lying comatose on comfortable loungers, walk up the stairs past lunchers on the terrace seated on those folding chairs that remind you of an English garden party, open the old pine door into the stübli, sit down and explain your problem. No problem. Have lunch and, while you eat, the helpful staff will write you out another set of instructions.

Lunch comes from a splendid menu with something for everyone. There are five different röstis (they are justifiably proud of their rösti; the potatoes are boiled the evening before and left out on the roof to cool so the next morning they can be grated and cooked fresh to order), seven different fondues, many local specialities and snacks that most would call a meal.

The prices, also, will please, starting at only nine Swiss francs for a simple rösti with daily specials at 14 francs. All the food is home-made and this is a real home: the family Guler-Heller has lived here since 1934.

After lunch, try a bowl of the Alplikafi im Beckeli mit Rahm. The Beckeli is the bowl and the Alplikafi is a heady potion.

As you leave, if you forget your instructions, do not worry; you will probably come back. Walkers get here easily by taking the Schatzalpbahn up and strolling across.

HAUTES CUISINES

RESTAURANT STRELLAPASS
❄❄

Ben Cartwright and Hoss are bound to be sitting on the terrace, because this is the Ponderosa on snow. The Strellapass is a long, low wood-built cabin with a rail outside for tethering your skis. You can sit at the long tables on the long terrace and toss sugar cubes to them. Inside, long benches covered in Indian blankets surround the band, who emit strains of country music from an assembly of instruments any antique shop would be proud of.

As you sit and sup your bowl of chilli, you are distracted by a pair of duelling Alpen horns, which hang from the ceiling, together with Mary Poppin's umbrella and a four year old dried ham to keep them company.

Had you chosen the delight of lying stretched out in the sun beside the partner of your choice, you would have elected sunny corner. It is at the far end of the terrace and partitioned off from the self-service lunch crowd. There are double sun beds with swivel tables upon which to rest your drink from the ice bar, or perhaps your choice from the barbeque - grilled salmon, chops, steaks and a selection of salads. These enticing, blanket-covered palliasses are five Swiss francs an hour or 20 francs for the day.

On Thursday evenings here they produce the world's largest frying pan, one metre in diameter, and cook up a form of fondue and creamed macaroni, a must for everyone who has not had their full ration of cream cheese that week.

The place offers good value, good views and good byes to those starting the easy long run back down to Davos. Walk up to the top of the mound above the restaurant and look down at the view of Arosa nestling below.

WEISSFLUHGIPFEL
❄❄

Take an hour and count the peaks. Try to believe that there is another world out there, somewhere beyond the rank upon rank of snowcapped mountains standing to attention before you. Every Alpine view is amazing, fantastic, awe inspiring and breathtaking, and this one is just the same. Well, maybe this one has an edge, but you will need to come here to experience it.

The Weissfluhgipfel restaurant sits on this site with the confidence of a Swiss bank. Although pleasant inside, a touch like an English provincial tearoom, its real virtues are the terraces which cling to its sides, projecting over the descending snow fields which surround them. There is even a large conservatory, which protects the viewers of views on windy days.

The menu offers fair fare, and a variety of victuals not commonly found one and a half miles above sea level. There is a special vegetarian menu as well as every type of Schwein and Fleisch. There is even an Aerobicteller, which may sound like a dancing bank clerk, but is actually a Swiss way of marketing chicken salad. And für die Kinder, we once again meet the Donald Duck, the Mickey Mouse and the Alf (who is Alf?).

The prices are average in this much above average place.

The wines start at around 25 Swiss francs for a bottle of white Italian and a Dôle is about 18 francs for half a litre. Intriguing is the Château Madame, a light red wine, or is it a

HAUTES CUISINES

red light wine, from Bordeaux. Answers on a postcard, please.
Back to the terrace and the view. After a while it has a mesmeric affect upon you and in order to break this spell, or enhance it, we recommend a café from the Spezialitäten list; perhaps a Schümli Pflümli, which apart from having more umlauts than a Dalmatian has spots, contains substances made from fruits, topped with coffee and covered with cream. Lick it and you will know how the cat felt. Drink it all and you will forget.

The restaurant is at the top of the Weissfluhgipfel cable car and as easy for walkers as climbing into bed.

HAUTES CUISINES

LES DIABLERETS
1200m. - Top Station 3000m.
SWITZERLAND

Les Diablerets is one of the prettiest and least spoilt villages to be found in the Alps, characterised by elaborately carved chalets, elegantly painted and lovingly cared for. Despite its vast lift system, which now connects with nearby Villars, Les Diablerets manages to remain small, quiet and friendly. Although not reachable on skis, Gstaad encompasses the resort in its super ski pass for the area.

Night life is limited, much of it taking place in the hotels rather than in the noisy discos of some of its neighbours, encouraging an early start for the slopes which, because of their height, offer reliable snow conditions.

The nearest international airport is Geneva with a transfer time of about one and a half hours.

AUBERGE DE LA POSTE
❆❆

There is something gently reassuring about the Auberge de la Poste, rather like a comforting elderly relative, all old fashioned elegance, baubles and charm. Indeed, the Auberge is the prettiest building in a pretty village with green shutters, gilded wrought iron sign and gaily painted window boxes. But twee it is not. Dating from 1789, it wears its trimmings with quiet self confidence. Set in the centre of the village, the road passes outside, it provides a stark contrast to the concrete block-house-cafetaria style of the restaurants attached to the lift stations on the glacier.

While the trip from the top of Les Diablerets may be too time consuming for lunch, as a place for a pre-ski breakfast or a post-ski supper, the Auberge, run for the last five years by Mme Crecq-Pichard, has no equal.

Inside, the restaurant seats between 50 and 60 people with a further 20 to 30 catered for in a separate bar area. Seating is available outside and an open car park area opposite provides an unobstructed view of the moutains. The décor of the ground floor restaurant is plain and simple, the chief decoration being provided by rows of cow bells, something of a Les Diablerets motif.

The restaurant's specialities are fondues, ranging in price from 13 to 20 francs. A three course plat du jour provides good value at 18.50 francs.

The service, on the occasion of an inspection, was adequate rather than enthusiastic. The only note of criticism, captious rather than substantial, was the absence of a lock on the door of the gent's loo. A tightly wedged foot was needed against intruders.

HOTEL DE L' OURS
VERS L' EGLISE
❆❆

Memento mori! A situation next to a grave yard is, it could be argued,

HAUTES CUISINES

not the most advantageous location for a restaurant for skiers, especially those of a nervous disposition, but the paucity of provision of decent food on the pistes coupled with the undeniable charms of a pretty building in a village of pretty houses tend to overcome any piffling objections visitors may have. Besides, one can always eat inside.

Hotel de l' Ours is easily found at the bottom of lift 22 at Vers l' Eglise, making it handy for walkers if a trifle tricky for skiers who can discover their attractive approach through trees turning icy when the weather turns warmer. A charming wooden building, it is old, if not quite as old as the Auberge de la Poste (qv), dating from 1833 and for the past 30 years it has been owned by the Isoz-Ducret family.

There is a comfortable dining room with seats for around 40 and another room as well. The food is always cooked to order, so no hastily rushed meals are possible, and there is a good dish of the day (or a half dish for smaller appetites) together with a selection of omelettes, croûtes and salads. Prices are lower than those you would pay for inferior products on the mountain.

Summed up by an inspector as being wholesome and good value, the Hotel de l' Ours, although requiring a diversion from the piste, does represent, by way of compensation, the chance to get away from crowds and to enjoy a relaxed lunch in a very good restaurant at prices that will encourage you to ignore the graves.

HAUTES CUISINES

FLAINE
1600m. - Top Station 2480m.
FRANCE

Like Topsy, it has growed. Originally opened in 1969, sitting in a large bowl in the middle of the Grand Massif, it has very effectively linked with its neighbours of Les Carroz and Morillon and Samoëns to provide a breathtaking variety of skiing, nearly 200 miles of it in all.

Skill in reading a piste map and judgment of time and distance are necessary to ensure both maximum enjoyment and minimum chance of being cut off in one of the satellite villages when the lift system closes for the night (a taxi ride adds nothing to the day except further expense).

Flaine has no pretentions to Alpine charm, but its value for money efficiency ensures it a place in the hearts of those who return year after year.

The après ski includes a golf practice area, good skating, swimming, a gymnasium; unusually there is a library with English books, and even a 'drive on ice' school, which provides thrills for the participants and smiles for the spectators. There are the usual discos and a fair selection of bars.

The nearest airport is Geneva and the transfer time is about two hours. The linked resort of Samoëns is listed as 88th in the list of French Historic Monuments, a unique classification for a ski resort. Samoëns is a true Savoyarde village but not a convenient place for skiers to stay.

Les Carroz, on the other hand, is fast developing as a traditional Alpine resort and offers much of the charm that is lacking in Flaine and is increasingly popular with British skiers.

The village of Morillon is slowly emerging from its agricultural heritage and has a natural appeal although limited accommodation and most develoment here is taking place at Morillon Grand Massif which seems to be repeating some of the architectural mistakes of Flaine.

HOTEL RESTAURANT AU RENDEZ-VOUS DES SKIEURS
❋❋❋

Those for whom reading a piste map is as easy as reciting last year's Wisden backwards, will arrive here on purpose. Those who find the piste map for this vast area as comprehensible as the wiring diagram for a nuclear submarine, will arrive by accident. Samöens is one of the smaller resorts which make up the Grand Massif area and is generally populated by the French.

Au Rendez-vous des Skieurs is an unprepossessing building on the piste at the bottom of the Chariande red run beside a wooden, chalet-style self-service restaurant called La Chariande. The dining room is approached by way of an outside staircase and then one passes through what the French call a solarium, a sort of conservatory with bronze glass all round (ugh).

When you come in and sit down, it has that distinctive atmosphere of a French provincial hotel, but then that is exactly what it is. Bus timetables, sports posters and the tarif des boissons line the walls and a large television provides excitement and disappointment when the ski racing is on. The oil cloth covered tables and the refectory-like setting do not suggest 'le grande bouffe', but instead, le grand value, a promise satisfyingly fulfilled.

HAUTES CUISINES

The menu du jour is 52 francs and offers a hearty main course, such as blanquette de veau with rice, a salad and fruit or ice cream. For 70 francs you can start with a quiche lorraine and have a plateau de fromage before your dessert.

People who stay here ski back for lunch, no surprise there. Pisteurs and ski instructors make up the friendly clientèle, who hang on the bar for an aperitif before lunch and, maybe, a digestif afterwards. The wine list, too, offers excellent value, with a Provence Costiere de Gard at 36 francs a bottle and a very palatable St Emilion at 90 francs.

The à la carte menu offers steaks, grills and an excellent, locally caught trout, cooked en papillotte with thyme and locally cured ham (delicious). At 48 francs it reminds one what good value France can be.

The Rendez-vous has been here since 1933, the first restaurant on the mountain, and the affable M. Molland, the grandson of the founder, carries on today.

So brush up on your wiring diagrams or take a guide, but make the effort. It is well worthwhile.

LE BLANCHOT

❆❆❆

The open white bowl that is Flaine is a natural setting for pine log cabins with great, stone fireplaces and sunny, open verandas.

High above the village, smiling down on the tree-clad slopes that give the post-modernist architecture of Flaine its human touch, sits Le Blanchot, the White Hare, and inside, in a glass case above the bar, sits a white hare. He gives the impression that he does not entirely welcome the brightly coloured poeple who have invaded his domain but the staff at Le Blanchot make up for it, by being busy, chatty, smiling and enthusiastic. Madame Ambroise has a young team working for her in this her fourteenth season.

The menu favours the carnivore, with beef steak, faux filet, entrecôte, escalope, côte d'agneau and confit de canard. Even the starters, with the exception of the onion soup and the tomato salads, are local charcuterie. It makes a change from the often cheese based diet of many savoyarde mountain huts.

Normally, there is a plat du jour and normally it is under 60 francs and normally it makes a change from steak, steak or steak. The food at Le Blanchot meets that midday need and pretends nothing more.

A litre of local wine is 50 francs, starters are in the 20 to 40 franc range and main courses run between 60 and 90 francs. A good lunch will cost about 100 francs a head with wine, taxes, service and smiles tout compris.

Find Le Blanchot by skiing down from Le Grand Platières on the gentle Serpentine blue run. It is on the piste just beside the Plate chair lift.

A reminder that not everything is on tap is a notice saying that due to water shortage the loos are for customers only.

HAUTES CUISINES

LA CASCADE

❆❆

The chalet La Cascade restaurant is on the way back to Flaine Forum below the start of the Grand Balacha Téléskis on the Azurite piste. This is the run behind the back of the téléphérique station. The Cascade is tucked away on the left and most people ski past it which is why you can always get a seat in the sun on the huge terrace or by the wood fire.

The food is very good - with lots of variety, a good cheese board and a wide range of desserts. You serve yourself but this is no canteen. You don't have to queue for long, there is a drinking fountain where you can collect a fresh carafe d'eau. There is even a microwave in case you get carried away with the sun bathing and let your lunch get cold.

It is a good place to stop on the way home for a vin chaud, but be warned, you will be sorely tempted by the tarte aux myrtilles on the bar. This large modern wooden chalet has the best loos on the mountain - but for patrons only.

LE CHALET DE MICHET

❆❆❆❆

Take one large, old stable, sweep out thoroughly, clean down the ancient stone walls, polish the huge wooden beams, tile the floor and you have the beginnings of an idea. Now decorate it with old savoyarde dressers, rustic tables and chairs, put an old, long case clock in one corner (but do not wind it up; time means nothing here), and, in the centre of the room, set a large circular fireplace, surmounted by a great copper chimney that rises through the roof. Now the idea has become a place to go, a refuge on the mountain.

In this case, the mountain is minutes from the village, and whilst the energetic take the giant bubbles to the summit to work up an appetite skiing down, the more relaxed stroll gently from the late 20th century to the considerably more charming 19th.

On a cold day, one can sit inside in a room laid out for conviviality and enjoy the 'menu' for 89 francs. Start with a salade variée, followed by a main dish that changes daily, always good, always substantial, and finish with the home made pâtisserie, or a plate of local cheeses. On a sunny day, sit outside on the terrace, choose a starter from the buffet, salads, crudités or a bowl of taboulet, then choose what you want from the charcoal grill. Steaks, brochettes, or local, spicy or plain, sausages.

Michet also provides a carte rapide skieur, which applies to the pace one wants to take lunch rather than the speed one skis.

The prices are excellent value and compare favourably with some of the many self-service restaurants which dot the area.

The wine list is varied. A litre pichet of the local Gamay is 78 francs, as is the light and easily drunk Crepy blanc.

In the evenings, M. Wilcker and Mdme Descombes, who have run and owned Michet for the last seven years, produce a special menu of local dishes such as tartiflette, raclette, fondues and pierrade, as well as a well balanced à la carte list. A children's menu (steak hachée or escalope de volaille, frites followed by ice cream and a bill for 55 francs) is available lunchtimes and evenings.

Reservations are recommended. Tel:50.90.80.08.

HAUTES CUISINES

CHALET DES MOLLIETS
LES CARROZ

❄❄❄

The weathered timbers that support the frontage of this foresters' hut have a random feel about them, as if they, like the trees around them, have grown rather than been carefully placed. Inside, the random factor is at work again: no architect's slide rule or builder's level has had any part in the construction of this gem on the mountain.

Four years ago, Patrick and his two partners, Gerald and Philippe, transformed this chalet alpage into one of the cosiest of mountain restaurants.

Whether you have skied down the breath taking black, Corbalanche, or the picturesque blue, Marmotte, you will feel the need for a small reward. Take off your skis, loosen your boots, and walk into the dark interior. Blink, as your eyes accustom themselves to the light, and, as you walk past the table at the door, count, one, two, three. . . six . . . eight . . . eleven, yes eleven different, delicious, home made tarts, together with a huge, freshly made Black Forest gâteau, and a bowl of îles flottantes, so light that they may indeed float away.

Philippe is the chef, and, as a man from Beaujolais would, he takes great pride in his cooking. Everything they serve, they have cooked, and all they cook comes from les recipes de Beaujolais.

Like the place itself, the lunch menu is small, simple but satisfying: a range of salads from 20 francs, a main course of jambon frites for 35 francs, and excellent T-bone steaks for 85 francs. There is not much more, but then, of course, there are the desserts. Should it be the tarte noisette? or the banane? the cannelle, the poire, the marron, chocolat or even the griotte? If indecision is a failing, then do not visit the Chalet, although at 20 francs a portion, the self indulgent could well have more than one.

Perhaps, afterwards, purely for digestive purposes, one might take a glass of local Genepy or a marc de Savoie. The wine list boasts a number of vins de Beaujolais (en directe de la propriété, of course), and the local wines, a Gamay or white Chignin, start at 65 francs.

The really lazy can get there by car, and it is very popular in the evenings, when dinner is from a larger menu and lighting is from a candle. For those who prefer to eat with their sunglasses on, there is a large terrace.

L'IGLOO
MORILLON

❄❄

Almost hidden by the tall pines that crowd the slopes of Morillon, this recently rebuilt chalet breasts a ridge that overlooks the wide open pistes below.

The chalet was rebuilt because in 1990 it was struck by lightning and burnt down. Jean-Luc, the patron, promises that lightning will not strike twice. It will, of course, take time for the fresh yellow pine to mellow to the colour that gives these chalets their cosy charm, but in the meantime, Jean-Luc carries on where lightning left off.

He offers a daily plat du jour for about 60 francs and a variety of salads at around 35 francs. The soupe du jour at 25 francs is both warming and filling, as are the crusty baguette sandwiches at 20 francs. The wine list, although not

HAUTES CUISINES

long, produces a litre of robust red for 40 francs. Jean-Luc's prices are very reasonable in comparison to many, and, given time, the Igloo will once again grow into a chalet ancien. He will cook savoyarde specialities, but 'phone him if you want something complicated.

You will find him at the top of the Vielle chair lift up from Morillon, or you can ski down Le Sairon from La Vielle. Tel: 50.90.14.31.

LES SERVAGES
LES CARROZ

❄❄❄❄

At the bottom of the bouncy red Timalets run down from La Kedeuze, just above the télécabine station in Les Carroz, sits a small, welcoming chalet alpage. Les Servages is savoyarde style at its best. Outside, its toy town appearance does not lie: inside, it is small, friendly, and really quite chic, with a low, wood beamed ceiling, locally quarried stone walls, and a big, wood-filled fireplace.

Lunch here is not for hurrying, and, indeed, the portions discourage anything other than contemplative enjoyment.

Savoyarde outside, savoyarde specialities inside. The menu extends from the simple, but delicious, fondues or raclettes, to the more complicated Pela des Aravis, a compilation of sautéed onions and potatoes, covered in local Reblochon cheese, cooked slowly and served with jambon cru and a salade. If that sounds as though it lacks serious gastronomic weight, then a more doughty contender is the farcement de Marnaz, a slightly sweet, potato cake made with plums, raisins, bacon, eggs and flour, which is cooked in a bain marie for about four hours and served with a dish of charcuterie and green salad. Honest. Several other specialities adorn this excellent menu, with prices ranging from 80 to 100 francs.

The diet conscious will order the salade Servages, or the salade montagnarde, both of which are combinations of the best, fresh produce arranged in quantity on the largest dish they can find. Steaks, lamb and duck make up the rest of the menu.

The dessert list is short, but added to daily with home made tarts and the best meringue you can find.

A comprehensive wine list, sprinkled with a few wallet stripping specials, seems quite appropriate.

If serious lunch is on your list, be assured. Les Servages is as serious as they come. But even if you just want a cup of tea, a glass of cold beer, or a hot choclate hidden behind a cumulus of cream, it will look after you just as well. The delightful Arnelle Linglin will offer you the same, elegant greeting and hope you will come back. The odds are in her favour.

Walkers have no need to worry. Being at village level, Les Servages is easily reached.

HAUTES CUISINES

LES GETS
1170m. - Top Station 1850m.
FRANCE

The most southerly of the resorts of the Portes du Soleil, Les Gets is about 6kms from Morzine and in general a rather more charming village made up of chalet style buildings.

The skiing is extensive and some of it greatly challenging. Many of the runs are through the trees and extremely picturesque. The snow record is quite good and the sunshine record is excellent.

Most accommodation is in one of the 20 hotels although there are chalet apartments as well.

Les Gets is famous for its Mechanical Music Museum, worth a visit on a bad day. There are cinemas, ice skating and even a tourist train.

There is a good variety of restaurants and bars and there are three discos

Linked resorts are Morzine (qv), Nyon, Avoriaz (qv). (Portes du Soleil)

Les Gets is about one hour's drive from Geneva.

CHEZ NANNON
NYON

❋❋❋

Built by Pravecis' great grandfather, this 150 year old savoyarde chalet looks both hors de service and hors de combat, your first instinct is not to lean on it. But once inside the smouldering smell from the wood stove concentrated by the low ceiling and the smallness of the room immediately tells you otherwise.

People make the short pilgrimage here mainly for the "pommes de terre au Reblochon". This mountain dish is a fricassee of potatoes covered in Reblochon and served with a big dish of local charcuterie, and a crisp green salad. It takes longer to eat than it does to cook and thats a while.

All cooking is done on a wood fire and the necessary interior electric lighting is supplied by a petrol generator in a shed at the back. There are standby oil lamps for the occasions when the petrol runs out or the staff forget to run out to refill it.

The small team in this time-warp kitchen share the responsibilities well. Francois Baud makes the speciality and the crêpes, Michael Precevis makes the plat du jour and the fluffy omelettes. The soup is always hot and filling and served always with the local cheese of "Abondance" and a basket of farmhouse bread all for 25 francs. The speciality is 85 francs but still manages to be good value at this price.

A stuffed Chamois trophy hangs on the back wall and lace fringes with coffee pot decorations hang over the small windows.

Local ski instructors, pisteurs and the lift attendants are regularly to be found sitting in a corner testing the quality of the vin chaud or the local marc.

The mountains are full of secrets and surprises and Chez Nannon is the best of both.

As with the electricity, water is at a premium and the sign on the loos often suggests they are out of order. The water comes from a source which they hope to enlarge, but meanwhile ask nicely and the loos are yours, but don't tell everyone.

Chez Nannon can be found by taking the Trones chair up from Le Grande Pre or the Raverettes drag from the top of the Nyon Telepherique.

HAUTES CUISINES

LA CHANTERELLE
COL DE L'ANCRENAZ
LA CÔTE D'ABROZ

❄❄

Hidden on a tree-laden slope at the bottom of the red Marmottes run and the black Chevreuil (both from the summit of Mont Chery) and, sensibly, just above the bottom of the Chery Nord chair lift, is La Chanterelle. Small and pine built, it has seating inside for 28, all of whom sit close to the open log fire in front of which lies Loulette, a Bruneaux de Jura hunting dog as friendly as his owners.

The menu offers home cooked food at homely prices. Naturally, the omelette aux chanterelles, locally picked, is a speciality at 36 francs, as is the tartiflette, an oft found savoyarde favourite at 56 francs for one, but only 72 francs for two if ordered beforehand. Steaks, sausages and crêpes make up the rest of the menu. There are also good sandwiches for the hurried or desserts of sweet crêpes for the idle. Whatever you choose, disappointment is unlikely.

The wine list starts at 34 francs for a litre of red or white house wine, or what they call a quart de blanc for 16 francs (sorry, this is not two pints but a quarter of a litre).

A prettily situated terrace doubles the capacity on a fine day and the English are welcomed with open arms. The red run is very easy, so even those who normally restrict themselves to blue will not be troubled.

To order your tartiflette for two, call 50.79.03.57.

LA CROIX BLANCHE
LES CHAVANNES

❄❄

La Croix Blanche is the oldest establishment in this skiers' hamlet having sat here for 47 years, although only for the last six under the care of M. and Mme. Christian Anthonioz. The pleasantly weathered exterior has, in recent years, been extended, but while it retains the same style, the new pine looks somewhat out of context. Time will solve this problem. Meanwhile, the extension provides a 'quick' restaurant and bar in addition to the rather grander restaurant which is open for lunch from midday. So, whether you want to be served with a good sandwich of ham, sausage or cheese for a reasonable 16 francs, or a magret de canard sauce poivre for 92 francs, you are in the right place.

As with other good restaurants at Les Chavannes, its access by road and good views of the pistes ensure its popularity with all generations both skiing and non-skiing.

One can stay here very comfortably for from as little as 240 francs full board. For a quieter holiday, on or off skis, this could be the solution. Tel: 50.75.80.66.

LE GRAND CRY
LES CHAVANNES

❄❄❄

Amidst the tall pines of Les Chavannes sits Le Grand Cry. Upon

HAUTES CUISINES

entering you are immediately aware of a jungle of potted vines, succulents and rare house plants, all in perfect condition, obviously cared for.

The same care is happily extended to the customers who sit at rustic tables, hand-painted in the local style. The kitchen is under the command of M. Patrick who, although welcoming the British, is not overwhelmed by their lunching habits. He provides a wide and interesting menu with some dishes using the locally collected morilles and chanterelles. However, he says that the British eat the soupe à l'oignon, 28 francs, the croûte au fromage (a large portion for 57 francs) or saucisse de Strasbourg avec frites, 33 francs, but ignore the locally caught trout, the sole cooked in sorrels and frequently leave without trying the wonderful homemade tarte tatin, a richly caramelised, upside-down apple pie.

When the sun shines the large terrace outside is packed with the sun and sandwich seekers alike. Those who care more for taste than their waist, plough through the dessert menu with over 20 different coupes de glaces and 20 different crêpes.

Although the richer dishes on the menu are of richer prices, there is something for every taste and every pocket. Park your skis, sled or car outside.

LE GRIFFON
LES CHAVANNES

❄❄

Les Chavannes is a clutch of houses situated at the top of the Chavannes bubbles 300 metres above Les Gets. It is the departure point for three drag lifts and a chair lift and also the arrival point for hungry skiers at lunchtime. There are four restaurants here and the one that warmed our hearts, and whose open log fire warmed our limbs, is Le Griffon.

A relatively modern but traditional savoyarde building, it has limited atmosphere but it offers a reasonable menu at prices starting at 30 francs for an omelette, rising to 76 francs for a decent-sized entrecôte swathed in Roquefort sauce. The plat du jour is usually about 50 francs and will not leave one feeling hungry.

There is a children's menu of main course and dessert for 47 francs.

Wines start with the cuvée du patron at only 35 francs or 42 francs for a Côtes du Rhône.

There is a nice terrace for sunny days, but for early in the season, arrive early, get the table by the fire, loosen your boots and enjoy the home cooking and warm smile of Annie Bergoend.

In most weather the restaurant can be reached by road and is, therefore, popular with families with non-skiing members. The restaurant seats about 60 people with nearly the same number again on the terrace.

LE SOLEREY
MONT CHÉRY

❄❄❄

In savoyarde patois, Le Solerey means a place on which the sun shines and for those on a diet of vitamin D the top of Mont Chéry provides exactly that. The view is superb, too, as the ranks of mountains march off into the distance. On a clear day Mont Blanc can be seen, along with her little sisters,

HAUTES CUISINES

the Aiguille du Midi, the Aiguille d'Argentière and the Aiguille Verte.

If vitamins are not your thing, then in the basement below the restaurant is the Musée de Ski. If ever one needed a reminder that skiing today is safer, easier and more enjoyable than 30 years ago (let alone before the First World War when some of the skis and bindings on display were made), then wander around here. Ninety years of skiing crowd this museum in miniature.

When you have exhausted the view, the museum and enjoyed leaning against a bar by the big open fire, take a rustic chair at a rustic table and peruse the menu. Lots of choice and the word 'homemade' appears frequently. Three course prix fixe starts at 76 francs.

Whether you gave the time and the appetite to opt for a savoyarde speciality like vacherin chaud, a combination of Swiss cheese, boiled potatoes and smoked ham, or the brasserade garnie, the pierrade garnie, a raclette or a fondue; or plump instead for a simple salad, omelette, pasta, trout, steak or good old lamb chops, you will not be disappointed.

Elizabeth and Guy Anthonioz have been here for fourteen years and, as has been remarked before in these pages, the quality and care of a family-run establishment is hard to beat.

One night seven years ago, the whole roof of their restaurant home blew away, to be found a day later in the valley. Dismayed, but undeterred, they rebuilt the restaurant and continue to welcome the skier, the sun spotters, the tired and the hungry.

Their prices are reasonable, starting at 35 francs for a hearty, traditional mountain soup, and the wines start at a very reasonable 39 francs for a bottle of Cep de Vigneron. They also serve a good Normandy cider, dry or sweet.

If you are in a hurry to get there, take the Mont Chéry bubble followed by the Super Chéry drag lift, which arrives at the door. If you prefer a little ski before lunch, take the Pointe de Chéry chair and ski down. On one visit the mist hung low and visibility was down to 20 feet. As the party arrived Elizabeth said: "Ah, les Anglais. When the weather is bad it is always the English who venture out." Mad dogs or intrepid skier, Elizabeth welcomes them all.

HAUTES CUISINES

GRINDELWALD
1050m. - Top Station 2490m.
SWITZERLAND

One of Grindelwald's many attractions are its 180 kilometres of prepared ski runs covering every degree of difficulty. It lies in the heart of the Bernese Oberland and is linked with Wengen. As every Swiss school child will tell you, the Bernese Oberland is home to that magnificent group of mountains the Eiger, Mönch and Jungfrau, with their beautiful shapes, gigantic mass, immense rock faces and the splendour of the glaciers. This is Heidi country, a traditional Swiss resort with farmers doubling as ski instructors in the winter when their cows are biding time, waiting for the snows to melt. It has been known for people to return home with half a kilo of cheese in their pockets after skiing with an instructor for a week.

The journey by train to Grindelwald is a bonus to your holiday, as you pass blue lakes, picturesque villages and, always in view, the snow-covered mountains.

There are three points from the village from which you can ascend the mountains: a six-man gondola on the First side of the valley; a four-man gondola to Männlichen; or by train to Kleine Scheidegg. The train will also take tourists to the furthermost point, the Jungfrau Joch, which is 3454 metres high, travelling via a tunnel hewn through the notorious north face of the Eiger to the high Alpine wonder world of the Aletsch Glacier. The station here is the highest in Europe and the views are breathtaking.

Grindelwald offers excellent heliskiing on the Ebnefluh and the Petersgrat, as well as good off piste skiing.

For non-skiers Grindelwald offers a wide range of other sporting and leisure activities. There is one discotheque called The Spider, but dancing also takes place at many of the bars and hotels, with music played by small groups. For many the centre of chic is Herbie's bar in the wonderful Hotel Regina.

BAHNHOF BUFFETT

❄❄❄

Somerset Maugham is credited with the remark: "If you want to eat well in England, eat breakfast three times a day". Well, if you want to eat well in Switzerland, then station buffets are always a safe bet. After all, a country that takes its profusion of railways so seriously, would naturally take its stations seriously too.

The Bahnhof at Scheidegg is really a miniature Crewe, with trains arriving from three directions and leaving the same way. There are tracks to the left and tracks to the right, and those wonderfully serious station staff with kepis reminiscent of Beau Geste on snow. Ski pistes also arrive and depart from this cosmopolitan cross roads, with the same profusion as the trains, but without the same, rigid timetable.

Inside the station, the buffet has a nostalgic air: the romantics among you will fill your notrils with the sense and scent of travelling that modern modes of transport are rapidly eroding. The hungry will fill their nostrils with the smell of Röstizzas cooking. Röst what?

The menu proudly proclaims that there are 27000 restaurants in Switzerland, and this is the only one where one can enjoy a Röstizza, a combination of Rösti and Pizza, which, so they say, is

HAUTES CUISINES

low in calories and fat, and rich in vitamins. Well, that as may be, but there are four to choose from, the vegetarian Fiorentina, with tomatoes, spinach, onions, marjoram and mozzarella; the campagnola with vegetables, oregano, mozzarella and beef; the bellavista introduces turkey and garlic, and the casalinga hached beef, tomatoes, mozzarella and marjoram.

If these new culinary delights fail to raise your interest, the menu goes onto a wide choice of tasty, but less individual, dishes, and every day there are four or five new dishes. The prices range from four Swiss francs for the soups, 13 to 16.50 francs for the Röstizzas, pastas for around 15 francs and a hearty rumpsteak for 20 francs.

There is a reasonable selection of wines and the prices, like those of the menu, are, if anything, below average for the mountain.

Although owned by the railway, the restaurant is run by Sylvia and Horst Schärer, and, as always, that family feeling shows.

Finding it is no problem; finding your way away will depend on how many 'coffees' followed your lunch.

RESTAURANT BORT
FIRST

❄❄❄

Before being replaced last season, the old chair lift that sidled up the mountain from the village to First was one of the great experiences. The canvas-covered chairs had given 40 years of service, as had the vast, blanket-lined coats that engulfed you on the 25 minute ascent, slipping in and out of way stations like a fairground ghost train. The new bubbles are faster and warmer, but, just like their predecessors, they let you on and off at Bort.

This traditional, old mountain hut has been serving skiers and walkers for generation upon generation. Whether sunny or snowing, Bort is always full. The true afficionados claim that here is the best rösti in the valley and certainly it is excellent. Brought to the table straight from the pan, it sits like a loaf of soda bread turned golden by the heat, a nob of butter on top slowly melting as you decide who gets which bit. Some choose it to accompany the Bratwurst, some a steak, some a pork chop, and some just take it on its own.

Outside, the early birds get the seats that back onto the hut and bask in the Alpine sunshine, looking across to the silent Alpine horns, the Schreckhorn, the Wetterhorn, the Grossfischerhorn and the perfect triangle of the high Finsteraarhorn.

The ski down to here is on a black run from Egg. When the snow is good, it is not much more than a winding red, but if it is icy, take care or take the bubble. The same applies to the scenic run back to the village.

EIGERGLETCHER RESTAURANT

❄❄

If one thinks of Switzerland as a giant train set, then the trains of the Jungfrau region are, without doubt, the most exciting. The green and yellow trains of the WAB link Interlaken with Mürren, Wengen and Grindelwald, and the peak of their achievement is Kleine Scheidegg at 2061 metres. From

HAUTES CUISINES

here the Jungfraubahn takes over, and for the real heightseers, it will take you up to the Jungfraujoch station, which, at 3454 metres, is the highest station in Europe.

Here one can take lunch in the restaurant, visit the extraordinary ice cave and stare down at the spilt milk of the Aletsch Glacier as it flows away for nearly 20 kilometres. The railway, a remarkable feat of engineering, was opened in 1912 and picks its route right through the north face of the Eiger, with two stations actually inside the mountain. The first is the Eigerwand, and a window allows views that would otherwise only be available to a climber half-way up this treacherous route. The second stop is at Eismeer, at 3160 metres, where another window opens across the glacier.

The first stop, however, is at Eigergletscher, and it is here that most skiers detrain to take either the famous Blackrock run down to Falboden, or the more gentle Punchball down to Salzegg. Before attempting either, most take some refreshment in the station restaurant and look out across the glacier which gives this place its name.

The restaurant has stylised murals of the region adorning its walls, and has long been a favourite lunch stop for skiers. The menu offers all the regional specialities and excellent house rösti. The wines list has usually more than just Swiss wines and the special coffees are just what one needs before the black run down Blackrock. Lunch, including wine, should be less than 30 Swiss francs a head.

In 1992, the family that were running it left, and a manager was installed by the railway. Some respondents were less than flattering about this, so let us hope it was just a settling down period.

On a sunny day, the terrace is in great demand as those not inclined to ski down, settle down to absorb the vista and the vitamin D.

HOTEL RESTAURANT WETTERHORN

❊❊

One of the nicest and prettiest runs in this valley is the Stepfi run. It takes skiers all the way from the top of the Schilt drag, around the valley, underneath the Grosse Scheidegg and down into the forest, following a gentle, undulating and winding path. It ends at the foot of the Wetterhorn in front of the restaurant, which looks up to its namesake and across to the wonderful Oberen Gletscher.

This ever-moving eruption of glacial ice has brought people to Grindelwald to sightsee, walk, climb and paint for nearly two hundred years. Even Turner came here as part of his grand tour. For all that time a hostelry has stood on or near the spot now occupied by the Wetterhorn Hotel, and it has served the painter, walker, climber and now skier with good local food and wine, and delivered it with a local smile.

People ski here for lunch to indulge in the excellent fondue, although the menu offers all the regional dishes, both hot and cold. When it is cold or snowing, the stübli inside offers comfort and warmth, and regulars seem to find regular tables.

Opposite the hotel stands an ancient cable car, which in the years before the first world war, carried parties of people up the Wetterhorn so they might more easily walk across to the Gletscher. It took four years to build this, the world's first working

HAUTES CUISINES

cable car, and it opened on 27 July 1908, carrying a group of notables the 450 metres up to the Enge station, which a keen eye can still pick out. The advent of world war one brought a decline in the fortunes of the cable car company and, like grandfather's clock, it stopped short, never to go again, in 1915.

So by now you will have had a wonderful ski, surrounded by magnificent peaks, had an excellent lunch, admired one of the great sights of Europe, the Oberen Gletscher, and had a history lesson. If all this has been too much then the ski bus will collect you from the door, but if not, another interesting ski back to the village awaits you.

HAUTES CUISINES

GSTAAD
**1010m. - Top Station 1970m.
SWITZERLAND**

Old, established, stylish and discreet, Gstaad is better known for its residents than for its skiing or indeed for the length of its season, which, due to its low altitude, can end earlier than some of its neighbours.

Popular with non-skiers who like to play the 'who's that in the sun glasses' game as they sit around in the restaurants or stroll up and down the main street, Gstaad boasts some of the smartest window shopping in Switzerland. The accommodation is mainly in chalet style hotels or in chalets or apartments.

Night life is, as one would expect, amongst the choicest in Europe with jeans cheek by cheek with dinner suits.

The skiing is saved by good connections with other resorts with six other stations included in the Super Gstaad Ski Region pass.

The nearest international airport is Geneva. Transfer time is two hours by road - private helicopters are quicker.

CHEMI STÜBLI

❅❅

Anyone familiar with a British road map will remember how to find the Chemi Stübli: straight up the A1 and you have arrived. Alternatively, it is to be found at the bottom of the A2 Lengebrand-Gandlonene drag with which the A1 Sesselbahn Reid-Lengebrand connects.

This geographical distinction apart, it is to be noted for "the best hausgemacht Wurst with Rösti in the area" according to one regular Gstaad visitor. The Wurst is served with a delicious onion sauce and can be followed by a wide choice of desserts. An exceptionally potent house coffee will reduce the incautious to a state of agreeable somnolence.

The restaurant enjoys beautiful rustic surroundings and is consequently extremely popular. Booking is recommended, but you have in the process to gamble a little with the weather: you must specify whether you wish to sit inside or out.

HAUTES CUISINES

LES HOUCHES
1000m. - Top Station 1970m.
FRANCE

A satellite village in the Chamonix region, Les Houches lies below the main ski area off the road to Geneva. Once a farming village, it has become over run with chalets and hotels. Although it is relatively low, its snow record is good and there is some attractive skiing through the trees. The scenery is quite spectacular and more than makes up for the lack of charm in the village.

There are two main cables up from the village, one up to Bellevue and the other up to Prairion where there are excellent runs down to St. Gervais (qv).

Wherever you are the views are dominated by the magnificence of Mont Blanc, an inspiration for those who choose to ski down the famous Piste Verte race course. There is also some excellent off-piste powder skiing and down in the valley there are good cross country trails.

A bus connects Les Houches with Chamonix, but taking a car is an advantage in such a large ski area.

Nearest airport is Geneva, which is less than two hours away.

LA CHALETTE

❄❄

If ever there was a little hut on the prairie, this is its mountain cousin. On top of the Bellevue, it looks the kind of hut one might find in a large garden. Wooden-built, and giving the impression that it is used to store the garden tools and the lawn-mower. Well, no tools here. Inside, La Chalette has little more than half a dozen tables and, although half the hut is a kitchen, it has a short and simple menu.

The soupe du jour at 28 francs is wholesome and warming. The plateau de charcuterie at 50 francs allows you to help yourself to a variety of local mountain sausage. There are omelettes natures, fromage or jambon, and to finish you may want to try the assiette de fromage. If cheese and ham are not on your diet, there is a salade d'endive or a salade de tomates.

As for wine, they have both kinds, red and white. It comes in a pichet and half a litre costs 25 francs. The local red comes naturally chilled and is friendly and fruity (much like the local white).

For all its limitations, La Chalette is a good, friendly, cosy and genuine mountain refuge: mountain food for mountain people and mountains all around.

HOTEL RESTAURANT LE PRARION

❄❄❄

If a room with a view is your desire the Le Prarion is the place for you. Situated at the cross roads of the pistes above Les Houches, Le Prarion is a restaurant, a hotel, a cafe and, in poor weather, a welcoming refuge. A log-fed fire dominates the pine-clad dining room and the large windows let the magnificent views join you at your table. The whole place has a family-run feel to it under the direction of Yves Hottegindre, the son of one of the founders.

In the restaurant proper, there is always an interesting choice of menus offering both local and classic French cuisine. The prices range from 80 francs for the fondue savo-

HAUTES CUISINES

yarde, to 170 francs for a full seven (yes, seven) course menu. The food and the portions have a traditional French quality which ensures satisfaction for both gourmet and gourmand. The wine list offers a selection of interesting fine clarets and burgundies from 1978, as well as younger, reasonably priced local wines. There is a perfectly drinkable red house wine for only 48 francs a bottle.

Non-skiers will love it here. A one minute walk from the Prarion bubbles, the restaurant is an excellent example of what value can still be found in France.

If you want to be first on the piste in the morning, you can stay the night for as little as 80 francs in the dormitory, or half-board in a room with bath for 305 francs (this includes a ski pass). Opened in 1928 by Gabriel and Julie Orset, 60 years of practice makes almost perfect.

HAUTES CUISINES

IGLS
890m. - Top Station 2250m.
AUSTRIA

One of the satellite resorts that surround Innsbruck, Igls was the venue for the 1964 Winter Olympics. It is a popular, attractive village and is still relatively unspoilt and is consequently a quiet and peaceful spot that has not yet succumbed to the throb of the discotheque.

The bob run is popular and something of a challenge, particularly among the Italians many of whom favour the resort. The skiing revolves around the famous down hill course where Franz Klammer first carved his fame. The nearby resort of Axamer-Lizum, which has all the charm of a National Car Park, does extend the skiing greatly as well as extending the skiing season.

Fly to Igls via Munich or Innsbruck.

GASTHAUS HEILIGWASSER

❄❄❄

The Holy Water Guest House, to give the translated form, enjoys the benisons of an adjacent church (hence the name), a pretty view up the valley to Arlberg and the arboreous comfort, so reassuring to those not born on a mountain, of a surrounding, snow-dusted forest. The church was built in 1665 to commemorate the appearance of the Virgin Mary to a party of local children. A statuette marks the precise spot and, in the summer when the snows melt, holy water seeps from the rock on which She stands. It is not for any guide writer to quibble over matters of such moment. It can only be observed that She chose a beautiful place.

Like many blessings the Gasthaus has to be sought quite carefully. As you ski down the Famillien piste, watch for the church spire through the trees. You will then see the sign for the Gasthaus. A gentle walk uphill, quite possible with skis on, will take you along the 100 metre path to the restaurant from which a large Alsatian, all bark no bite, will rush to greet you. Walkers reach the restaurant by taking the lift to the middle station and then strolling for 15 minutes through the snow.

The Gasthaus Heiligwasser has been owned by the Thurnbichler family for 70 years and the present incumbent, Peter, has honed the staff to a fine edge of efficiency. In cold weather a wood fire greets you; in warm weather the large, sunny terrace beckons.

The food is as traditional as the setting, the family ownership and the architecture: roast pork, Wiener Schnitzels and a big range of home-made pastries. It is good solid food, well made and well presented. The usual wines and beers are offered. Prices are average for Austria. Perhaps the best testimony to the quality of the Heiligwasser, which despite its name no longer offers rooms to guests, is the look of contentment and happiness, albeit not quite holy, on the faces of those who call there.

HAUTES CUISINES

ISCHGL
1400m. - Top Station 2870m.
AUSTRIA

Do not bother to set your alarm clocks, as you are woken in the early hours before dawn by the sound of church bells in this wonderfully picturesque, old and charming Tyrolean village.

Located in the Silvretta range, which separates Austria from Switzerland, you can ski to the Swiss duty free area of Samnaun to pick up your duty free bargains. On the way the scenery is spectacular and, as you look back, you can see the village set in a broad, sun-filled bowl and surrounded by towering mountains. There is good skiing both on and off piste mainly suitable for intermediates, with good ski touring for the advanced skiers.

There are nine restaurants on the mountain, five of which are self-service, and three of which are outlined below.

The nearest international airports are Munich or Zürich.

Linked resorts are Samnaun and Galtur.

LA MARMOTTE GOURMANDE
ALP TRIDA

❄❄

One of the joys of skiing in Ischgl is the ability to pop over to Switzerland to pick up the duty free. Alp Trida, just across the frontier from Ischgl, is included in the ski pass and is a delightful area for medium and advanced skiers, quite apart from the delights of cheap booze. Moreover, not only is it warmer on this sun-trap side of the mountain, but there are fewer queues when, finally, you arrive. It is, however, a hike from Ischgl.

There are three restaurants in the Alp Trida area, all run by the same group. By far the best is La Marmotte Gourmande, which, happily, is the first you reach on your journey from Ischgl. It is a large, traditionally styled building with a self-service on the ground floor and a serviced restaurant on the first floor. There is a balcony where lunchers may gently roast over their rösti.

The food is outstanding both in terms of quality and presentation but, despite the Swiss location, prices are reasonable. Starters range from five to eight Swiss francs with main courses ranging from 12 to 25 francs. Dishes encompass the Italian and French as well as the indigenous specialities. The onion soup and good quality rösti are recommended. The wine list is more internationally flavoured than the Swiss norm and, for those celebratory occasions, champagne is available.

The only complaint received concerned the location of the loos in the basement, requiring those on the first floor to walk off their food while searching for a place to powder their noses. Otherwise, this greedy rodent is commended to hungry skiers everywhere.

PANORAMA RESTAURANT

❄❄

In a branch of the restaurant industry that sui generis offers good views, it takes chutzpah to call your establishment the Panorama but, being situated at the top of the Idalp lifts (handy for skiers of all grades

HAUTES CUISINES

and non-skiers to boot), this large, modern building, long on location but short on atmosphere, more than justifies the liberty. Like many restaurants in the area it is schizophrenic, providing both serviced and self-service areas. The upstairs, serviced establishment is not small; downstairs the self-service is vast with seats for 450, meaning that tables can be well spaced and lunchers are spared the sensation, common to many mountain eateries, of eating out of a stranger's lap. The food upstairs is good and the prices are reasonable. Spaghetti is 90 schillings and a steak will cost about 280 schillings. A quarter a litre of wine will set you back 30 schillings. But really, the whole point of the place is the view, so grab a window seat or a spot outside.

PAZNAUNER TAJA

❄❄❄

Situated at the top of the lift up from Bodenalp, the Paznauner Taja is as attractive as it is unprounceable, a difficulty compounded by its listing on the piste map as Paznauner Taya. But Taja is what the owners, the Canal family, call it and they should know. Built as a farmhouse in 1830, converted to a restaurant in 1987, it is, to quote an inspector, a joy to find, warm and cosy, at the end of a hard day's ski. The serviced restaurant is on the upper of the two floors, so one lunches among beams and rafters. If you want to catch the midday sun while avoiding the hoi polloi, there is a tiny balcony on which you may eat, but arrive promptly, it fills up very quickly.

The staff are very friendly and operate efficiently from the circular bar in the centre of the restaurant which seats about 120 people. The self-service is located on the ground floor.

Food is as traditionally Austrian as the architecture with Tiroler Gröstl mit Spiegelei und Kraut Salat at 110 schillings being a particular favourite. House wines are priced at 38 schillings for a quarter litre.

Only one minor gripe: piped music, but otherwise this place is a must even if you only have time for a hot chocolate in the afternoon.

HAUTES CUISINES

KITZBÜHEL
760m. - Top Station 2000m.
AUSTRIA

One of the oldest and most famous of Austrian ski resorts, and certainly one of the most fashionable, Kitzbühel is a beautiful old town with a true Tyrolean atmosphere. Although its altitude is rather low, snow conditions are usually good until the middle of March.

With the excellent lift system extending the skiing into the nearby resort of Kirschberg and the ski safari system bringing in the villages of Jochberg and Pass Thurn, the skiing area extends to 100 miles of downhill pistes. A car would be useful but driving and parking in Kitzbühel brings its own challenge as does the famous downhill course on the Hahnenkamm.

We have not, in this edition, included restaurants at Jochberg. Reports would be appreciated.

As befits an international resort, Kitzbühel boasts a casino to add to its list of après ski distractions, which include swimming pools (included in the lift pass), bowling alleys, curling and ice hockey, squash and indoor tennis. The many bars and restaurants help to round out the perfect offering for a ski and après ski resort and at prices that compare more than favourably with other centres of its standing.

The nearest airports are Munich and Salzburg.

BERGASTHAUS FLECKALM

❋❋❋❋

It was a close run thing: enthusiastic skiers, avid for a spot of lunch, bore down across a marginal, and officially closed, red piste 25 upon Bergasthaus Fleckalm, while a brave taxi driver laboured up a snowy track to deliver famished non-skiers from Klausen. On this occasion, the result was a dead heat. And, as in Alice in Wonderland, there were prizes, seats for lunch, for everyone. Walkers, as opposed to car and taxi riders, are not advised to try Fleckalm: it is a long way up.

The Bergasthaus is quite big, but the dining area is divided into different rooms, all with low ceilings which creates a womb-like intimacy. Piped music intruded.

The menu is long and, in the way of things in Kitzbühel, solidly nourishing: thick soups looked capable of standing up a broom handle rather than a mere spoon. Main courses tend to the regional steak, pork, ham and sausage norm, but fondues at 210 and 230 schillings are offered as well. Mountainous portions challenge the surrounding peaks.

A beautifully flavoured Schweinskotelett came, at 105 schillings, topped with slices of mushroom and a whirl of whipped butter, flavoured with a hint of garlic. There were, beside it on the plate, enough roast potatoes to have averted the Irish famine of 1845. With this dish was served a salad of carrot, beetroot, lettuce and potato. Very few wines were listed. The house red was young, pale and light. Only two or three puddings were offered, but then only the very determined or the terminally hungry would get that far. A popular dish is Kaiserschmarren, which some lunchers made their entire meal: torn-up pancakes, sprinkled with icing sugar and served with apple or plum sauce. It is offered by many restaurants in the resort.

HAUTES CUISINES

A friendly dog nosed around in search of titbits and affection, a pleasant diversion: when the restaurant is crowded, service is just a little slow; but given the comforts of Fleckalm, this is forgivable. On a bad day it is a hole in which any hobbit would be happy to settle.

LANDGASTHOF AND RESTAURANT OBERAIGEN

❋❋

Through the white-out something loomed in the gloom. Was it a cow shed, a group of trees or an optical illusion? No, it was the Landgasthof and Restaurant at Oberaigen and very welcome it was, too. Like the Sonnbergstubel, only 200 metres away (qv), it is reached from the Bichlalm chair with the option of a halfway jump-off or an easy ski down from the top. Non-skiing sybarites can motor up. Rooms can be rented. Tel:0536.2351.

The restaurant describes itself as 'gemütlich' and justifiably so. It is simple and elegant with a large deck edged with wrought iron lamps. Two, smaller, bar areas lead off the main room.

The menu is more modest (in terms of cost as well as gastronomy) than that of its neighbour, with sandwiches offered at prices ranging from 28 to 42 schillings. Two soups were offered at lunchtime, followed by roasts, Wiener Schnitzels and Tiroler Gröstl mit Spiegelei (sausage with fried egg). A children's menu costs between 44 and 88 schillings. The wine list offered four white wines, including an Italian, Soave, and four red, also featuring an Italian, in this case Valpolicella. The presence on a side table of Mouton Cadet and other French wines was suggestive of more lavish standards in the evenings.

The existence of two such establishments as the Oberaigen and the Sonnbergstubel so close together demands a visit from anyone staying in Kitzbühel, even if the skiing in the immediate vicinity is neither very extensive nor demanding.

MELKALM

❋❋❋

The Hahnenkamm cable car leads to a valley of temptations only tenuously connected with skiing. On leaving the station, a gentle trickle down blue 21 to a 'T' bar (suggestive of rum already) leads from the top, via a short ski to the Sonnbühel (qv) and then the Melkalm, past which only the iron-willed will travel without a break.

The Melkalm is an elaborately carved chalet, sporting a pretty balcony and a narrow deck, blessed on sunny days (definitely not needed on the day of the visit) with big overhead blinds. The view is said to be wonderful.

Inside, one passes through a small bar area to a restaurant with tables and chairs, some arranged booth style, for 35 to 40 people. As is common in the area, the restaurant is heated by a big square, green tiled stove, the top of which consists of a large, white, hemispherical mound, dotted with tiles, reminiscent of a giant steamed pudding.

The menu carries a number of dishes of the day including a blessedly light, salmon trout on a bed of creamed leeks, served with parsley potatoes and salad at 180 schillings.

HAUTES CUISINES

There is pasta, on this occasion tortellini with a cheese sauce rather than spaghetti with a meat sauce, and for those who want a lunch that is light on the wallet as well as the stomach, there are cold sandwiches for between 40 and 55 schillings. There is, also, a selection of omelettes and salad.

Frau Polzelbauer is bustling and helpful and the whole establishment is spotless.

At lunchtimes, red and white wines are served by the quarter litre.

THE OCHSALM (OXALM)

❆❆

"Double, double, toil and trouble," muttered the inspector as he forsook the unseasonal witches' brew of snow, cloud and wind outside (it was almost April), to find himself confronted by a giant, copper cauldron in the Ochsalm's entrance hall. Too shiny for a blasted heath, Macbeth would have recognised it for all that.

After so much weather outside, Ochsalm was huge, warm and inviting. Like Gaul, it is divided into three parts: a restaurant, with carpets, to your right, seating about 45 people; a plainer restaurant to the left, closed on the day of the visit, and a large bar area at the back with stone-flagged floor, massive low rafters and places for about 100. In the corner of the bar, two guitars resting against the wall, threatened a sing song.

The efficient and very hard-working staff come kitted out in national costume. On a snowy Saturday morning they were stretched to keep happy the numbers who sensibly preferred drinking and eating to skiing.

On offer was a plat du jour (alright, Tages Karte) of Leberknödelsuppe at 38 schillings, Rollschinken with potatoes and Sauerkraut at 105 schillings. Spaghetti bolognese (is there, anywhere, a mountain restaurant that does not serve it?) and steak sandwich weighed in at 90 and 115 schillings respectively. For vegetarians, a mushroom schnitzel, served with rice and salad is available, useful in an area where specialities run to peppered steak or varieties of pork. Desserts included impressive looking, homemade Sachertorte and apple pie.

A very limited range of wine and beers is offered, although for the extravagant, Moet et Chandon is listed at 1200 schillings. Taking a champagne bath in the cauldron is not advised - it comes expensive. By way of compensation, lots of hot drinks, rum grog, hot chocolate with rum, tea with rum, and many others including traditional Glühwein, are available.

On an easy blue run, piste 26, down from Ehrebachhohe, Ochsalm can also be reached by a narrow road, mostly open in winter, up from Kirchberg, a village which, like Marlow on a clear day, is said to be discernible from the narrow terrace. Rooms are available to overnighters and overindulgers.

SONNBÜHEL

❆❆❆

"It is one of the best restaurants on the mountain," said Kevin about the Sonnbühel. He had been working in Kitzbühel for two months, in catering, and knew a thing or two about restaurants. He chewed his lip reflectively. "It's also one of the most expensive." As subsequent

HAUTES CUISINES

researches established, this is not quite true - read on. But Sonnbühel is a place to be taken seriously, in every sense.

It is easily reached from the Hahnenkamm cable car. Down from there on piste 21, gently blue, to the 'T' bar, straight up and then ski 150 metres to the traditional, wood-tiled restaurant.

On the menu there is the customary range of Austrian soups, including on this occasion, for those who enjoy skiing alone, garlic soup. Handy for keeping trolls away, too. There are cheaper dishes for those who do not want an enormous lunch: little dumplings in onion soup are 65 schillings, or Tirol fried bread with a fried egg insulates against the cold in return for 105 schillings.

Solid succulence is offered in the form of black pudding with sauerkraut on fried bread at 105 schillings, or beef goulash with fennel dumplings for 115.

Peter, the friendly proprietor, has two wine lists. There is the ordinary list, which suffers the Austrian bias of little wine but lots of spirits, and includes what are termed 'specials': mixed drinks that range from 'bellinis', through the odd 'speedy' and 'bullit', up to, and including, the 'holy ghost'. There is, additionally, the special wine list with a total of 13 wines, mostly white, that start off at 240 schillings and reach 310 schillings.

The main dining rooms, there are two, are reached through a small bar that is decorated with dolls, hats, pen-and-ink drawings and the odd stuffed elephant (small). There are bedrooms for between 26 and 30 people. To reserve, call: 053.56.27.76.

SONNBERGSTUBEL

❄❄❄❄

Hock the jewels, wipe the smile off the face of your piggy bank, and hie you to the Sonnbergstubel for a bottle of champagne. The list is for the discriminating, it includes Krug, Louis Roederer Cristall, Taittinger and Veuve Cliquot, and for the economically advantaged: prices top out at 2800 schillings a bottle.

If this creates a certain impression of the restaurant, this is only partly true. Yes, there is an air of, well, glitz. The walls are decorated, discreetly, with signed celebrity photographs and in one corner there hangs a framed Roger Whittaker gold disc. But on the other hand, it is one of the prettiest and most seductive dining rooms to be found anywhere. It is quite small, tables for around 30, with a big open fireplace in the corner; is arranged on two levels, raftered and beamed delightfully and in one corner is supported by a huge, round, plastered pillar. With pink clothed tables and neat flower arrangements, it is a wonderful place in which to while away the hours.

It is open both at lunchtimes and in the evenings and bookings are recommended. Tel: 053.56.46.52.

The menu is quite short, which some find reassuring in a busy restaurant. The house speciality is pheasant breast, larded with bacon, and served with red cabbage and dumplings. A steal at 220 schillings. In addition to the customary sausages and goulash, there is a simple roast chicken with salad for 155 schillings. If you feel tempted by an unusual little savoury, a tasty try-out at 25 schillings, toy with puréed kidney lard on fried bread.

Avoiding a second mortgage on

HAUTES CUISINES

your house, there are slightly more modest wines to choose from than the champagnes. Anyone tempted, nonetheless, by the prospect of bubbles in their vino, will be relieved to learn that the Sonnberg lies below 2000 metres, beyond which height, Berkmann's law, champagne should not be drunk.

The restaurant can be reached by road or on skis. Out of Kitzbühel on the Pass Thurn road, one turns off for Bichlalm and then takes the single chair lift. Halfway up, at Oberaigen, there is a jumping off spot for those who want to get their noses down quickly (the restaurant is 150 metres away); or skiers can carry on to the top and then ski down a blue piste. A resident, and friendly, Alsatian will emerge to greet selected visitors.

HAUTES CUISINES

KLOSTERS
**1130m. - Top Station 2850m.
SWITZERLAND**

The Prince of Wales cable car sums up a great deal of the appeal of this elegant old resort in the Grisons. Some of the varied skiing here is thought to be among the best in the world, with two distinct areas offering everything from beginners' paradise to extremists' excitement. And if that is not enough, the linked resort of Davos redoubles the offering.

There is an exciting toboggan run down from Gotschnaboden, as well as the normal skating and curling rinks, sleigh rides and swimming; and there is nearly 40 kilometres of well prepared and picturesque langlauf tracks.

Accommodation is split between elegant old hotels and comfortable chalets and chalet apartments.

The après-ski offers a good selection of bars, restaurants and night clubs at prices to suit most pockets. Zürich is about a two hour drive or train ride away.

BERG-UND SKIHAUS
SCHIFER

❋❋

Red-smocked waiters and waitresses give a traditional quality to this solidly built Haus. It is owned by the Davos-Parsenn Bahn company and so lacks that family feel, but still remains friendly.

There is a large, sunny terrace outside and little stüblis inside for colder days. A nice fireplace is filled with logs, ready for a change in the weather.

The menu is long and every day there is a changing list of specials. There is always a vegetarian choice, and there seems to be a sausage for every occasion. Röstis run riot. Ursula, an export Swiss who lives and works in Cyprus, praised the Nüsslisalat forêt noire, freshly made with sautéed mushrooms and apple. She has been coming here since childhood, and every year returns for two weeks in Davos to renew her Swissness.

The setting is a pretty one, surrounded by tall old pines and larches and one minute's walk from the bottom of the Schiferbahn.

BLOCKHÜTTE EREZSASS

❋❋

In a hundred years time, this will be the place to come. When the Swiss build new huts, they use old plans and leave the rest to time. This is a large, all-encompassing rest stop. It has a restaurant, a shop, a self-service restaurant, a pleasant outdoor bar, and a feeling of being busy, busy, busy.

The menu is long and comes in Swiss-Deutsch, English and French. Somehow it tastes better in Swiss-Deutsch. Here you will find an alternative to the ubiquitous rösti. It is called Maluns and comes with cheese and apple sauce. "What is it?" we asked the waiter. "Oh, it is like rösti," he replied.

Pizzas proliferate here and one to test the digestion is the Vesuvio. It comes with mozarella, ham, tomatoes, peppers, olives, capers, onions, garlic and herbs. The eruption comes later.

The prices compare with most huts in the area. The Swiss here have a cartel on pricing and most dishes are within a franc or two of the same elsewhere.

You will find this investment in the future at the bottom of the

HAUTES CUISINES

Schiferbahn, but with so many older and more interesting huts around, you could leave it for fifty or more years.

CONTERSER SCHWENDI

❋❋❋

If our inspector had been able to read Gothic script, he would have translated the beautifully painted inscription above the door of this hut of huts. But all he could make out was Skihaus Schwendi 1931, and that is all you need to know. As you ski down through the trees on what an American called "the good old 24", and the rest of us call the Kublis run (18 kilometres of wonderful gliding through a winter wonderland), you will glide to the door.

There is some suggestion that Schwendi is short for Swiss Wendy House and, indeed, if an indulgent Swiss parent wanted to give a spoilt child the perfect little Swiss chalet, a Schwendi would be it. Outside, there is a broad, wood-floored terrace. Inside, there is an unplanned simplicity, a stage set for the smiling Swiss hospitality that Romeo Fleckenstein and his young staff provide.

On a cold day, try to get the table in front of the big, enclosed radiator, and decide on a slow lunch. Start with a light soup, the heavy ones are a meal in themselves, so go for the bouillon and then try the Chäsgetschader (practice your pronunciation first in front of the mirror), which is a step of bread soaked in white wine and covered in cheese and grilled, before being served with a little garnish. It will anchor you in a gale.

Drink a glass or two of red wine (the Hügelwein is very reasonable at 17 Swiss francs a litre) and then think about a Linzertorte with cream. The whole lot will come to about 20 francs, excellent value anywhere, but up so high, wonderful.

Next door, there is a real Wendy Schwendi, where Andrea presides over her ice bar with a rod of smiles and a mountainous personality. After you lunch, snack, drink or rest (strike out whichever is not applicable), continue on your way down to Klosters or all the way to Kublis.

SKI HAUS SCHWENDI

❋❋

Ski Haus Schwendi was built four years ago to replace the smaller and more charming Alte Schwendi which still stands beside this larger, more modern version. These days, the pretty, smiling waitresses who work here live in the old hut. There is a party every night according to Ciska, a blushing blonde beauty.

This is a popular place with the young. Outside, Vroni sits at Vroni's bar dispensing smiles of beer and schnapps. The wide terrace is paved with colourful ski suits, whose occupants find meditating in the sun the perfect way to spend the afternoon, peering through their sunglasses at the

HAUTES CUISINES

intrepid who ski down the corkscrew black run through the woods (number 51). Others come on the gentle path, marked 21. Both run from the top of the Gotschnabahn.

The menu holds few surprises: perm any combination of cheese, meats and potatoes, although there are always two Tagestellers with a touch of imagination. Whatever you have, you will not leave hungry; the portions cover the plates in depth.

The prices start around five Swiss francs for soups and the main courses land in front of you for about 11 francs.

Afterwards, the cafe Lutz will make Luzerners nostalgic and slightly squiffy, and the helter skelter ride back down to Klosters will burn off some of those carbohydrates.

HAUTES CUISINES

LECH AM ARLBERG
1450m. - Top Station 2450m.
AUSTRIA

Thought by many to be the model for the classic Tyrolean resort, Lech revels discreetly in its royal connections, its relatively gentle skiing, offering flattering undulations to those whose investment is in their ski suit rather than their skiing.

The village is delightfully traditional, with even new buildings being constructed in traditional ways with traditional materials. Most accommodation is in hotels and very little of it is to be found on the pages of tour operators.

The resort links up with the nearby villages of Zürs and the hamlets of Zug and Oberlech. The ski circuit this provides offers a varied days skiing with good stopping points for drinks or lunch. The problem is that the circuit can only be done in a clockwise direction so queues can be a problem. Most people come to this area by car, which enables them to enjoy other nearby resorts such as Stuben (qv), St. Christoph (qv) and, of course, St. Anton (qv).

Lech is a sunny, stylish expensive resort, popular with the Germans and Austrians and where, although English is spoken, it rarely comes without an accent.

The nearest airport is Zürich and transfer times are long.

GOLDENER BERG STÜBLI
OBERLECH

❆❆

"Grüss Gott! "Grüss Gott!" The traditional welcome of this part of the Vor Arlberg meets you at every corner of this friendly small restaurant on the hotel inhabited pistes of Oberlech.

The area of Oberlech, like Lech itself, is a relatively modern imitation of an Alpine tradition, but the sincerity of its imitation flatters rather than offends. Indeed, Lech itself has been imitated by some ski resorts in the New World.

The Goldener Berg is a gem of 14th century originality and is, therefore, immensely popular with skier and stroller alike. Here one can lunch fast or at leisure. The menu offers good variety and the sensible arrive early for a table; even then, the conversations you attempt will be shared with your chic by jowl neighbours.

The prices are comparable with the area and generally cheaper than its Swiss equivalents.

PALMENALP
ZUGERBERG

❆❆

One of the problems one encounters in Lech is the old: "Where can I take my minder?" question. You cannot leave him in the car or hotel; equally, they look so untidy standing around outside the smarter restaurants concealing their love for you and their job with a bulge in their ski suits. In this democratic age it is good to be seen talking and occasionally eating with them.

Problem solved. The Palmenalp is a new kind of restaurant on the mountain, full of high style, with linen-covered tables, comfortable seating and convivially-sized, snug corners. The decor is of the traditional mountain variety, with lots of wood, but this time with the occasional imitation palm tree thrown

HAUTES CUISINES

in. Some believe they would be better thrown out.

Outside, a hanging verandah overlooks the valley, the village of Zug, and eyeballs the Madlock, where skiers cross over from Zurs.

Pizza lovers say that the pizzas here are everything a pizza should be: crisp of base and covered in everything that makes a mouth water. There are several different options and they are all 75 schillings. A big plate of meaty and juicy spare ribs comes to 90 schillings. Most of the food is of this snackish variety and most of the prices are very reasonable.

Rows of glasses line one counter and in them are figs and slices of pear. Later these health-giving fruits will be cruelly drowned in vodka or schnapps, and then gleefully gulped.

What makes the Palmenalp a 'new kind of moutain restaurant' is that, with all its luxury and its pretensions, it is in fact self-service. If there have to be self-service restaurants, then this is the model. Palmenalp can be found at the top of the Zugerberg chair up from Zug and high above Lech.

SCHLÖSSLE

❋❋

There is Lech and there is Oberlech and there is a little ober, Oberlech, and it is here you will find Schlössle. Hotel restaurants line the pistes around here and most offer good value lunches, sunny terraces, waitresses in national costume, sun chairs, ice bars and spaghetti bolognese. Enough spaghetti must be consumed daily in the Arlberg and Vor-Arlberg so that if it were laid end to end, it would stretch from somewhere to somewhere else, and possibly that is what should be done with it.

Schlössle is one of a long line of hotel restaurants and we mention it only because it epitomises all the others. A long, all-encompassing menu, starts with the Tagessuppe for 30 schillings, and other starters range up to 80 schillings. Main courses range from 90 schillings for the inevitable spaghetti bolognese, to about 190 schillings. Good food, well presented and beautifully served.

There is a choice of Kinderteller, the Mickey, the Goofy, the Pluto and the Alf (who is Alf?).

Whatever you choose to have as a starter or main course, at least once while you are in the Arlberg have the Germknödel mit, or mit out, Vanillesauce, for dessert. In the land of the Knödel, the Germknödel has a special place: it is the largest of the species Knödel and, indeed, the only one which comes covered in custard (Vanillesauce). If you can imagine a giant, yellow spider with its legs pulled off, then you are getting close to a vision of our hero. What it contains is explained elsewhere, but you will try one or, at worst, you will know someone who has, and it is best to discuss it with them personally.

Meanwhile, Schlössle and its many like-minded Oberlech cousins continue to welcome, feed, water and satisfy the visitor.

HAUTES CUISINES

LENZERHEIDE/ VALBELLA

1500m. - Top Station 2865m.
SWITZERLAND

On either side of the road at opposite ends of the lake, the twin resorts of Lenzerheide and Valbella sit on the route to the Julier pass.

This is an area greatly favoured by the Swiss and in particular by families with children. The skiing is excellent for those up to intermediate standard, but with few challenges for those whose adrenalin needs constant pumping. The lift system is good and allows well planned circuits to criss cross the valley.

The village is very friendly and in the evenings it is relatively quiet with most activity going on in the many hotels.

The nearby hamlet of Parpan has a timeless air and a couple of good inns popular at both lunch time and in the evenings.

The linked resort of Churwalden is a little lower down the valley and has its own ski area, the skiable link is steep and best left to good skiers.

Zürich is the nearest airport and the transfer time is about two hours.

ALP NOVA

❄❄

Sitting at the top of the Pedra Grossa four man chair, the Alp Nova is newly built but using old timber, and the interior has all the feeling of an old mountain hut.

The menu is as extensive as one is likely to find in the mountains but the prices are among the dearest in the valley. There is a short children's menu where the ubiquitous chicken nuggets make their appearance.

Outside, the terrace provides a five star view up and down the valley and across to a veritable brass band led by the Weisshorn and the Rothorn, accompanied by the Lenzerhorn and the smaller Schwarzhorn.

BERGHAUS TGANTIENI

❄❄❄

Whether you go up by the three-man chair, ski down from Piz Scarlottas, or even travel there by road, the Tgantieni is a popular lunch time meeting place, providing big, sunny terraces, an interesting, round outside bar, and even a sunbed platform where one can stretch out for six Swiss francs. Although the sunbeds seem a little expensive, the menu does not.

In fact, the menu is among the cheapest in the area, with the Tgantieni Rösti with bacon, cheese and fried egg costing only 11 Swiss francs. There is also a range of good, cheap snacks and sandwiches as well as the more substantial Schweinssteak Crap la Pala. This serious pork steak comes covered in all kinds of things such as mushroom sauce, bacon, and cheese and is served with spinach noodles. Its name is inspired by the view from the restaurant of the famous Crap la Pala peak, at 2151 metres not the highest local mountain but there is something about it that sticks in the memory. For the real Alpine flavour, try the small stübli off the main restaurant.

In a family skiing area like Lenzerheide, children are very important and the Tgantieni recognises this with its special children's menu. The discerning child can choose from the Mickey Mouse

HAUTES CUISINES

Teller, the Donald Duck Teller or, for the precocious, there is the Bimbo Teller; although it sounds like a tabloid exclusive, it is in fact a panfried schnitzel with frites.

There are desserts to delight and coffees to confuse, including the locally famous Puuvekaffi, which ranks alongside the Schümli Pflümli as a kind of alcoholic Day Nurse.

The Tgantieni is also a hotel with about 30 comfortable rooms and it does mean that you are first on the piste in the morning. Normally staying half way up a mountain means missing out on the night life in the village. In Lenzerheide it does not.

The evening menu is different from lunch and includes that famous speciality fondue chinoise, popular all over Switzerland and totally unknown in China.

One can always tell a family-run restaurant and the Tgantieni has all the trade marks. The family, the Pargan-Simonets, can feel pleased with themselves.

CREST 'OTA

❄

Situated at the top of the beginners' slope and at the bottom of an attractive blue run through the trees down from the middle station, the Crest 'Ota is a large, well run restaurant popular with skiers of all grades and accessible by road to non-skiers. It is also at the top of the Dieschen drag.

A large, sunny terrace and spacious interior ensure that there is always seating. The menu is large, as is the wine list, and there are always good daily specialities. But inside it is the sort of restaurant where you need to bring the atmosphere with you.

SKI HUT MOTTA

❄

Ski Hut Motta can be reached either by taking the steepish run down from the Rothorn (it is marked black but in some other resorts it would be red) or by skiing down the easier run to the Weisshorn chair lift, at the top of which the hut is sited. It is a small, pine-clad hut surrounded by a large sun terrace on which self-service is available.

The menu is not inspiring, but the solid nature of the fare brings a warm glow on a cold day. The shortness of the menu does remind one of the difficulty of getting supplies to a restaurant 7000 feet up a mountain.

As one arrives a carved wooden legend proclaims "beer by the metre" and why not? Inside one can get a rum punch without alcohol, but why?

The staff are friendly and efficient and the all-important loos are good, clean and free.

The knowing come here mid morning for their glass of sekt on the terrace or, for five Swiss francs more, you can enjoy a good glass of champagne, soak up the sun and the view and plan a fuller lunch elsewhere.

ROTHORNGIPFEL

❄❄

This small stübli is to be found inside the cable car station at the top of the Rothorn. It is warm and friendly inside with a good sun terrace and excellent views across the valley. Young, smiling staff produce good mountain food. Their

HAUTES CUISINES

speciality is called Why Not? a collation of scampi, rösti and hollandaise sauce. The brave are tempted by Kafi Yeti as drunk by Dr. Jekyll. Those in search of vitamin C plump for the Wodka feige mit Schlagrahm, two of which do wonderful things for the memory: they erase it. There is a good selection on the wine list, starting at a relatively modest 20 Swiss francs for the Veltliner.

SCARLOTTAS HUT
PIZ SCARLOTTAS

❄❄

There has been a hut at Piz Scarlottas since the 1940s, perhaps even earlier. The current one, built three years ago, is owned and run by the Rothorn lift company, and is large with a fresh, white pine interior.

Open from 8.30am when an early skier's breakfast may be had, the hut is busy all day. It sits at the top of the Scarlottas chair, and offers a variety of runs down. It is a good example of the modern Alpine hut, a combination of Swiss quality eating, friendly service and a view that you would never find on a motorway service area. On a cold day it provides a welcome refuge. However, on a well planned day, it is not where the skiing trencherman would plan to stop for lunch.

RESTAURANT SCUNTRADA
FADAIL

❄

At the bottom of the beginners' slopes below the Alp Nova chair sits the Scuntrada. On a sunny day the terrace is crowded with families at the learning stage of skiing. It seems popular, too, with the recently injured, lingering over their drinks, bandaged for all to see, perhaps as a reminder that even the most experienced are still learning. It is also particularly popular with those learning to snowboard.

The menu offers the local fare and the wine list is small but adequate. There is an outdoor barbecue for grilled bratwurst. It is a good place to visit for a cafe fertig at the end of the day.

STATZ ALP RESTAURANT

❄❄❄

More like a holiday resort than a mountain restaurant, the Statz Alp is big – no vast. It has one of everything and two or more of somethings. It has a huge terrace served by a huge, outdoor star-shaped bar. It has a barbecue. It has a range of deck chairs (five Swiss francs to rent) and it has eight life-sized carved and painted cows who stand and contemplate the crowd.

Inside, it is equally extraordinary. Its lavish use of wooden logs must have depleted half a forest. There is a souvenir kiosk, a self-service restaurant with six separate dining rooms and a little stübli where, exhausted by sight seeing, one can sit in comfort and order from an adequate menu at not unreasonable prices. Whilst waiting for your meal, you should consider the surroundings. Larger than life, carved wooden women, whose genesis must lie somewhere between Wunderkind and Alan Jones, support the roof. There is always an art exhibition lent by a local gallery and

HAUTES CUISINES

changed from time to time. There is live eine kleine lunchen Musik.

While it breaks almost every rule one might set for a 'good hut', there is something about this spread of vulgarity that makes it a must to visit, but perhaps only once.

There is also a gourmet menu in the 'Gourmetstube'. The food is of the best quality, well cooked and well presented, but somehow 'Gourmetstube' is not quite justified and the set lunch at 65 francs could certainly be given a miss. For once, perhaps, the most tempting proposition is to join the barbecue queue and take lunch outside.

STATZ DAMIEZ

❄❄❄

Much smaller than its near neighbour the Statz Alp, the Damiez offers much more of the tradition associated with good mountain restaurants. The interior has a big open fire and an array of cow bells hanging from the rafters. A stern-eyed, stuffed Steinbock stares intently across the room.

The menu has four different röstis providing for the hungry, the very hungry and those who have not eaten for a week. Good homemade soups, raclette, spaghetti and the possibility of frites with everything ensure that nobody leaves feeling peckish. The house coffee is Hanueli which, if not taken in moderation, could ensure you never leave at all.

The wine list is unambitious but, like everything here, it is reasonably priced.

Outside, the terrace provides whatever the weather supplies with a good view thrown in. On a sunny day the wise book a table in the sun. Tel:081.35.1500.

RESTAURANT TSCHUGGA
ABOVE PARPAN

❄❄❄

Swiss secrecy, it seems, is not restricted to banking. The Restaurant Tschugga is another example. Someway off the beaten piste, it lies among pine trees, a short but stimulating walk above Parpan. On first sight, it confirms that the basic design for a Swiss mountain chalet has never been improved upon.

For the Salzgeber-Juon family who own it, it is their home, their farm and their restaurant. Their eggs could not be fresher, travelling as they do, a mere 20 metres from the chicken to your table. The enveloping silence of the mountain is occasionally interrupted by one of the chickens announcing the arrival of another egg, or perhaps a passing comment from the cows and horses that inhabit the same, adjacent barn.

The menu is short but the house speciality, the Käsefondue Tschugga, ensures that lunch will not be. The prices are below most others on the mountain; perhaps a bribe to encourage you to walk up.

On a cold day the small Stübli is cosy and an early arrival is recommended to ensure a table When the sun shines, the terrace is a glorious sun trap looking up to the Schwarzhorn and the Joch. The experienced locals leave their skis in the village and, after a hearty lunch, rent a toboggan for two Swiss francs and glide back to the village, leaving the toboggan for later collection.

The Käsefondue Tschugga comes bubbling in a pot heated by a small burner. A basket of fresh bread, in the correct sized cubes, accompanies and the first taste tells of the

HAUTES CUISINES

schnapps traditionally included in a fondue recipe, and, better still, that the cheese is homemade. The rösti deserves a mention if only for the wonderful waxy potatoes it is made from.

To be sure of a table you can phone them on 081.35.15.33. It is approached on a marked path running out of Parpan past the marked parking place.

RESTAURANT ZEMAN
PARPAN

❄❄

Whether approached on skis, by car, bus or on foot, the Zeman is all one expects of a Swiss restaurant: stuccoed walls painted with vines, cheerful red chairs around tables covered in equally bright colours. Cheerful waitresses with pouched aprons offer an unhurried welcome.

The Kofler-Collet family who own and run the Zeman offer a reasonably priced menu including, of course, a good raclette and the inevitable rösti, this time topped with cheese, ham and a fried egg. The Tagessuppe is only five Swiss francs for a stomach-warming bowl. If you can prove your child is under six years old, there is a half portion of fresh fried frites for only five francs.

The wine list is exclusively Swiss but reasonably priced.

The view of the tree-clad slopes is impressive. The long Heimberg T-bar is only 20 metres away and the gentle slopes are a favourite with learners. The little village of Parpan is quiet and restful and popular with cross country skiers.

HAUTES CUISINES

LIVIGNO
1820m. - Top station 2800m.
ITALY

In olden days when skiing was shocking there were the three separate communities of S. Maria, S. Antonio and S. Rocco. Now, heaven knows, anything goes duty free and the influx of skiers has caused them to merge into the resort we know as Livigno. This obvious attraction apart, Livigno lies stretched out along the valley, making congestion a problem and parking a headache.

The resort is divided into the East and West sides of the valley with high and wide slopes along each. The lift system is not the best planned one can encounter and the pistes are frequently poorly marked. There are a number of lifts that do no more than return you to your starting point.

There are not a large number of restaurants of quality on the mountain; but there are many popular places at the foot of the nursery slopes.

Despite these reservations, Livigno represents good value for money, especially for the bibulous.

RISTORANTE COSTACCIA

❄❄❄

Different establishments employ varying means to lure customers to their tables. At the Costaccia, which Cusini Giovanni has owned since 1973, they use an old trick, but one that works: the smell of fine food cooking. Outside this, admittedly rather dull looking, building on both the ground floor and on the first floor balcony, there is an enormous barbecue grill. Skiers in search of lunch, like the Bisto kids of old, need do no more than follow their noses towards the smell of grilling meat.

Apart from the products of the grill, there is polenta and pasta aplenty from which to choose. Much favoured is the pizzocheri valellinesi (brown noodles with potatoes and vegetables) at 8000 lire. Those wholly seduced by the olfactory lure of the barbecues, will opt for a mixed grill for 17000 lire. Ice cream features strongly among the desserts.

The wine list is long and varied and spans most of Italy.

There is plenty of space both inside and out but an early arrival is recommended if you want to lunch outside. Costaccia is rightly popular. And there is an added bonus. Apart from the swish of skis on the adjacent piste, the susuration of well trained staff about their work, the only sound to be heard is the conversation of happy munchers. No piped music.

This agreeable spot can be found just below the top of the Costaccia chair lift on a comfortably blue run.

RISTORO TEA BORK (BORCH)

❄❄❄

Ristoro Tea Bork or Borch (as far as the spelling goes you pays your money and you makes your choice;

HAUTES CUISINES

either seems to do) is one of our favourite places in Livigno. It needs to be good because it is neither easy to find nor reach, a situation exacerbated by a piste map which fails to mark all the resort's restaurants. The persistent will discover it half way between the bottom and the mid station of the Carosello 3000 cable car, just off to the right. Take a red run from the mid station or a black from the top of the drag lift that starts just below the mid station.

It is a small restaurant (seats inside for 30 and around 40 outside), converted from an old farmhouse with what our inspectors described as lots of character and a fine, clear view back down the valley to Livigno. It is perfectly situated to catch the best of the midday sun, so remember the sun block.

The staff are efficient but not officious and the food delicious. Try the gnocchi with sage at 7000 lire or the popular sausage and chip platter at 10000 lire. Chips arrive with trimmings of mustard, tomato sauce and mayonnaise, just to impress the diet conscious. Also offered are the customary pastas together with goulash. The usual local wines at the usual prices are listed.

The farmhouse is two hundred years old and has a vivid history. The two brothers who own it, Gigio and Alberto Mottini, will recount, to carefully selected audiences, how their father single-handedly held at bay the might of the Wehrmacht in the last war. These days the Germans are guaranteed a more friendly greeting.

HAUTES CUISINES

MAYRHOFEN
630m. - Top Station 2280m.
AUSTRIA

Mayrhofen sits low in the Ziller valley and has long been a popular resort with summer visitors. Its developement as a ski resort has been more recent and lifts and cable cars have not fully kept pace, to date, with the pressure of numbers. As a consequence queues are common and the pistes, when reached, offer more for the beginners and the intermediate skiers than they do for the advanced. The upper slopes generally provide good snow but the low setting of the resort means that snow in the village tends to disappear quite early.

There are three main ski areas: the Ahorn, which has gentle slopes ideal for the beginners; the Penkenjoch, which is more demanding and attracts the majority of skiers, and the Horberg -Gerent area which provides some powder.

Nonetheless Mayrhofen has good hotels shops and facilities for non-skiers which together with active night life makes it popular with many people.

The nearest international airport is Munich.

Mayrhofen is linked with Finkenberg.

ALMSTUBERL

❄

Mayrhofen is not a resort over endowed with restaurants. Good serviced restaurants are impossible to find on the pistes and so, if you are looking for somewhere to lunch on the mountain, then the Almstuberl by the middle station on the Finkenberger Almbahn is one of the better places to go. Old style architecture, complemented by good views from the large terrace, raise it above the self-service norm. There is a reasonable range of indigenous food and the prices are par for the course. Piped music everywhere and clean loos.

HILDE'S SCHITENNE

❄

Like the Almstuberl (qv), Hilde's is self-service and is easily reached on piste number eight. It has no great views to offer visitors but, instead, draws them inside with low beams, wooden tables and a large, central stove. There are seats for around 75 people and twice that number on the terrace outside. The food is acceptable both in terms of quality and price with a Leberkäse with chips costing 70 schillings. Generally summed up by visitors as "a self-service but a nice one". The clean loos cost one schilling and piped music entertains.

HAUTES CUISINES

MEGEVE
1100m. - Top Station 2350m.
FRANCE

The grand old dame of French skiing, Megève is a delightful, traditional old village. The narrow streets are lined with restaurants and shops of the more expensive kind, and the little square in front of the church has a line of horse drawn carriages awaiting your decision. The centre of Megève has been kept car free and this adds enormously to the intimacy which it projects.

The skiing here is extensive without being challenging. However the Mont Blanc ski pass covers 14 different resorts with over 400 miles of marked pistes all of which are not more than an hours drive from each other and some of which link together.

Megève, because of its altitude, is a resort to visit early in the season when the delight of cruising around the many restaurants and hotels that dot the pistes can be enjoyed to the full.

The night life here is as you would expect - "très chic" but certainly not "très cheap".

A car is a great asset here to make the most of the extensive opportunities that surround you, and it can be left in one of the three underground garages. More reports from here please.

Linked resorts. St Gervais (qv), St Nicholas-de-Veroce.

About one hours drive from Geneva.

CHEZ ERNESTINE
❄❄

Chez Ernestine is another of those simple, small, unpretentious establishments that make skiing in many resorts a joy and the stopping to eat or drink even better. An old farmhouse on one floor, with limited provision for lunchers, no more than 30 places, it offers the mixture of spaghetti, salads and reasonable plat du jour, 60 to 65 francs, that many people find entirely to their taste.

What sets Chez Ernestine apart in this worthy catelogue are the superb views towards Mont Blanc and the Aiguilles du Midi. A splendid sun trap, there are few more delightful places to spend a lazy afternoon with a drink.

It can be reached by skiers of most grades on the blue Clementines run.

LE RADAZ
❄❄

"Poets," observed G. K. Chesterton, "have been mysteriously silent on the subject of cheese." The great man was right, but possibly few, indeed any, poets have visited Le Radaz, a farmhouse/restaurant set in meadows, easily reached on foot or ski, still open to welcome walkers in the summer, at which time, the air fragrant with mountain flowers, Le Radaz makes its own cheese.

It is, as you will by now have inferred, an old style establishment ("traditional, two cats, one dog," noted our inspector), but quite small, seating but 40 people in the dining room and fewer more on the deck outside. On cold days, the interior is warmed by cast iron stoves.

The menu is also quite small, majoring on salads, omelettes and local cheese. There is a good plat du jour (last season, roast pork, salad and chips for a user friendly

HAUTES CUISINES

65 francs) and the house salad of ham, cheese, endive and egg is only 35 francs. A popular local dish is the tartiflette for 65 francs.

The clean loos are unisex, the proprietors Paulet and Brigitte are but the most recent of a long line of Blancets to own the restaurant, and it can be found on the blue Pre Rosset run. Get there early. It can become very busy.

HAUTES CUISINES

MERIBEL
**1450m.-1700m. - Top Station 3200m.
FRANCE**

A long time favourite with the British, Méribel continues to get better and better. Every year brings an improvement to the lift system and an extension to the already vast ski area, nearly 70 miles of it just in Méribel.

The area splits into two, with Méribel-les-Allues, the chalet dominated traditional part and Meribel-Mottaret, the newer but quite attractive development at the head of the valley.

The local architecture is very pleasing and whilst the village seems to lack a centre there are a few good bars and restaurants and now a discotheque or two.

The connections to the rest of the Trois Vallées are excellent and this area remains one of the ski paradises of the world.

The nearest airport is Geneva but the transfer time is about three and a half hours.

Linked resorts are Courchevel (qv), Val Thorens, (qv) and Les Menuires.

HOTEL ARDRAY-TELEBAR

❄❄❄❄

If a little indulgence is required, the piste-side restaurant of the Hotel Ardray-Télébar is the place. A large chalet set among the pines and snows of Méribel, it has one of the most charming dining rooms one can find.

The low, beamed ceiling of the restaurant has that meringue plasterwork that seems so peculiarly Tarentaise. The large, stone fireplace is always lit in the winter. Burnished copper competes with glowing brass to mellow the gentle lighting.

The kitchens are under the skilled hand and watchful eye of M. Monnet the proprietor, and the salon is steered quietly by Mme. Monnet. They have been here for 39 years and have every year improved their offering.

There is a daily menu at about 180 francs for four well prepared courses, or there is the plat du jour on its own for 90 francs. The à la carte menu offers excellent variety at prices that, while not cheap, are certainly cheaper than many lesser establishments in this area.

The wine list starts at a surprisingly low 45 francs for the table wine.

Recently, M. Monnet's son Fabrice has joined him in the kitchen, ensuring, one hopes, another 39 years of hospitality and fine food.

RESTAURANT L'ARPASSON

❄❄

L'Arpasson is an example of the chalet-restaurant-bar-self-services that seem to pervade the Méribel Mottaret area. It boasts a three-floored service area for skiers.

Upstairs, the restaurant is small but enjoys panoramic views through huge, plate glass windows. The main floor consists of a terrace and a pleasant bar, while below lies the self-service area.

The menu is for meat eaters: even the salade L'Arpasson has bacon in it. Starters are terrines, jambon or escargots, followed by main course steaks, lamb or duck, all of them served with vegetables. A three-course meal off the à la carte menu

HAUTES CUISINES

would cost about 170 francs including wine. There is, however, a daily plat du jour at 65 francs, and on Sundays cous cous at 70 francs.

The loos are one franc, perhaps reflecting water shortages or the number of non-customers who use them.

L' Arpasson is at the top of Tougnete I, the middle station.

LE RESTAURANT LE CHARDONNET

❄❄❄

Compared with the lift station beside it, the architecture of Le Chardonnet is a rest for the eye, wooden and slightly church-like (those modern churches, you understand). Inside, the temptation to use flock wallpaper has been resisted and wooden walls, lined with wood, separate the large, triangular windows. The almost inevitable stuffed marmotte grins down at his new home. Le Chardonnet is named after the man who built it and it is now run by his daughter, Mme. Gregan, and her husband.

The carte offers more variety and imagination than many mountain restaurants and the smell of cooking as you enter is an improvement on some, particularly French, olfactory greetings. There are two fixed price menus. Six courses are offered for 220 francs on the "menu detente", including the house speciality escargots aux amandes. The "menu skieur" at 122 francs is a simple and quick four courses that will get you back on the slopes without slowing you down. If neither of the menus amuse, there is a wide choice on the à la carte and a daily plat du jour for about 60 francs.

Some people rave about oeufs Pas du lac, a dish described as containing eggs, smoked breast, tomato puree and Alsatian sausages. Smoked breast of what? you may ask and hope that the sausage comes from Northern France rather than the dog next door.

There is a good selection of homemade tarts, including pommes and myrtilles and at 25 francs a portion they are worth a try. The pièce de résistance is a coupe de glace or, to be precise, a selection from 14 coupes des glaces that come in as many flavours with all the traditional accoutrements and topped with a mountain of whipped cream. If you want to open a child's eyes, this is the place to come.

The house wine is 54 francs a bottle and quite drinkable.

The restaurant is easily found at the half way station of the Pas du lac bubbles.

RESTAURANT LE CHOUCAS

❄❄

There are many good hotel-restaurants that line the pistes of Méribel, but few of the small mountain refuges where the truck cannot unload outside, nor the boy pop down the road for another loaf of bread. On the mountain there must be carefully planned provisioning, all cooking needs to be done on the premises, and sometimes the reality of a disappointing day when it snows and the skiers stay below, needs to be faced. This is the constant uncertainty of running a mountain restaurant and one that Le Choucas deals with as it happens.

Small, pine-built and of a contemporary design, it nonetheless suits the Tarentaise tradition. Its terrace

HAUTES CUISINES

commands a spectacular view down to Méribel and inside one sits on long benches at pine tables to take a snack or lunch.

The menu offers few surprises, listing the usual charcuterie, spaghetti and croques monsieurs. There is always a good soup for 30 francs. The house special is oeuf Choucas, two eggs, bacon, tomato, sausage and, of course, cheese. The actual method of preparation is a secret the chef claims he wishes to keep. At 42 francs it is certainly worth a try and represents the best value on the menu. There are different homemade tarts every day, and with afternoon tea or chocolate there is nothing better.

The wines are a little more expensive here than other places. The house wine starts at 60 francs and the pleasant local Chignin Blanc at 80 francs.

You will find Le Choucas and their slightly indifferent service just below middle station on the Burgin-Saulire bubbles.

CÔTE BRUNE
MOTTARET

❄❄

Supermarkets since the pioneering days of Jack Cohen have specialised in loss leaders: those tempting, cheap items that lead you to buy on impulse other goods with high margins that otherwise you might have ignored. The Côte Brune has refined this technique to a point of fiendish subtlety: instead of tantalising the senses with low prices they have sited the dessert display in such a manner that anyone walking to the loos has to pass, and invariably, stop, stare, and more than often order one.

The desserts on offer include fresh fruits of the forest, fruit salad, chocolate charlotte, îles flottantes, three types of chocolate gateau and raspberry tart - and all for 35 francs, and all rich, rich, rich.

The rest of the menu, working backwards, is varied but not cheap but for those wanting something fairly basic and good value, dishes such as chicken, chips and salad are offered. The other great advantage of the Côte Brune is that you can eat there at almost any time of the day.

The restaurant is at the bottom of the Méribel Mottaret so walkers can reach it easily. The corresponding disadvantage is that the view is not great. It is a traditional building with tables and benches outside for fine days and efficient and friendly staff inside for all days. Very good food and highly recommended.

LE RHODODENDRON

❄❄❄

The bar of the Rhododendron is a beer drinker's dream. The counter is at the right height for the elbow; there is a rail at exactly the right height for the foot, and above the bar are ranks of glass tankards of half litre size (the actual bar top is 1923 metres above sea level - there must be a bet in there: "How high would you say this bar is George?"). When you have pocketed your winnings, you can climb the stairs to the little restaurant attelier where one may escape the bustle of the self-service below and take lunch in comfort.

It is a small restaurant with a small menu. Starters consist of charcuterie and salad; main courses are entrecôtes, escalopes and good

HAUTES CUISINES

côtes d' agneau aux herbes. The speciality is a Tarentaise favourite, the crozet, a pasta dish with cheese, cream and ham, and at 30 francs it is the skier's friend. The wine list is okay, with the house wine at 48 francs a bottle and, for a change, there is an excellent dry Normandy cider at 44 francs a litre.

There is a large terrace outside, which looks down to the Méribel Altiport below, but this is the preserve of the self-service. The whole place has a comfortable, professional feel. Janine Jung has been running it for 23 years and is not afraid to continue for another 23.

The Rhododendron sits at the top of the Altiport chair at the junction of the Renard run and the Boulevard blue.

LE CHALET TOGNIAT
MOTTARET

❄❄

The flags of all nations that line the route to the Chalet Togniat do not encourage the impression that one is about to make the restaurant find of the season. After all, if the Eighth Army, the Marine Corps, the Foreign Legion and the Wehrmacht have all been there before you, what can you expect.

What you get is a huge chalet with an intriguing bar, painted in the charming Tyrolean style which is so alien to this part of France. The dining room too, an offshoot of the inevitable self-service area, has a folklorique ceiling.

If you are not yet put off, then you show some style, for the smiling staff make up for every other deficiency this giant motorway filling station may possess. Inge Girre and her helpful staff bring a yodel to the throat and, suddenly, the riddle is explained: Inge is German and all the painting is her own. Outside, a large terrace catches the sun, and those who sit there try to work out how many flags they can recognise. The small, stübli restaurant has a short, simple menu and a good three-course meal with wine will cost about 150 francs.

The Togniat is just below the top of the Combes chair up from Méribel Mottaret.

MÜRREN
1640m. - Top Station 2970m.
SWITZERLAND

A veritable time warp, Mürren clings to a high shelf overlooking the Lauterbrunnen Valley, approached either by train or by cable car. This hideaway village has changed very little over the years.

Its history is entwined with that of the British Skier ever since Henry Lunn came here in the early 1900's. The skiing is not extensive, although the run down from the famous revolving Schilthorn restaurant is one that no serious skier should miss.

Every year they organise a famous "inferno" race, where over 1000 skiers descend all the way from Piz Gloria to Lauterbrunnen, a long and difficult race where they ski across snow, rocks, grass and each other.

Accommodation here is in one of the dozen or so hotels or in one of the many delightful chalets or apartments. The nightlife is livelier than one might imagine with live music in a number of the hotels.

The adjacent resorts of Wengen and Grindelwald greatly extend the skiing area and are easily reached by the little trains that knit the region together.

Nearest airports are Zürich and Berne.

HAUTES CUISINES

RESTAURANT PIZ GLORIA
❄❄❄

Remarkable feats of engineering are fairly commonplace in the Jungfrau area of the Bernese Oberland: for example, the WAB railway that connects the area so well or the incredible Jungfraubahn which climbs through the Eiger and up to the Jungfraujoch, the highest station in Europe. And then there is the amazing revolving restaurant which crowns the Schilthorn so spectacularly.

It first came to universal attention in one of those James Bond films, when Bond and a villain had a fight on top of it, and tension was raised as each fell, only to be saved by possessing fingernails sufficiently strong to support his body weight as they both dangled from the precipitous sides of the restaurant. Had one been dining there at the time, these melodramatics would only have obscured the views and so would have been extremely unwelcome.

Getting there is made easy by the network of cable cars that start at Stechelberg in the valley bottom, and rise through Gimmelwald to Murren, to Birg and thence to Piz Gloria itself, exactly 10000 feet above sea level. Skiers come up here for the exciting and testing run back down to Mürren (or even to Lauterbrunenn when the snow is good), and it is the start of the famous inferno race, when as many as a thousand lunatics set out to race down to the valley.

Sightseers come for a unique panoramic view that is fed to them in digestible eyefuls by the revolving restaurant. Lunch here feeds all the senses.

The menu offers warming soups from 3.50 Swiss francs, salads and cold plates at between 13 and 19 francs, and a wide selection of hot dishes from 17 francs, including an excellent rumpsteak Café de Paris, for 28 francs. There is a vegetarian dish for 16 francs, and children get fed up for 9 francs, with a choice of escalopes with French fries or noodles. Wines are inevitably Swiss, as is the friendly and efficient service.

The restaurant was refurbished in 1991, and there is now a private room available for up to 20 people, and even a conference facility for up to 200 people for those truly high level talks.

The trip up is included in the Jungfrau region ski pass, but the trip down again is not, although people with skis, who have taken a look at the run down and decided that lunch is best left undisturbed by the tumbling mogul field at the start, get a discount.

If you are staying in Wengen or Grindelwald, it can be worth 'phoning to make sure the lifts are running before making the journey. Tel:036.23.14.44.

OBERGURGL
1930m. - Top Station 3040m.
AUSTRIA

Obergurgl and Hochgurgl have long been the centres of charm providing very high, sunny slopes with good snow (Which has not prevented cautious Austrians from investing in snow machines) and pistes to satisfy most grades of skier. There is the added advantage of being able to ski right to your doorstep.

Access is not particularly easy (it lies 50 kilometres from Insbruck) but this offers the bonus, once there, of relative security from

HAUTES CUISINES

invasion by weekenders. Night life is centred on Obergurgl, which is the liveliest of the two resorts. Decent hotels make it a good area for families.

The nearest airport is Munich.

WURMKOGL
HOCHGURGL

❄❄

The Wurmkogl discourages casual visitors lacking a proper sense of occasion. It lies at 3000 metres, at the top of the Wurmkogl drag lift and departure is down a black run. But it rewards richly those who make the effort, fortifying them for the descent with superb views across into Italy or back towards the village.

It is quite small, ten tables in all, but cossets with sheep skins thrown over benches and entertains with stuffed animals on display. Given the size and vertiginous location, the menu is limited. But the soups are nice, the sausage succulent and the Glühwein goes down smoothly.

The atmosphere is distinctly and pleasantly homely. When the food you have ordered emerges from the kitchen, you fetch it from the bar. Anything less like a conventional self-service would be hard to imagine.

The loos are rustic: a hole in the floor through which the snow is visible ten feet below.

For good skiers the Wurmkogl is highly recommended, for the views, the relaxation, the intimacy of the interior. Entertainment is provided by the local radio station.

DAVID

❄

A small, stuccoed house at the bottom of the Steinman lift, David is walkable from the village or skiable down a red run. It is, thus, popular and an early arrival is recommended. Neither especially traditional nor modern, the restaurant is quite small and specialises in homemade pizza and soup and snackish fare for the peckish in a hurry.

The pizzas range in price between 65 and 90 schillings and the soups run from 22 to 45 schillings. Tiroler Gröstl and spare ribs are also listed. There is the usual selection of beers and wines. While lacking the ambience and variety of the Nederhütte (qv), it makes a change for those who have had too much Tyrolean music. It is, in addition, open for fondue parties in the evenings.

HAUTES CUISINES

NEDERHÜTTE

❄❄❄

The Gamper family, owners of the Nederhütte, lay great emphasis on tradition, which, on Thursdays, takes the form of a hut evening in the course of which raclette and fondue are served and entertainment is provided by the Nederlumpen duo, who, with accordion and Lederhosen, provide, one is assured, both atmosphere and fun. From 4.00pm on Mondays, Wednesdays and Fridays, there is "high life" with après ski entertainment, at which point the Nederhütte hots up.

The humble luncher is denied these amenities, but the restaurant, low, wooden and bedecked with a charming sun terrace, has much to offer by way of compensation. First, it is easy to reach: straight up the Gaisberg lift and there it is, and an easy ski takes one back to the village. Secondly, the staff are quick, but not pressing, yet manage to be friendly. Thirdly, the food is rather good.

The menu is as traditionally mountainous as can be, from spaghetti bolognese, 80 schillings, via various rösti to the famous sweet dumpling, the Germ Knödel. A slight change on the usual is worked by offering spare ribs, 120 schillings. Dedicated devourers of protein will settle for the goulash soup at 45 schillings and then tuck into a steak at 180. More snackish fare is available in the form of baked jacket potatoes with cheese at 85 schillings. There is a wide range of beers, rather less wide ranging wine, but the Glühwein gives a good glow at 46 schillings. Tradition is not sold cheap.

There is a special menu for children, an English menu for the linguistically disadvantaged and piped Tyrolean music in case you cannot make it on Thursday to catch the Nederlumpen duo. The Nederhütte is a nice one.

HAUTES CUISINES

LA ROSIERE
1850m. - Top Station 2640m.
FRANCE

Set high, 1850 metres, in the south facing slopes of the Isère valley, La Rosière is a quiet resort of pleasant views and varied, if ultimately not very challenging, skiing. The snow and sunshine record are excellent.

Popular with families, it provides the opportunity of skiing across to La Thuile in Italy (qv) and trips by car to more populous spots such as Tignes (qv).

LA TERRACE DU YETI

❄❄

Our inspector was unequivocal: "a must for all skiers" he wrote, and demonstrated both his discernment and commitment by eating lunch there six days out of seven. Fortunately, it is also handy for non-skiers, being located at the bottom of the lift system.

La Terrace du Yeti is, in fact, part of the original Hotel Petit St. Bernard and provides quick service, quality food (house speciality is pizza) and rapid but friendly service. It seats about 60 people, has a decent sized bar, and, given its position, is well placed to provide tea or more powerful fortification on the way back from a day on the slopes. It also boasts clean loos and a view over the Tarentaise.

HAUTES CUISINES

SAALBACH/ HINTERGLEMM
1000m. - Top Station 2100m.
AUSTRIA

Saalbach and Hinterglemm were two small villages, set on the floor of a steep valley. They spread towards each other, as each developed as a ski resort, and have now effectively merged. Attractive and charming, hemmed in by the steeply rising valley walls, they offer extensive, if not very demanding skiing, with the possibility of skiing a complete circuit taking in each side of the valley.

There are a huge number of hotels, nearly 400 in all, but the centres are effectively pedestrianised and parking is well organised.

There are pleasant shops and restaurants in the resorts and some agreeable places to eat on the slopes but a large number of self-service cafeterias as well.

For those with a car Zell-am-See is not far away and the nearest airport is Salzburg. More regular flights are available to Munich but the drive is longer.

BARNALM

❆❆

The restaurant is small, pretty and unpretentious. The menu is big, heavy and designed to fuel an army of skiers through two blizzards - at least.

The Barnalm sits at the top of the fast, triple chair lift leading towards Bernkogel, that departs from the middle of Saalbach. A big, broad motorway cruises back to town. Those wishing to enjoy the resort's ski circus can tag on to the adjacent 'T' bar after their break.

Prices are very reasonable: roast pork, dumplings and Sauerkraut represent good value at 100 schillings. That mountain benchmark dish, spaghetti bolognese, unravels for 76 schillings. Also on offer are stewed pork lights, for the adventurous foreigner, and spare ribs. A world champion salad, ingredients unexplained and, on this occasion, unexplored, is served with bread for 89 schillings. If in a celebratory mood and the schillings are smoking a hole in your ski suit, smoked salmon with champagne is conjured up in return for 420 of the local currency. If you, instead, are feeling hard up and your palate needs a kick start, try Schmalzbrot mit viel Knoblauch und Zwiebelringen - brown bread, lard, onions and garlic, and yours for only 40 schillings. Puddings include the famous Kaiserschmarren - torn-up pancakes, icing sugar and apple or plum sauce.

The wine list is par for the Austrian course: limited, although champagne is available without the accompanying smoked salmon.

The terrace outside runs around three sides of the restaurant offering views of either Saalbach itself or close neighbour Hinterglemm.

ROSSWALDHÜTTE

❆❆

The Hasenauer family's restaurant looks deceptively small as you approach on blue piste 28 from Hasenauer Kopfl. No family member was available to explain whether or not they had taken the lease on the mountain as well. In fact, this nicely carved, modern chalet which sits right beside the piste, contains a large tiled restau-

HAUTES CUISINES

rant with a plain wooden bar and a big tiled deck outside for sun bathing and eating.

The Rosswaldhütte offers excellent value for money around the usual Austrian themes. Soups include Nudel and Gulasch. Main courses encompass a cordon bleu pork dish at 125 schillings, a Wiener Schnitzel, salad and chips at an undemanding 115 schillings, while the inevitable spaghetti bolognese is a mere 70. Anyone desiring only carbohydrate with a dash of colour, can opt for chips with ketchup for a modest 35 schillings. Other snack dishes offered include home-cured ham with bread.

The staff wear local costume and the entire enterprise has that welcoming, friendliness that family restaurants so often provide.

WILDENKARKOGEL HÜTTE

❄❄❄

The Seidl family have a sensible, economical approach to the demands of outside catering at their Wildenkarkogel Hutte: standing on a flat area of packed snow, the restaurant's terrace is deemed to be any patch that catches the sun and on which their customers wish to place a sun chair. Tables and benches are grouped a little closer to the centre of the action, the kitchen.

For non-skiers, the place has a potent attraction. They just have to get down the valley from Saalbach to the bubble station at Vorderglemm and then take a ride up. It is a good, high point to meet skiing friends, while for the latter, there are many blue and red runs leading away from their most recent meal.

The building is self-consciously rustic in tone (ceiling open to the rafters, big, crudely finished beams supporting, at one point, a small farm wagon) and it teeters on the brink of being twee without actually going over the edge.

It encourages early visitors (breakfast that includes ham and cheese is available for 90 schillings) while snack dishes such as chips and ketchup are also listed.

For more substantial meals, pastas that include spaghetti, canneloni and lasagne, are offered, all at 90 schillings.

A children's menu, essentially smaller portions of popular dishes such as spaghetti and Wiener Schnitzel, is useful for family outings.

The usual soft drinks, spirits, beers and robust hot drinks are available. The wine list is small.

HAUTES CUISINES

SAUZE D'OULX
1500m. - Top Station 2820m.
ITALY

"I was told this place was the Benidorm of the Alps," expostulated one visitor, disappointed with the lack of action at the Andy Capp Pub or the local discos. In truth, Sauze, an old, attractive village to which much modern and functional development has been added, built its reputation on being a good, cheap ski.

In recent years snow has been thin and in mid-March 1992 trips across to the linked resort of Sestriere (q.v.) were necessary to find reasonable skiing. Much money has, however, been invested in snow machines.

In common with some other Italian resorts, there is heavy reliance on long drag lifts where a chair would be more welcome, while many of the chairs provided are of the single variety. That said, there are many attractive runs through trees and a touch of that festive, family atmosphere that Italian resorts seem, effortlessly, to provide.

For the demanding skier, there is not a wide range on offer, but for others there is much to satisfy. Piste marking is, at best, indifferent.

There are not many attractive bars or restaurants on the mountain but one attracted our attention, while one restaurant in the resort cried out for inclusion.

PIAN DELLA ROCCA

❄

Pian della Rocca, a log cabin style restaurant and bar, situated two short chair rides up the mountain face, is a stark and welcome contrast to the concrete hotels and cafés of Sauze.

Every effort has been made to provide both a functional and attractive setting: for example, there is room for up to 60 inside but different sizes and shapes of tables help keep the atmosphere intimate and friendly.

The deck outside overlooks gently wooded slopes on one side and craggy mountain peaks on the other. One thoughtful device which other proprietors may note, is the ledge for drinks on top of the fence which surrounds much of the deck.

The menu is basic, polenta and pasta, so more suitable for a pit stop rather than a major lunch event. But the view may keep you for hours.

English was spoken well on the day of inspection. Even the now ubiquitous alsatian responded well to being thus addressed.

A place, then, to visit perhaps several times in one day, when either skiing down criss-crossing red runs or while travelling up a slow lift system to higher peaks of Pia de Moncrons or Mt. Bourget.

HAUTES CUISINES

RISTORANTE DEL FALCO

❄❄❄

Ristorante del Falco is a restaurant that has taken wing and deserves to succeed which, to judge by the numbers sighted there last season, it undoubtedly will.

In the old village of Sauze d'Oulx, just off the square by the tourist office, and occupying a stone vaulted basement once the host to cattle rather than human diners, the Ristorante del Falco has a simple, unpretentious elegance in which popular yet honest and well prepared Italian food is served.

The Liverpudlian owner, Vince Hawkins, has owned businesses in Sauze for 10 years and so he is no newcomer, nor fly-by-night, to the town. He has fitted out his new venture with a small bar where customers can wait for a table (sometimes necessary, but not too long) and an old fashioned open oven where pizzas are cooked to order. The restaurant seats around 40 people on two levels.

A small selection of starters that include avocado, mozzarella and tomato salad, and sautéed wild mushrooms, is complemented by pasta and excellent meat dishes. Many customers, however, prefer to choose from among the 17 varieties of pizza on offer. The dough is perfect and the fillings fresh.

The wine list is not large but is competitively priced. Puddings include classics like tiramisu. The restaurant provides good value (our inspectors ate three courses for 52000 lire, for two) and offers an interesting counterpoint to other aspects of Sauze night life.

HAUTES CUISINES

SESTRIERE
2050m. - Top Station 2820m.
ITALY

Sestriere is one of the very first purpose-built resorts, a joint venture between Mussolini and the Agnellis, who between them demonstrated a preference for function over style.

Set fairly high, around 2000 metres, with a high top station, Sestriere has some good skiing without matching the best on offer in France or Switzerland. Moreover, piste marking is generally very poor.

The lift system relies heavily on drags rather than chairs and where a modern, excellent, new chair has been installed, the 1991-1992 piste map failed to show it. Piste maps also followed the deplorable custom, all too common in Italy, of failing to mark the sites of restaurants and bars.

The efficient cabin link with Sauze d'Oulx (qv) effectively extends the range of both resorts offering many runs, but, again, without matching the best elsewhere. Last March, only one good mogul field was open.

BAR CONCHINETO

❄

Having tackled an optional black mogul field from Mt. Sises (2600m), gentle pistes carry skiers down through attractive wooded slopes. If you are lucky, and it has to be luck the pistes are so poorly marked, you will ski across Bar Conchineto. Tucked down in a gulley to the left of a bending motorway, Bar Conchineto is a delightful find on a mountainside completely barren of restaurants and bars.

Built in traditional style of wood and stone, public access is on one floor split into two sections, one bar area and one restaurant area. One queues to order food and drink at one hatch where a ticket is handed over; queues and collects drinks from a second hatch; and queues and collects food from a third.

Furniture both inside as well as outside on the long, narrow deck, is solid pine. The atmosphere is basic and hardy but also jolly and good natured.

Food portions, whether of variations of polenta or chops and chips, are large. A group of English 'lads' one inspector encountered expressed themselves very well satisfied with quality and quantity.

The fare at Bar Conchineto is refreshing after some challenging skiing. Do not go expecting four star waiter service and you will not then be disappointed.

Two words of caution to those uninitiated in the art of the 'hole in the floor' loo. Take care.

LA GARGOTE

❄❄

La Gargote is situated at the foot of the Garnel 'button' lift across the main road from Serestriere village. The village is set across the valley in a long strip so further drag lifts can be viewed to both the left and right of the restaurant. The windows by the main entrance look back towards Serestriere itself, a privelege whose value will vary according to your aesthetic judgment of the local architecture.

A white-washed plaster building, more Mediterranean than mountain, with big, arched windows, La Gargote offers an attractive venue

121

HAUTES CUISINES

for skiers or non-skiers and a secure room where the former may deposit their skis.

Tables and chairs, protected by glass screens, are provided outside for warm days. Inside there is a tiled floor, wooden ceiling and seats at simpler tables and benches for about 40 people. Self-service facilities are offered to al fresco customers.

The menu is very short. On the day of inspection there were two starters, one of which was a salad, two primi patti, including the house polenta Gargote which was not tried, two main courses, veal and chicken, and two desserts or cheese. Prices were quite high, 15000 to 17000 lire for a main course, but then La Gargote aspires to be more than a run-of-the-piste establishment. There was no plat du jour.

The staff are friendly and attractively kitted out in coloured tops printed, discreetly, with the restaurant name.

The loos were spotless and so hi-tech that one inspector failed completely to understand how to make the taps work.

In a resort not over blessed with mountain huts, La Gargote is a welcome place at which to call.

HAUTES CUISINES

SERRE-CHEVALIER
1350-1500m. - Top Station 2780m.
FRANCE

Serre-Chevalier is actually the name of a mountain, the first peak to be originally skied, and from this the resort grew.

The two bowls lying either side of the Serre-Chevalier peak afford wide open undulating skiing which leads down to the main village of Chantemerle, which together with Villeneuve and the smaller hamlets make up the area known as Serre-Chevalier.

Le Grand Serre Chevalier includes Briançon and Le Monetier which are all linked with a network of well maintained lifts between the valleys affording a large skiing area which is growing from year to year in efficient and up-to-date facilities. The skiing area is wide and open, appealing to the intermediate skier, but for the more competent there are steeper runs just above the snow bowls and a vast range of safe and easily accessible off-piste skiing.

The French have for a long time favoured Serre-Chevalier, therefore there are many apartments owned and let by the French. But there are also good modern 2 and 3 star hotels built around a modern shopping centre with many bar-restaurants. Villeneuve has a tractor drawn train which provides free transport around the village and across to the old town.

French families tend not to disco in the evening, but for the young, these can be found.

Briançon (1325m) is an old fortified town with a maze of cobbled streets. From the ramparts one can see across the valley floor to the Briançon ski area. Well worth a visit.

Le Monetier Les Bains is an old spa village and is situated on the western side of the resort and is a quieter old style village. Le Monetier has the highest chair lift in the system at Pic de L'Lyret 2830m.

There are approximately 45km of prepare trails for ski de fond along the valley floor from Briançon to beyond Le Monetier.

There is much to ski in Le Grand Serre Chevalier and this would keep even the most avid skier occupied, but if another adventure is wanted, Montgenèvre on the Italian border is to be found half an hour's drive from Briançon, and is well worth a visit.

L' ECHAILLON

❄❄❄

Take the Côte Chevalier chair lift in the Villeneuve valley; from the top take the red Fangeas run; half way down execute a smart right (be very careful as it is easily missed) and there lies the Echaillon. The Fangeas piste may also be reached from the Rouge button lift.

The restaurant is of the wooden chalet type, making a welcome change from the locally predominating brick. It is situated just below the tree line in a nicely secluded position away from the main pistes and junctions and offers a large sunny terrace. The patron is welcoming and attentive, as are his many clean and tidy waiters.

The chalet interior is a large, vaulted room simply decorated, with a central fireplace, a long bar and seats for about 100 people. Large windows offer panoramic views on three sides.

The cuisine is of a high standard with a fair-sized choice on the menu. The plat du jour is good value and more adventurous than most mountain restaurants, offering

HAUTES CUISINES

for example, mousse de rascasse. Portions are ample and appetisingly presented.

The house wine, Réserve de L' Echaillon, is cheap and of commensurate quality. The other, more expensive wines, on the list are recommended.

It is a good place for those who enjoy lunching, but beware, one is not close to lifts down to the valley floor: when you leave L' Echaillon, there is skiing still to do.

Loos are his and hers and situated at the bottom of a narrow spiral staircase.

JACQUES A

❄❄

"If you've got it, flaunt it!". So said Zero Mostel in the movie "The Producers". Never bad advice if what you have is what people want, and everybody wants a warm and friendly reception and cheerful service, and that is what you get at and from Jacques A.

In the three years he has been here, Jacques has imprinted his own brand of hospitality and, in no time at all, this has become the place to meet those you know and those you do not. Take your drink and sit by the fire and watch. They come, they go, they linger, they come back. It is as if something is going to happen and no one wants to miss it. So while you wait to find out, try a lunch here. It may not get into the Michelin guide, but you can eat well here for a lot less than it costs to mend a puncture, and feel better for it.

Outside, the view takes in Serre Chevalier, a lot of trees, people skiing, lifts and, of course, mountains, so no great surprises there; but it sure beats the M25 at rush hour.

Find your friends at the top of the Chantmerle on the Serre Rocher piste.

LE PI MAI

❄❄❄❄

'Dear Lord, may I hang up my boots and rest here forever'. Thus spake a normally sane inspector. The day she arrived was marked by flurries of fresh snow and, inside, the smell of the larchwood fire, promising a lunchtime of warmth and conviviality. The restaurant is run by Mimi and Riquet Charamet and even offers bedrooms for those overcome by an outstanding meal or who wish to emulate our inspector and hang up their boots.

The menu is small but adventurous. The specialities being 'Les Grillades au Feu de bois de Mélèze et son Gratin', a selection of dishes cooked over an open larchwood fire encouraged by a chef-operated blow pipe. Other establishments may fan their coals with bellows, but only here does the chef blow hot and not cold. The serious trenchermen among you may see fit to start with the 'Salade Grande Serre', a mixture of white and red cabbage and braised Jurancon duck. Those with a richer appetite may wish to start with foie gras or even the local jambon cru. Those who know, complete their meal with a portion of Visitandines, a recipe of Mimi's grandmother. The wine list is small, but well chosen, and quite reasonably priced.

The restaurant seats fewer than 40 people and so, on a cold day, an early arrival is advisable.

On a sunny day the terraces surrounding the chalet provide as

HAUTES CUISINES

much vitamin 'D' and ultraviolet as you can absorb.
The restaurant, an old-style chalet, can easily be approached on the green Fréjus run from the top of the Ecole Fréjus chair lift or by the picturesque red run from the Cole de la Cucumelle. Afterwards, a gentle run back to Villeneuve takes one through the tree-clad slopes on a picturesque piste to the village. In an area overtaken by self-service, Le Pi Mai should not be missed.

HAUTES CUISINES

SOLDEN
1380m. - Top Station 3060m.
AUSTRIA

With the linked, but very much smaller, village of Hochsolden, Solden offers a large ski area to visitors. The village itself is not noted for character or traditional charm, being spread out along the main road. However, most people who go there enjoy it for the night life and social amenities. There are, we know, many good restaurants on the mounatin, too, but regrettably when our inspectors called in March, the weather was so severe that the resort was closed. In these difficult circumstances they were unable to cover much territory and were forced, instead, to spend several hours in the Hainbach Alm, an experience which left them enthusiastic about its qualities. Their report appears below. We would, therefore, greatly welcome reports from readers about their favourite restaurants on the pistes of Solden which will form the basis of our reports for next year.

HAINBACH ALM
❄❄❄

The Hainbach Alm has a special attraction for wine lovers: a giant wine barrel, complete with tiny crystalline stalactites, in which up to a dozen people can make themselves comfortable for a morning or afternoon drink, or lunch. This vinous phenomenon is to be found by the Rotkogel lift just below Hochsolden. The restaurant is arranged on two floors, although the upstairs section is cramped, and has a modest deck outside.

The menu is small, but inexpensive. Spare ribs to insulate against the cold are 80 schillings, goulash soup is 40 schillings, with less robust soups starting at 30. A half litre of Pils to chase it costs 30 schillings.

The Hainbach Alm is owned by the Grüner family, and their well trained staff coped with competence and good humour despite being faced for five hours with the demands of a packed crowd of stranded and increasingly relaxed skiers.

HAUTES CUISINES

ST ANTON
1300m. - Top Station 2650m.
AUSTRIA

This is the honey pot for the young skiers who want their challenge equally divided between the snow and the high life. The clientelle are an international selection who come to test their knees and their stamina. The village has less charm than one usually associates with Austrian resorts and whilst a car is useful to visit other local resorts, such as Zürs (qv) and Lech (qv), it is a problem in the village.

The skiing is the best in the Arlberg, a region that once gave its name to a style of skiing and is the home of many down hill racers. In recent years there has been a considerable amount of investment in new lifts and in snow making equipment, even though St Anton has one of best snow records in the Alps.

The skiing links up with St Christoph (qv), a hamlet of hotels just up the pass and now with Stuben (qv), opening up the exciting Albona ski area for St Anton visitors.

The Après ski is almost as extensive as the skiing, many bars and restaurants, most with music ensure a lively time. For the fitness conscious there are swimming pools, tennis courts, squash, skating and saunas.

The nearest airport is Zürich with a transfer time of two to three hours.

BAHNHOF RESTAURANT

❄❄

Learning to ski uses more effort, energy and concentration than almost any other recreational sport. At certain times it is as unclimbable a peak as the surrounding mountains. Compound this with the feeling that while you are falling on the beginners' slopes everyone else is flying down the mountain, and an occasional sense of despair is justified.

How good it is then for one of the more popular mountain meeting spots to be at the bottom of the beginners' slopes. The Bahnhof offers the additional attractions of good food, good prices and good company. It is the locals' local with the traditional village table; the qualification for sitting at it is at least five generations in the valley. The other locals who gather here are the season ticket holders; those who the jealous among us refer to as ski bums.

Continental railway stations always seem more romantic than their English counterparts, so added to the friendly atmosphere is another ingredient: in this case the announcer may well say, "the train now leaving platform one will return tomorrow".

Lunch is generally served between midday and 2.00pm and dinner is available until 10.00pm. Wiener Schnitzel is a popular dish and the quality of the beer has been praised by assiduous drinking inspectors.

THE KRAZY KANGURUH

❄❄

This place is a legend even outside St. Anton. Almost every skier you know has either been here or knows a man who has. With this in mind, most people arrive for the first time expecting something, but what?

Nice as it is, it is probably not the decor. Funky as it is, it is probably not the music. Excellent as it always is, it is probably not the

HAUTES CUISINES

Glühwein. And it is certainly not the haute cuisine.
Maybe, just maybe, it is because between 16.00 and 17.00 hours every day, the place implodes with the young, bright, boisterous English, Swedish, Australian, German and even Austrians, rubbing shoulders, brushing cheeks, buying rounds and generally letting the day off with a caution.
They come here to meet, eat, drink and date. The eating is from a list as short as it is specialised: taccos, nachos and bonitos; the truly cosmoplitan take a hamburger and fries. These can be washed down with some of the excellent beer that comes vom Fass and overflows the big goblets.
To ski down here, start up at Gempen, or at least pass it on your way. Pleasant blues lead you to the rock and roll.
To ski away from here, back to the village, leave alone and before it turns icy. Mass exodus at 1800 or 1900 has produced mass collisions on the way down.

RODELLHÜTTE

❋❋❋

If mountain restaurants were to be measured by ticks in boxes, then the Rodel Alm would come way up the list with more ticks in more boxes than most others.
This log-built cabin captivates all the senses that are heightened by the extended test that is skiing. Here the great log fire, sensibly placed in the centre of the hut, warms the chilled extremities. The seating brings rest to the tired limbs, the moody, gas-lit interior turns the flush of effort into a mountain tan, and the menu provides the fuel necessary to venture forth once more. Here one makes friends with the speed of schnapps, large quantities of which are dispensed by people who can not only spell gemütlich, but really know what it means.
Many who arrive here in poor conditions are disappointed when the weather improves, thereby removing their excuse for not leaving. In the evenings, many walk up here to fuel their courage before taking the 15 minute toboggan run down to Nasserein where the toboggans are collected.
Those who ski down here do do from Kapal or Gampen and look forward to the Tiroler Gröstl at 95 schillings or the Schweinehaxe served with Sauerkraut and the inevitable Knödel for 125 schillings. Snackers who want to soften the constant drip of schnapps, pad out with a good Bratwurst.
Herr Alber, who has been here for the past 14 years, always provides a warm welcome, and has done almost everything to make sure his guests enjoy themselves. The 'almost' refers to the loos, which, although good and clean, need to be approached from outside the hut, and on cold days even metal monkeys may think twice.

ULMER HÜTTE

❋❋

Shiplap shingles give this old established hut a distinctly colonial feel

HAUTES CUISINES

from the outside. Smallish windows and polished wood give it an intimate feeling on the inside. Established in 1903 for climbers, it has long been a favourite stopping place for those skiing down from the Valluga.

The Getränkekarte (this is German for the get drunk card) is much longer than the Speisekarte (this is German for what you should have eaten before you get to the get drunk card). There are six different types of schnapps, including Vogelbeerschnapps, which translates as either for bird brains or that is how you are after drinking one.

The menu is simple and good value. The ever-filling Gulaschsuppe with bread is 45 schillings and main courses run from 80 to 120 schillings. If you can leave a little space then try the hot apple strudel with custard and cream.

Oustide, an ice bar is surrounded by wobbly tables and equally wobbly drinkers.

There are not many places to stop on this part of the mountain and so the Ulmer Hütte is very popular. You may, therefore, have to wait for a table, but not to be served.

HAUTES CUISINES

ST CHRISTOPH
1770m. - Top Station 2650m.
AUSTRIA

Not so much a village as a small group of hotels, St Christoph is just up the pass from St Anton (qv) and just before the turn up to the Flexen pass and on to Zürs (qv) and Lech (qv).

Hotels have been here for hundreds of years as a refuge for those taking the often perilous journey through the pass.

Hospitality therefore is second nature to these people and every visitor is aware of it.

The skiing links into St Anton (qv) and Stuben (qv) so is extensive and exciting.

Nearest airport is Zürich

HOSPITZ ALM

❄❄❄❄

"When the bombs start falling do not forget the corkscrew". This must be engraved on the mind of all who work at the Alm, for in their air conditioned nuclear shelter, protected by a ten inch thick steel door, is one of the finest collections of good wine in the world. Certainly, at an altitude of nearly 1800 metres it must be unique. For here lies nearly half a million pounds worth of some of the finest Bordeaux that one can imagine, some in bottles of 18 litre size that tower above the relatively commonplace imperials, jeraboams and double magnums that lie in elegant state in this treasure trove.

From 1921 Château Latour, the rollcall starts. There are few names of import that do not say "here sir". There are 26 vintages of Yquem and 13 of Petrus; and although the clarets reign supreme, no lover of Burgundy is going to feel left out.

St. Christoph is not a village, certainly not a town; if anything, it is a hamlet of hospitality. For the last 707 years there has been a Hospitz here to greet the weary traveller and 707 years of tradition is very hard to beat. The Hospitz Alm is the first restaurant you see as you ski down from Ulmerhütte or Galzig. Outside, you will, if the weather is right, see a terrace covered in colours of the rainbow lazing around the ice bar, dazzling each other. Do not be seduced into staying outside for there is more within. As you enter you will encounter a glass case, well more a glass menagerie, inside of which are live sheep, bored and baaing and a goat, bearded and bright-eyed. Certainly makes a change from a stuffed marmotte. Stop, gape and continue into the dark and inviting interior. The wood butcher has been and his cousin the interior decorator was close on his heels. Stone pillars support wood beams, which support more wood beams. A large stone fireplace is usually ablaze. Discreet lighting and the world's largest bunch of dried flowers hang from the rafters. The large space is laid out well, with many cosy and comfortable corners, which induce a reluctance to leave.

HAUTES CUISINES

At lunch there is a light menu, reasonably priced: a good risotto and a recommended Arlberger Spinätzle. In the evening there is a considerably enlarged card to tempt you to indulge and dig deep into your pocket and your dreams as you blink over the wine list.

People make the journey here for birthdays, weddings, anniversaries, coups d'états and, probably, minor coronations. Those who have seen the wine cellar are tempted to run in shouting "War! War! Quickly, to the cellars!" Do not get left in the rush.

HAUTES CUISINES

ST GERVAIS
820m. - Top Station 2350m.
FRANCE

St Gervais is an old spa town that lies between Megève (qv) and Chamonix (qv). It offers good hotels shops and cinemas. The skiing is insufficiently demanding for the advanced, but the two main ski areas, one on each side of the valley, offer pleasant pistes for everyone else.

There are a good number of excellent hotels, bars and restaurants and being where it is, it connects in to the Chamonix ski pass which offers an unrivalled amount of all kinds of skiing. A car is useful to take most advantage of this.

The resort is about an hour from Geneva.

CHALET REMY
LE BETTEX

❋❋❋

The Didier family have owned this old, small and charming chalet for more years than they care to tell and have created a restaurant which is well worth the necessary diversion from the piste. Off the pistes between Le Bettex and les Communailles, it requires a short walk before you encounter this elegant establishment, low of ceiling with polished panels on the walls and plain planks for a floor, which celebrates, as the owners put it, "la vie de chalet sous le grand soleil des Alpes".

The menu is wide ranging but the salads are particularly recommended as is the wide selection of wine and beer. The Didiers ensure the special atmosphere that family ownership creates maintains a satisfactory balance between warmth and efficiency.

Outside, having made yourself comfortable on the patio, views of Mont Blanc can be taken with a drink from the bar.

Rooms are available in the summer as well, when skiers are replaced by ramblers and fishermen who also enjoy comfort and a sight of Mont Blanc. For reservations, call 50.93.11.85.

L' IGLOO

❋❋

Most skiers are sane, sensible creatures who know why they are in a ski resort: in the day they ski, stopping from time to time for essentials such as food, booze and loos; in the evenings they eat, drink, dance and indulge in those sorts of activities that happy, healthy groups of people on holiday always pursue, like embroidery. However, there are two nocturnal activities that are definitely the preserve of the less sane and sensible: one is torch lit descents (burning cinders and wax in hair, on ski suit and so on) and the other is toboggan racing. If you enjoy watching others making fools of themselves or putting their lives at risk, then the Igloo is as good a place to see them do it as any. Toboggan races back to the resort start from here.

On the other hand, if you want somewhere charming for lunch that serves a mean steak or salad at reasonable prices then the Igloo looks after your needs rather well. Located at the top of the Princess gondola and the Princess lifts, it is easy to reach for non-skiers who can catch up with their ski-wearing

HAUTES CUISINES

friends as they descend the Mont d' Arbois piste.

A traditional building on two floors, the Igloo can accommodate up to 150 people. Nonetheless, it is well to arrive early; it gets very crowded although this seems not to affect the commendable speed of the service. The house speciality is steak and very good steaks, too.

If you prefer to lounge on the terrace, there are sun chairs to make you comfortable and a fine view of Mont Blanc to discourage you from moving. If you insist on toboggan racing, then top up on the excellent mulled wine, plunge and pray.

HAUTES CUISINES

ST. MORITZ
1800 m. - Top Station 3300 m.
SWITZERLAND

A traditional haunt of the British, who are now largely supplanted by more recent wealth, St. Moritz is justly famous for its beauty, its lakes and non-skiing activities, notably tobogganing. A large town, not noted for being cheap but not as expensive as some may fear, it boasts such well known centres of luxury and grandeur as the Palace, as well as more modest establishments. Quieter and less ostentatious is the linked resort of Celerina.

The skiing is extensive and varied, providing flattering intermediate slopes as well as more demanding slopes for the skilled and experienced. A car is useful for access, however, because the ski areas are scattered. The pistes are also well stocked with restaurants; a selection is reviewed below.

The nearest international airport is Zürich.

SKIHÜTTE ALPINA

❄❄❄

Spaghettata. Is it a new form of pasta, a recent discovery of how to combine the slimming delights of flour, water and pattatas, or a spelling mistake? Switzerland has four official languages and 40 unofficial dialects. The languages are Swiss-Deutsch, French, Italian and Romansch. Romansch, which is the language of the Engadine, has its roots somewhere between the stars and schoolboy Latin, and is both entrancing and unintelligible to the ear. Spaghettata is son of Romansch and, sad to relate, is spaghetti. In this skiers' hut there are seven varieties.

Rustic upon rustic, wood upon stone. Inside, the walls are browned with the smoke of a thousand Swiss cigars and the almost caressing atmosphere encourages one to stay a while. Outside, stepped terraces permit unobstructed views up the valley and across the lakes.

Back at the menu, and away from the pasta all of which are around 15 Swiss francs, the Swissness reverts to dishes 'mit Rösti' with the exception of a rather expensive chilli con carne at 20 francs. Filling snacks abound at around 10 francs.

The real interest comes after lunch, for the same menu that contains, clearly described, für Kinder dishes at between seven and nine francs, also contains clearly described nicht für Kinder: adult delights of digestifs that include ovo alpina with rum and cream, cafe schümli with plum schnapps and whipped cream and cafe Grischa which comes in a rustic ceramic pot with spout for sipping through. In Italy it is called a Groller and is a great way to raise the temperature and lower the quality of the conversation. Needless to say, those involved do not notice this and leave with a feeling of well-being and love for their fellow man. This is a good way to leave here but not necessarily to start an afternoon's skiing.

The Skihütte Alpina is located between the Corviglia and the Fis-Hang drag lifts.

RESTAURANT ALPETTA

❄❄

The snow-making machines that line the piste down from the Murtel, mean that the snow is always perfect on the gentle cruise to Alp Margem. You will glimpse

HAUTES CUISINES

this stone and wood-built chalet sitting above the trees that line the run down to Surles.

This small and cosy restaurant has withstood the worst of the Alpine weather for many years and provides the skier with oft needed refuge in the face of ever changing mountain climes.

Inside, the central stove is warmly welcoming. Surrounding it, comfortable booths encompass round tables for six or eight people. On a cold day, get there early. Outside, a barbecue and and ice bar, with strong Aussie overtones, is always busy on a sunny day and long tables are crowded with noise and colour.

The menu is as fresh as the food, written daily on small blackboards that hang always just where you cannot see them. The list is short, reflecting the smallness of the kitchen and the sensible ambitions of the chef. Particularly popular is the Hörnligratin, yet another way of disposing of Switzerland's most famous mountain, the cheese mountain. It comes bubbling in a shallow dish and soon dispenses with any pangs of hunger; it also dispenses with 14 Swiss francs.

The wine list matches the menu: short and Swiss, but quite adequate and reasonably priced.

After lunch, a short walk back to the piste helps both the digestion and the limbs before the rigours of the afternoon.

RESTAURANT CHASELLAS

❄❄❄❄

Restaurant Chasellas is not for every day, unless that is, your pocket runs to it. It epitomises charm, elegance and style in a resort of style.

Madeline Ruedi, who runs this small establishment, manages to do so without that sense of elitism that so often occurs with lesser but more pretentious restaurants. Her polite and friendly team of bright young things make one as welcome in ski boots at lunch as they would the fur coated that fill the place for dinner every evening.

Although it sits on the piste at the bottom of the Suvretta chairs, it bears none of the trademarks of the more usual boot-bruised hut. Solidly stone built, its exterior belies the feminine touch that gives dining here something extra. There are flowers on the table, nice linen, customised banquettes around the walls and chairs that do not have a time limit.

Ici on mange français. The gourmet menu, which is even more so in the evenings, offers much traditional fare, but with an à-la-carte opportunity to escape the rösti trail. The restaurant is famous for its côtelette double d'agneau, which most of us would recognise as a Barnsley chop, but somehow in French it tastes better and costs more. Ris et rognons de veau, an unusual moutain dish, can follow your foie gras in a calvados sauce, if richness is what you seek.

The wine list offers fair choice with a balanced combination of French and Italian wines as well as the usual Swiss.

Regulars book their table on cold days for the restaurant is small and people tend to linger (tel:08.23.38.54), but on sunny days the large stone terrace outside seems to absorb all who come. The view across the valley, and the unhurried service, relax the limbs that the day's rigours tense up.

Prices run a little higher than most mountain stops, but everyone leaves feeling enriched by the

135

HAUTES CUISINES

experience even if a little poorer, although compared with restaurants in the town, it reeks of value.

RESTAURANT FRITZ

❋❋❋

A designer hut is how one person described the Fritz, and for the smarter set of St. Moritz, it is certainly designed to please.

Although half the restaurant is taken up with self-service, somehow it manages to resemble a buffet rather than the normal sliding rail, but then, belonging as it does to the Suvretta House (qv), this does not surprise. Pass through the 'self' area and a cosy service restaurant hides behind a polished wood door.

The menu, under the supervision of Robert Jagisch, is thoroughly good value. Perhaps that is why the smart set are so smart. Soups and starters are from seven Swiss francs and main courses range from ten francs upwards. Specials from the ever-changing day card run from 16 francs up to 50 francs, with a Swiss version of bouillabaisse at 27 francs and a huge entrecôte at 48 francs. Those who believe that Europe runs from Calais to the steppes of Russia, will be intrigued by the spaghetti Doctor Shivago (although the inspector was not Russian to try it himself).

The wines are mainly Swiss, but the carafes start at 13 francs for half a litre.

Outside, two terraces caress the snow and are crowded with the young bp's who know how to balance a glass, flick their hair and check out who else is there, faster than you can say Fritz. But say it, remember it, you will like it.

The restaurant Fritz is situated at the base of the Randolins chair on the plateaa Noir.

FURTSCHELAS

❋❋

At first sight, the building that surrounds the top station of the Furtschelas cable car reminds one of an abandoned airfield, best left abandoned. On closer inspection, you will find a big and busy, and somewhat charmless, self-service restaurant. Do not be put off. Carry on past the unusual, for this sort of place, open fire and, at the far end, behind a solid wooden partition, hides Bedientes restaurant.

Big windows let light and views stream in. The snow-covered lake of Segl looks like a giant white motorway heading, as it does, towards the Italian border. One gets the feeling that this gesture to elegant eating is not the ambition of the management. The single waiter, sweat on brow, has to do the work of three to keep the demanding lunchtime skiers happy. But to be fair to Fritz, he probably grew up in the mountains doing the work of four, so this daily challenge he meets with enthusiasm and skill and is always ready to discuss the menu and some of its more unusual dishes.

These dishes include chestnut soup, stuffed spinach beet leaves, Engadine specialities, fresh fish, good risotto and pasta. Rösti buffs will find several new ones here, including a calves liver rösti and a cream cheese rösti.

The wine list, like the food, has an Italian influence and the prices allowed lunch for two, including wine, to round out at 25 Swiss francs per head.

HAUTES CUISINES

After lunch, a tow up on the Grialetsch or the Chuderun drags gives you a short time for digestion before testing the knees once again.

GLÜNETTA

❊❊

The Glünetta is situated at the bottom of the new super lift below Piz Glüna. A modern restaurant, but nicely done in stone and wood, the respect for tradition extends to the cooking. The aroma of raclette greets new arrivals and at 10 Swiss francs it is hard to resist.
The more gastronomically adventurous can try rabbit sausage (the Glünetta makes a speciality of sausages), topped up with vitamins from the salad bar.
The restaurant is good value and understandably popular. When the weather is bad, arrive early. When the weather is fine, soak up the sun on the terrace and try the barbeque.

MARMITE CORVIGLIA

❊❊❊

Schizophrenia is not uncommon in the Alps and the Marmite is but one example: a combination of self-service (if you must. . .) and a serviced restaurant offering good food in more cosseting surroundings.
Lunch is recommended, especially given the ease of access for non-skiers, but the real delights of the Marmite are signalled by the array of desserts on the sideboard. It is a great spot for those with a sweet tooth and a sheer delight for those who wish to indulge in that great British invention, now a sadly declining institution, but a source of joy for all that, afternoon tea.
Easily reached via the cable car, nicely positioned above St Moritz, the Marmite is perfectly sited for visitors who, overwhelmed by carbohydrate and saturated with cream, wish to lumber slowly homeward for a bath and the contemplation of dinner.

PIZZA CHADAFO

❊❊

Like the Marmite (qv), the Pizza Chadafo is attached to a self-service restaurant. Cosy, a roaring wood burning pizza oven dominates the place, and with reasonable prices, 12 to 16 Swiss francs, this new establishment has a happy, Italian atmosphere. Long tables allow parties of up to 15 people. Worth a visit with friends.

SKIHÜTTE PARADISO

❊

Simple and basic and basically simple in both menu and architecture, the Paradiso is a long way from paradise, but for those who want to ski fast and be fed fast, this hut is the place to visit. Pasta fills the menu, be it spaghetti, macaroni or any other variety. If you like to eat breakfast all day, there is ham and eggs and bacon and eggs. Order, eat and away. The service is as crisp as the salad.
The slower take to the sun lounge area and pick at a char-grilled something. They sip through straws the drinks delivered from the ice bar, and lie in the sun exchanging

HAUTES CUISINES

gossip or catching up on their reading.
Although not expensive, somehow one feels there are places which offer more for the same, but if skiing outranks lunching, the Paradiso will not detain you. Ski here on the red run down from Munt da S. Murezzen.

ZÜBERHÜTTE

❄❄❄

Favoured by the carriage trade (the indolent, the traditionally minded and non-skiers can make the journey by horse and carriage), the Züberhütte is popular towards the end of the day as an agreeable stop at Chantarella. The waiters are cheerful in Alpine dress, there is live music to entertain and customers insufficiently exercised by their exertions on the pistes can dance. A fire in the centre of the room adds to the appeal. Drink, relax and enjoy.

HAUTES CUISINES

STUBEN
1400m. - Top Station 2400m.
AUSTRIA

A skier's secret, Stuben is a quaint little village with half a dozen hotels sitting just below the Arlberg pass, which takes all the traffic to its better known neighbours of Zürs (qv), Lech (qv) and St. Anton (qv).

Whilst Stuben offers sunny nursery slopes, it is the skiing on the Albona that brings serious skiers back time and time again. The skiing links up with St. Anton (qv) and St. Christoph (qv) by way of the triple chair up to Ulmer Hütte, so providing a tiny village with a huge ski area.

The snow record here is excellent and the season can run from December until late April.

The après ski is not too bad for such a small village with two swimming pools and a good selection of bars.

Although somewhat more expensive than St. Anton, it has a character all of its own and the many who return here year after year think it is worth it.

HOTEL POST
❊❊

The Hotel Post sits comfortably on the edge of this quaint little village. The dolls' house architecture of painted stucco and shuttered windows reinforces the mountain atomsphere and makes it difficult to imagine what it would be like without a covering of snow. Happily, in the winter in Stuben, this is an unlikely prospect. For some reason the snow here is always better than in the surrounding villages, lying deeper and crisper and even longer.

This haven of experienced skiers is also a haven of experienced trenchermen, and the Hotel Post swallows them all with confidence. The menu offers local specialities cooked to delight. The Kartoffelrahmsuppe warms the inner being and leaves just enough room for a Schinkenrahmspätzle. The menu confines itself to its core of confidence but does not ever bore, with daily specials adding variety to virtue. The wine list is a little lacklustre, but reasonably priced.

The wise and hungry arrive before one o'clock to be sure of getting a table in the delightful, panelled dining room with its beautiful inlaid tables. On sunny days, the overflow spills out onto the west-facing terrace where lunchers can look towards Switzerland, smugly satisfied that they are paying less for their potatoes than the Swiss. For those in a hurry a Kaffee mit something alcoholic may be taken in the bar where, in the afternoons, a fire burns making the reluctant skiers even more reluctant.

The Hotel Post is run by the affable Fritz Niki, who will proudly tell you that it has been here for 500 years; with a few alterations that is. Ski down from the Valluga, the Albona or the Walvager; walk here through the village.

HAUTES CUISINES

RASTHAUS FERWALL

❄❄❄

Virtue may be its own reward, but courage deserves a prize, and so, for those who take the wonderful off piste run down the Verwaltal, there is the Rasthaus Ferwall.

Sitting in an idyllic position on the edge of the forest at the head of the Ferwall valley, this hut meets most expectations of the hunter of taste and taste sensations. The interior has that cosy feeling that is most easily found in an old pair of slippers, and indeed, the open fire provides the ideal spot to rest your slippered feet, so stick a pair in your rucksack before you set off. Even without slippers, you will feel at home here. The russet wood interior draws you in, even on sunny days, when many take to the terrace.

The menu draws strongly on the local preferences, and whatever you choose will be freshly cooked and delicious. Many come here to hunt out the excellent wild game dishes, while others claim the ski here is worthwhile for the homemade Apfel Kuchen, with or without Vanillesauce.

Langlaufers also make a pilgrimage here along the track from the Albona. However you choose to arrive, the experience will not disappoint.

HAUTES CUISINES

LA THUILE
1450m. Top Station 2640m.
ITALY

To an old mining village, add a large hotel and ski developement and you have something that looks remarkably like La Thuile. Facilities for parking are good, the accommodation is reasonable but the sum total of the parts has yet to attract huge numbers of skiers. The scenery is attractive and there are some good runs even if experienced skiers miss great challenges. Set in the Val d'Aosta, La Thuile is linked with La Rosière in France (qv). Trips by car to Courmayeur (qv) and Chamonix (qv) are possible. The nearest international airport is Turin.

LA CLOTZE

❄❄❄

La Clotze is that rarity in La Thuile a restaurant with proper service. Attractive, traditional and wooden, it is an easy ski down piste number two or comfortably walk-able from the cable car.

From the rear of the restaurant, the windows look out over the valley, the front looks directly onto the piste. There is no terrace as such but tables and chairs can be spread on the snow when the sun beckons.

The food is very reasonably priced (lunch averages about 9000 lire per person) and consists mostly of pasta and toasted rolls. Plentiful supplies of lager and red wine are available to wash it down.

Beware the loos. They are of the hole-in-the-floor variety.

HAUTES CUISINES

TIGNES
2000m. - Top Station 3439m.
FRANCE

Tignes is linked with Val d' Isère (qv) and provides the opportunity to ski over more than 160 miles of pisted runs. It has the advantage over its sister resort of providing summer skiing on the glacier of the Grande Motte. The determinedly athletic can rush down the pistes in the morning and windsurf on the reservoir in the afternoon.

Tignes is a purpose built resort and there is nothing folksy, twee or traditional about its architecture. What you see is what you get and that is squared off blocks and chalets that would not look out of place on the periphery of any major industrial city. This perhaps summarises Tignes' approach to skiing: efficient, focused and effective. Between them Val d' Isère and Tignes provide superb skiing on and off-piste.

Tignes is quite a large town and is divided into five parts: Val Claret, Lavachet, Tignes Le Lac, Les Boisses and Les Brevières. There are bars and reasonable night life in the resort, but the whole raison d' être of the town is dedicated skiing. The nearest major international airport is Geneva.

HOTEL RESTAURANT ARBINA

❋❋❋

The restaurant at the Hotel Arbina is situated on the first floor and comes as close to providing a traditional ambience as anything can in high-tech, high rise Tignes. On the day of our inspector's visit these unusual charms had attracted Ali Ross and a party of followers, the Dorking Ski Club (lots of good slopes in Dorking), myriad French families and a diminutive puppy, believed to be French as well.

The food is traditionally French and a mouthwatering magret de canard was particularly enjoyed. Also praised were sumptuous salads and cardiac-arrest-inducing chocolate desserts. The three course menu is priced at 110 francs, while an à la carte lunch will probably cost around 200 francs. The food and well dressed service were of a uniformly high standard.

The wine list is biased towards red and champagne. There are 20 of the latter listed, so if it happens to be your birthday and you find yourself in Tignes and stuck for somewhere to go . . .

The Hotel is opposite the Aero-Ski cabins at the bottom of the Rosset -piste. It can thus be approached on foot, reached by motor and enjoyed in the evenings. Despite its setting at the bottom of the piste, it provides fine views which can be sampled from the sun deck where chairs and loungers peer across the valley towards the Grande Motte.

The restaurant is quite smart with green marble floors and a touch of formality in the atmosphere. If you find this off putting while clad in ski suit and boots, there is a small bistro downstairs. But for the serious lunch, the restaurant is the thing.

HAUTES CUISINES

LE TOUR
1450m. - Top Station 3880m.
FRANCE

Situated at the head of the Chamonix valley, this little village claims to be the snow capital of France. Certainly its record is excellent. The village is small and charming, the skiing is on wide undulating slopes resting below a glacier. Good for intermediates and ideal for families and those seeking quiet.

Le Tour is about two and a half hours drive from Geneva airport.

HOTEL RESTAURANT L'OLYMPIQUE

For those who like a long ski down before lunch, a descent from the Col de Balme to the village provides a drop of 700 intermediate and picturesque metres. At the bottom sits the Olympique, a modern but traditionally built hotel, bar and restaurant.

As well as an extensive à la carte menu (which, unusually for France, includes a choice of vegetables), there is a daily set menu, four good courses for 90 francs, or the plat du jour alone for 60 francs.

The house wine at 32 francs a bottle is excellent value and the list is long enough for everyone to find a favourite. The little wooden bar is cosy, warm and an excellent end of the day meeting place.

CHALET RESTAURANT COL DE BALME

The Chalet Restaurant is a small hut in the true mountain refuge style. It is popular with skiers and walkers alike, being an easy ten minutes stroll from the top of the Charamillon Balme gondola. The menu is simple with the star offering being steak frites for 48 francs. The wine list is very local and the prices are all quite reasonable. There are good cheeses and charcuterie and on a clear day there is a wonderful view across into Switzerland, where similar mountain fare can be consumed for nearly twice the price.

HAUTES CUISINES

LA TZOUMAZ
1500m. - Top Station 3328m.
SWITZERLAND

This small resort, just over the mountains from its glittering neighbour of Verbier(qv), has an almost suburban feel to it. Sitting at the bottom of the wooded slope down from Savoleyres it is a quiet family chalet resort overlooking the Rhône valley.

The snow here is usually good and there are many interesting trails down through the woods, but with the rest of the four valleys on your doorstep variety is not going to be a problem.

Linked resorts are Verbier (qv), Nendaz, Veysonnaz.

The nearest airport is Geneva, about a two hour drive away.

CHEZ SIMON

❄❄❄

Although four years ago Simon Laurenti doubled the size of his little restaurant on the mounatin, it is still tiny, but somehow he manages to squeeze in an almost unlimted number of people.

Originally a fromagerie, Simon opened it as a restaurant in 1984. In the original part one still sits around the great old copper vat in which, during the summer, the Alpine cheeses were made. The cosy, pine clad interior is always warm. Two great, iron, wood-burning stoves provide an aroma of smoking pine, which seems to relax the mind and discourage a hasty exit. This is the only smoking allowed in the restaurant.

The simplicity of the menu is appropriate remembering the name of the owner. The soup, potage fromage, comes steaming in a big bowl, with a slice of local cheese and a basket of bread. At 5.50 Swiss francs it is probably the best value to be had on the mountain. A good, crusty sandwich jambon is 3.50 francs and a serving of the home made apple tart is delicious and costs two francs.

For those with eight francs to spend there is the assiette skieur, a plate of local cheeses, Bagnes, Illiez, Jeur and Gomser, and local sausage with more of the crusty bread. Wash it down with half a litre of the local Fendant for 11 francs, or the sunshine-filled local Dôle for 12.50 francs.

The wine comes from Simon's son, Christophe, who runs a cave down in the valley. For 1993, Simon hopes to add to his repertoire by providing fondue outside on the long, wooden benches which surround the house.

Ski down to Chez Simon from Savoleyres to the bottom of Le Nord drag lift and, after your pit stop, lunch stop or just rest stop, carry on down the pretty, tree lined route to Tzoumaz.

Chez Simon is not marked on the local piste map.

HAUTES CUISINES

VAL D' ISÈRE
1850m. - Top Station 3440m.
FRANCE

Val d'Isere and Tignes (qv) offer between them an enormous range of skiing that can accommodate any and all grades of skier. The interconnecting lifts, high speed trains (at La Daille) and cable cars offer the opportunity of covering great distances without going over the same ground twice. The altitude of the upper slopes provides good snow guarantees. In all there are around 160 miles of pisted runs.

While not built in quite the same modern brutal style of architecture as Tignes, Val d'Isere does not win any prizes for Alpine charm. However, the hotels and chalets are plentiful and efficient, the restaurants and night life in the resort are busy and welcoming and the shops offer a wide selection of goods at not-too-exorbitant prices. Val d' Isere understandably breeds loyalty in its customers.

The nearest major international airport is Geneva.

LE CABANNE DES NEIGES

❄❄

Huge, French and friendly, is a description that applies equally well to this long-established mountain lodge as to its proprietor Jean-Pierre. The continued theatre of meeting, greeting and eating starts here in the mornings and continues all day. Those arriving on the cable car or on the smart new Solaise express with its plexidome, inverted goldfish bowls, change places with those who have skied down from Cugnai or the Col de la Madeline.

Lunch here is taken from a vast list and, while gourmets need not apply, the quality of product and preparation will hardly disappoint: good grills, crisp salads and delighful desserts. The chocolate cake alone has been known to bring some people here for elevenses, lunch and, yes, afternoon tea.

If variety and death by chocolate cake are not enough to tempt you, the prices surely will, with main courses at 30 to 50 francs. The carte des boissons shows some imagination with interesting ciders and bottled beers, as well as a reasonably priced wine list.

If you need more reasons to come here, then there is a crêperie with a full house of fillings, and outside there are tables for the multitudes and sun chairs for the 'not this afternoon' skiers. Here one can look across to the Rocher Bellevarde and look at the downhill course, expensively created for the '92 Olympics and a challenge to the best of skiers. On sunny days, the attraction of this spot brings many non-skiers up in the cable car for lunch and a lounge. The seaside was never like this.

On Thursday evenings it is party time, and for 130 francs you get the famous Brasserade. This table-top barbecue of strips of tender beef is accompanied by frites and salad and a good local wine; and just when you think you cannot eat anymore, they bring you a slice of tarte aux pommes and a cup of coffee. All this, on top of the vin chaud that greets you as you arrive in the cable car, has been known to make the 20 yard walk back to the cable car something of a challenge for many, although the fresh night air and the view of Val d' Isère lit up below, refocuses the mind.

Worthy of note is that the loos here are clean and free, increasingly rare in this area.

HAUTES CUISINES

LA CRECH 'OUNA

❄❄❄❄

The charm of the old is an excellent basis for a relaxing experience, and when it has been loved and cared for by a family for over 15 years, it gets polished to near perfection. The Usannaz family have tenderly tended this old farmhouse and have renovated it to provide the kind of restaurant that entices you inside, even on a sunny day.

Antiques decorate the walls, a log fire warms the lunchers and adds a flickering glow to the rustic interior. Here lunch will not be a hurried affair; here there is that touch of gravitas that gives French cuisine and hospitality a quality that is impossible to emulate outside France.

The menu is classical combined with local. The potée savoyarde is a perfect example: cabbage stuffed wtih minced meat, covered in bacon and served with winter vegetables, a dish deliciously designed for mountain living by mountain people. The main courses here run from about 40 to 120 francs, but the portions are such that only one practised gourmand will go through the card from soup to nuts.

The wines are well chosen to accompany the menu and local bargains lie side by side with classic Bordeaux and Burgundies.

Tha farmhouse is set among the trees and on the edge of the World Cup downhill run, and the views from the small terrace reach up to Bellevarde and out across la Daille and the steep and menacing cliffs across the valley.

The loos here have left people rapturous, but are only what you would expect in a first class restaurant.

Do not come here for a fast snack, but rather save your appetite for a long and enjoyable lunch.

Ski down here easily on the red or blue runs from the top of la Daille bubbles. Walk up from la Daille, energetic but worthwhile.

HAUTES CUISINES

VALMOREL
1400m. - Top Station 2403m.
FRANCE

An example to all developing ski resorts, Valmorel has banned skyscraper blocks. The old buildings have been restored and the new ones are in traditional chalet style, at peace with each other and the surrounding landscape.

The circuit offers 162 km of pistes served by 46 lifts including the satellites of St. Francois and Longchamp.

The skiing offers a full menu of delights, beneficial to beginners, interesting for intermediates and exciting for the experienced. The ski school is very well organized and ski évolutif is an option. Children of all ages are particularly well catered for. Like all real villages, as opposed to resorts, Valmorel has a friendly atmosphere; centred around the village square the facilities spread out, restaurants, nightclubs and pleasing shops. The Grill le Creuset is well recommended, with its 'cuisine au feu du bois' and Le Jeans Club is a lively discothèque for those who like their evenings cheek to cheek.

The nearest airport is Geneva and the transfer time is about two and a half hours.

ALTIPIANO

❄❄❄

The Altipiano is noteworthy for many things. Not the least of these is that the restaurant is entirely self built by the couple who own it. They levelled the gound, no mean feat in itself, and went on from there. They started more than three years ago. What makes this even more remarkable is that he is French and she is English, an example of harmonious international co-operation sadly absent during the construction of Concorde, the digging of the Channel tunnel or any discussion of the Common Agricultural Policy.

The result of these labours is traditional in style, comfortable for around 70 people seated, equipped with a small bar, blessed with clean loos and offers a comprehensive menu at prices that will not bankrupt you. People who build their own restaurants are careful with your money as well as their own. The selection of French wines is rather narrow, but the beer is highly recommended.

The Altipiano can be found at the top of the Pierrafort gondola. Fortified by the example of your prospective hosts, you take a black run from there to the restaurant. After a lengthy lunch and sun bathe (the views down to Valmorel and across the valley are excellent) gentle blues and reds lead back to the village.

HAUTES CUISINES

VAL THORENS
2300m. - Top Station 3200m.
FRANCE

Val Thorens is the highest resort in Europe and consequently thin on traditional Alpine charm.

That said, the development here has been done with more sensitivity than in other purpose built resorts, and for those who want to ski, ski and ski, here is a virtual guarantee of good snow and variety.

As the newest of the four resorts that make up the Trois Vallées, it has had the opportunity to learn from the others and to install the best and latest in lifts and in this way has created over 80 miles of marked piste, suitable for beginners and powder hounds alike.

The accommodation is either in hotels or apartments and there are many bars and restaurants to cater for all tastes. The sports centre has indoor tennis, swimming, squash, weightlifting, a golf driving range and even a climbing wall. If this is not enough there are snowmobiles and snow motorbikes to rent, quad racing, a cinema and hang gliding and paragliding; and for the nocturnal there are music bars and discothèques.

Linked resorts are Courchevel (qv), Meribèl (qv) and Les Menuires. The nearest airport is Geneva which is a three to four hour transfer.

LES CRETES
SOMMET DE TOUGNETE

❄❄❄

Les Cretes is one of those restaurants that generate enthusiasm in even the stoniest breast of the most press-on-and-be-damned-to-the-food skier. Our far from stony inspector wrote quite simply, "I love this restaurant". An old establishment as these things go in Val Thorens, it was built around 1964 and for the past eight years has been owned by André and Françoise Griffon, who tend to greet familiar customers on arrival, the beginning of the magic they appear to work on the area's skiers.

The menu has an abundance of local specialities together with the more familiar steak and chips. Popular are diots, pork sausage in a white wine sauce accompanied by potatoes boiled in their skins, for 63 francs. Vegetarians can opt for an excellent vegetable sausage for the same price. Crozets at 48 francs are squares of pasta served in a fine, creamy sauce with cheese. If something a little lighter is preferred, the house salad, served in large helpings, consists of good local ham, potatoes boiled in their skins, nuts and greenery - good value at 48 francs.

Wines, too, are reasonably priced. A pichet of savoyarde wine costs between 32 and 48 francs depending on choice; a drinkable Burgundy is 98 and Bordeaux varies between 72 and 75 francs. If you prefer your liquids without alcohol, a 1.5 litre bottle of Evian for 22 francs is one of the cheapest to be had locally.

The only mildly discordant note in this admirable story is the need to recount the absence of running water in the loos, which are, nonetheless, clean.

Les Cretes is small and cosy on the inside and has spectacular views from the outside. It is sited at the top of the Tougnete gondola above Méribel or can be approached from St. Martin de Belleville on the Pranunt chair. It is a trek from Val Thorens. It is worth it.

HAUTES CUISINES

LA MOUTIÈRE

❄❄

La Moutière is a small, rectangular building, surrounded by an enormous deck, draped with ladders (one steep one leads down to the loos, be careful, another steep one leads to the owners' accommodation above), festooned occasionally with fresh flowers (watch for seasoned Ski Club reps with their noses buried in a vase of roses while devouring the dish of the day) that houses a delightful restaurant with a narrow but first class menu.

Some 70 people can be squeezed inside for lunch and frequently are. Fortunately, there is an extractor to deal with the smoke and any other hot air generated by a morning's derring-do on the slopes. La Moutière is a not-quite-self-service restaurant. You queue up to order and pay; you then sit down and wait for your food to be brought. Anyone who prefers to spend longer standing up, can wait to fetch the food for themselves.

Skiing staples such as ham and eggs, steak and chips and steak haché and chips are all well cooked. The ubiquity of these dishes encourages one too easily to overlook their excellence. Some people think more along the lines of the late Dorothy Sayers who said that she never regretted Paradise Lost since she discovered it contained no eggs and bacon. There is always a dish of the day (examples include turkey breast with mushroom sauce served with spinach; lasagne, or rabbit with polenta) representing good value at 54 francs. The apple and myrtille tarts are justly renowned.

The wine list modestly restricts itself to pichets and bottles of local wine.

Regulars praise the staff for their speed and courtesy under the fire of enormous numbers even at the end of the season when they might be forgiven a certain battle weariness. Like many good mountain restaurants, La Moutière has an animal, in this instance a Siamese cat, who can normally be found resting on the hot water pipes near the loos.

To join the crowd, go up La Moutière drag lift and ski down to the bottom of 2 La Plateau drag.

HAUTES CUISINES

VERBIER
1500m. - Top Station 3330m.
SWITZERLAND

Forget all the chatter about Verbier's not-quite-Royal connections. The whole point of the place is skiing. Great skiing and lots of it. Part of the Four Valleys circuit served by more than 90 lifts, there is something to attract all types of skier from the nervous nurseries to the off-piste plungers. For the dedicated summer skier the Mont Fort glacier at over 3300 metres provides good runs. Most famous piste is the Tortin - long, steep, mogul infested and exciting.

A parapente centre as well as a ski resort, the sky above Ruinettes (ski station and restaurant) on a fine day is crowded with parachutes, gaudy as exotic birds. Lessons are offered to anyone seeking an alternative route to the valley floor.

On the mountain, a small number of huts provide good food, drink and an excellent atmosphere whether you are seeking a quick pit stop or a serious intake of calories.

Situated above the valley, Verbier has splendid views of the Mont Blanc and Combin ranges. For those who want to take a break from skiing, the village has excellent shops, restaurants and bars. Those whose legs need further, nocturnal, exercise can be found in one of the village's many nightclubs.

Within easy reach of Geneva (a two hour drive), Verbier is readily accessible by rail or road.

AU MOYEN

❈❈❈

Hi-tech and low tech, radio controlled but not robotic waitresses and a granite stove plus open fire, co-exist comfortably at Au Moyen, the busy, buzzy restaurant run by Heidi and Jean-Paul Luisier, which sits below the top of the Mayentzet and just below the bottom of the La Combe I chairs.

The food which is served in the crowded, yellow pine interior has been described as homemade and hearty which translates as regular mountain fare. A warming bowl of bouillon with little profiteroles is five Swiss francs. The homemade vegetable soup, almost a meal in itself, is 9.50 francs, while a fondue for two is 40 francs and very pleasant, too, on a day when there is time to enjoy the performance, that is fondue eating, and the view that is served with it.

An interestingly different dish is the carbonara de pommes de terre et connettes, a satisfying agglomeration of carbohydrates on top of carbohydrates, pasta on potatoes, covered in cheese and ham and baked in the oven and priced at 10.50 francs.

The waitresses are summoned by their personal bleepers when Jean-Paul has something ready in the kitchen to ensure that it reaches the customer fast and hot.

If it is just a mid-morning or late afternoon stop one wants, then the vin chaud is all one expects and the Irish coffe comes with whipped cream rising like the top of Mont Fort but a lot less challenging.

There is no house wine but a local white Fendant is 28 francs a bottle and, if you like an interesting red, try the Humagne, which has rather more to it than the average Dôle.

HAUTES CUISINES

CARREFOUR

❊❊❊

Inside, outside, upstairs or downstairs, Carrefour is every inch a chic mountain restaurant, popular with skiers, walkers and even those who choose to arrive by ski bus. It has sunny terraces on two levels and the restaurant spreads over two floors as well.

Sited at the top of Le Rouge, a favourite beginners' piste, at the end of the pisted path around from Savoleyres and at the end of good runs down from Attelas, it is truly the crossroads of Verbier.

Laure Gulielmina has owned and managed the Carrefour for thirty years and knows well her clientèle and their likes and dislikes. The menu combines the mountain favourites of croûtes and pastas with a wide range of daily specials such as salmon and game, stews and grills.

A good range of salads and cold dishes make a light, inexpensive lunch a reality. For the hungry and choosy, the tournedos aux morilles never fails to please. Small portions of spaghetti and tortellini provide a welcome alternative to frites for children.

Inside, the tables are elegant with linen. Outside on the terrace, hats and sun cream are necessary to the enjoyment of the views across Verbier and down the valley.

Prices run from seven Swiss francs for the home made vegetable soup to about 15 francs for a croûte or a pasta. Omelettes, which are excellent, start at ten francs.

There are Vaudois wines that break the monotony of the eternal Valais and prices start at 25 francs.

CHEZ DANY
CLAMBIN

❊❊❊

"Wave to the nice man in the parachute, dear," is a cry frequently to be heard at Chez Dany, which lies on the parapente route, swift into the valley, down below Ruinettes (qv). But friendly, low flying parachutists, are merely one of its many attractions. Some come for the food, some for the ambience, some for the view, but whatever the reason, Chez Dany is one restaurant you cannot leave Verbier without visiting. And while there, you should attempt, a word selected with care, the eponymous "Spaghetti Dany".

To prepare spaghetti Dany, first catch your spaghetti (a large quantity). Place it in a fire proof dish and cover with ham, then cheese. Place under the grill and then top it off with a fried egg. If you are reading this after a light, salad luncheon on a warm summer's day, then its powerful appeal may, momentarily, elude you. After skiing down a mountain, one's digestive system enjoys a different perspective on the matter.

For the gourmet seeking something a tad lighter and more subtle, there is a "salade ouindu", consisting of rabbit fillets, raspberry vinegar, olive oil and salad. Alternatively, there is a cassolette de champignons, a dish of paris mushrooms, pleurottes and shitake mushrooms with eschalottes, garlic, tomatoes and herbs.

Prices are reasonable. Three Swiss francs secures a bouillon and a mere 13 francs, the spaghetti Dany. Bacon and eggs are eight francs, a croûte is 12. For 22 francs you can enjoy a tranche de gigot d'agneau gratin avec salade.

The wine list is limited but good value.

Daniel Michaul opened his restaurant 12 years ago having spent five years trying to get planning permission. When he did, he did it justice. The chalet is perched on a ledge looking across the valley and up to les Dents du Midi. The terrace seats nearly 100 people, but somehow looks small as it winds around two sides of the chalet. Glass screens protect visitors from winds.

Approach the restaurant carefully because the route is sometimes difficult and always easy to miss. Ski down from Ruinettes to the bottom of the Fontanays chair. Then follow the path through the woods that leads back to Medran. Chez Dany is sign posted to the left. Follow a well skied path to a forest of skis. Behind them you will find Chez Dany, where Dany himself commands the kitchen and his wife Brigitte the rest of the proceedings.

LA MARMOTTE
SAVOLEYRES

❄❄❄

Undistinguished from above, La Marmotte lies below the bottom of the Savoleyres Sud drag lift on the Verbier side of Savoleyres. However, as you round the corner and remove your skis, a magnificent example of the local wood-chopper's art comes into view. Built in an 'L' shape on two sides of the wooden terrace, La Marmotte is another answer to the old question: "What do I do with my old mountain fromagerie?".

Inside, the wood butcher's art is at its best. Low beams force the tall to duck and two monumental granite stoves provide resting places for hats, gloves, scarves and leaning places for cold bottoms. Various objets of Valais history line the walls and a big-horned bull's head looks quite at home on the eaves. Our favourite painting hangs in the small, many-windowed stübli which looks out across Verbier. It is a naif oil painting of two famous Valaisanne fighting cows in full pitch. This is a surprisingly big sport in the Valais in the summer and many wagers are won and lost in contests all over the region.

The favourite dishes here are the röstis, three kinds, all served with a mixed salad. There are eight kinds of croûte and fondues aplenty. Our favourite has bolets, local mushrooms, in it. These are the preferred lunch dishes, although the menu offers steaks, chops, sausage and even good old eggs and bacon. They are all efficiently produced from a kitchen that is as modern as the original hut is old.

The ubiquitous tiramisu makes an appearance on the list of desserts and there are special dishes and portions for children. The prices range from 13 Swiss francs for a simple croûte, to 25 francs for a goodly steak. A half portion of spaghetti on the children's menu is 5.50 francs.

The wines are from the Valais. The local Dôle and Fendant are under 30 francs a bottle.

This is one of the most popular huts in Verbier and, despite seating 120 inside, it manages that dark, inti-

HAUTES CUISINES

mate atmosphere that is so appropriate on the mountain.

AU VIOLON D'INGRES

❄❄❄

Mention the proper name of this restaurant to even old Verbier hands and few will know what you mean. But say "meet you at Ruinettes" and all will know.

This cavernous restaurant with a separate, and even more cavernous, self-service below has all the architectural charm of some of London's less interesting underground stations. Yet, not to mention it would be to do a disservice to the many thousands of skiers who have enjoyed the potage du jour, followed by the assiette skieur, always different, always good.

Ruinettes, for that is how it shall ever be known, has been under the guidance of the Michellod family for nearly 40 years and is more an institution than just a restaurant. When weather permits, the sunny terrace is the place to be. Here you can idle away an aperitif, a slow, well digested lunch, perhaps coffee and a digestif, and watch the paragliders soaring up on a thermal that sits over the restaurant. Some suggest it may be caused by the heat from the kitchen as they efficiently produce good food for up to 1000 skiers a day. Others know the thermal by its local name, the fool's pump.

The menu can feed the modest with two eggs and ham for nine Swiss francs or the potage for four francs. The more ambitious take the assiette skieur for 17 francs, and the serious carnivores know the entrecôte Café de Paris for 33 francs will see them through a blizzard. The menu has little fault, and what it lacks in variety it makes up for in consistency.

The wine list, too, offers good value with one litre of Fendant or Goron for 26 francs. For something far more interesting, try the Syrah Vendage en Novembre, a luscious red wine, or the Gewürtzraminer Sarassin de la Tour, with its mellow, slightly honeyed taste.

Once, during a particularly cold January an inspector skied down from Atelas I. It was minus 15 Celsius and frost bite was gnawing at the fingers. Reaching Ruinettes with tears in his eyes, he fled to the gent's loo where he knew there to be a hot air hand dryer, which brought rapid relief. Whatever your reason for visiting Ruinettes, be glad it is there, for like everyone else, somehow, some way, you keep coming back. Walkers come up by foot or bubble. Skiers cannot miss it.

HAUTES CUISINES

VILLARS
1300m. - Top Station 2970m.
SWITZERLAND

Villars is a place to ski early in the season: it is set low, 800 metres, on a sun trap mountain ledge, with a splendid panorama over the Rhone Valley.

It is a charming place. Even if it has not quite kept pace with developments in such nearby resorts as Verbier, especially in lift investment, it has, nonetheless, retained a very Swiss feel of calm order and efficiency.

The town centre is dominated by the Palace Hotel, until recently owned by Club Med, and there are many newer hotels to attract discriminating visitors. There is little night life apparent after 10.30 pm and most evening activity appears to take place inside the resort hotels.

On and around the pistes there are a number of excellent restaurants and bars which complement an enjoyable day's skiing.

Geneva is the nearest airport and it is less than two hours away.

BUFFET COL DU SOUD

❄❄

A piste on one's doorstep is rare enough, but a mountain railway train stopping every 15 minutes must be good for business. For Bertrand Huber, proprietor of the late nineteenth century Buffet Col du Soud (also known as the Auberge Col du Soud), this would appear to be the case. Whether skier, walker or railway passenger, a friendly welcome awaits you at this popular restaurant.

Built into the side of the mountain by the Bretaye-Villars railway line and piste, the Buffet is traditional wood and brick, rising an imposing four storeys from ground level. Mounting a short, steep stairway, a quick turn to the right provides access to a deck offering seats for two dozen people and views up towards the Chaux de Conches peak (2027 metres).

Inside, the restaurant is clean and simple: tables and chairs can easily be arranged to suit any size of party from two to ten. A huge selection of cold sandwiches complements a good choice of warming and energy giving pastas. This is a good place to 'carb up'. In addition, and surprisingly rare in mountain restaurants, there is a special children's menu at sensible prices, with parental favourites such as fish fingers for 8 francs.

RESTAURANT DU LAC DES CHAVONNES

❄❄❄

When it is time to skedaddle, grab the ski-doo. Literally. Getting to and from M. and Mme Maury's restaurant presents challenges. Basically, trudge in, a little way, and drag out. But it is worth it.

Anyone desiring a quieter lunch than can be found at Bretaye, must catch the 'T' bar to Chaux Ronde and then follow the well marked red run to Lac Noir. At the bottom the challenge begins. The turn-off for the restaurant runs flat, requiring vigorous poling, skating or trudging according to whim; a welcome dip then leads to a short hill (definitely a walk up), followed by a sharp dip. And there you are.

The specialities of the restaurant are mushroom dishes and quiches, the latter most certainly not to be con-

HAUTES CUISINES

fused with the limp offerings that often go by that name.

The champignons en croûte, at 22 francs, came with a splendidly creamy sauce and a salad of frisée and lettuce. The quiche paysanne, 17.50 francs, was reported to be superb - a rich, cheese flavoured filling topped by shredded leeks cooked to al dente perfection. "I cannot eat anymore," complained the inspector (the portions are generous) and then proceeded to do just that. Plats du jour are available more cheaply. The wine list is short but there is an extensive list of eaux de vie and liqueurs. Rum grog is offered.

Outside, by the frozen lake, tables and benches are arranged to take advantage of the sun and the view of the mountains and trees. The lake sits in an natural bowl. A self service bar is set up outside to cater for sun worshippers and at reasonable prices.

Inside, the restaurant seats about 50 people and an open fire is laid if not lit. A boot room is located just off the restaurant, complete with pegs for jackets. There are, also, to be found there well laden bookshelves, presumably for those who find boot removal a slow and difficult process.

Dormitories, for 17 people, are available for those who wish to stay the night.

People tend to lunch late at Lac des Chavonnes and booking is advised. Tel: 025.352197.

Interesting testimony to the attractions of the restaurant is provided by an inspection which took place on 9 March 1992, the day before the British Budget. Sitting in the sun enjoying the attentions of a companion, was a British Member of Parliament who clearly preferred the Maury's food to the cares of state. Who can dispute his choice.

And the ski-doo? Well, when you leave, the restaurant will, for a small fee, tow you behind it to one of two lifts. If he is in the mood and thinks you will appreciate it (he will not ask), the driver will depart at full throttle testing your turning skills to the maximum. Great fun if you can stand it and a remarkable aid to digestion.

REFUGE DE FRIENCE

❆❆❆

The Refuge de Frience, a chalet building of wood, low beamed inside and bedecked with hanging baskets and old lamps, and claimed by many to be the nicest restaurant on the mountain in Villars, is something of a well kept secret: the piste map omits to list it, leaving it to the locals, the congnoscenti, the persistent and the plain lucky to find. It is located on an easy black run (the description of our inspector) below les Chaux, but there is a red run for the less experienced or anyone who has doubts about the concept of a black run being easy. Walkers may puff their way to it in five minutes from the car park at Les Fracherets.

The restaurant is open in the evenings as well, when it is extremely popular with the local population or visitors staying at nearby chalets. At such times access is only available by the road route and booking is recommended, tel: 025.68.14.26. The Frience is owned and operated by Leo and Emile Cramari, who have spent 12 years polishing the food, the service and the building so their appreciative customers, toasting their toes by the fire, are always keen to return.

The menu includes the customary mountain favourites: raclette au feu

HAUTES CUISINES

du bois, and fondues, but trout, caught in a local stream, are listed and are delightful. The wines list, mostly Swiss, offers red, white, rosé and two varieties of champagne. Prices, by Swiss standards, are reasonable, although some of the better wines are quite expensive.

Outside, a terrace doubles the 85 seater capacity and provides a pleasant view down the valley towards Villars and Bex. On an indifferent day there are few better places to provide an excuse for not skiing in the afternoon.

LE RESTO

❅❅

If the sight of pizzas being loaded and unloaded into a traditional pizza oven warms your heart and tickles your taste buds; if a restaurant offering such fare that can easily be reached on blue and red runs or even motored to by road catches your fancy, then it has to be said that Le Resto is the only place in Villars for you to visit.

Go to the bottom of lift 17 at Les Fracherets and there you will find this modern, but pleasantly finished, restaurant bedecked with an outside terrace whose tables and chairs on a fine day are crowded with skiers peering out over the valley. Inside, it is laid out on two floors with seats for 80 and a downstairs bar designed to make 25 people comfortable.

The pressure of numbers (there are a lot of people who fall into the definitions in the first two paragraphs of this report) can make service occasionally slow but the food is worth waiting for. A potent attraction for customers and an inducement to celerity on the part of staff is the provision of free drinks on those occasions when demand temporarily outstrips supply and waiting becomes tedious. Pizza prices range from 11 to 17 Swiss francs starting with a basic tomato and garlic and reaching to a hefty calzone stuffed with tomatoes, mozzarella, oregano, ham, mushrooms and egg. There are a number of croûtes, a limited range of pastas and, for anyone flush with the readies there is a steak de boeuf for 22 francs or a grilled pavé de saumon for 26 francs. Puddings are ice cream, sorbets or fruit tart with, for the determinedly healthy, a Bircher muesli maison for an invigorating seven francs.

Le Resto is also open in the evenings when a longer and more ambitious menu is available.

CAFE RESTAURANT DE SOLARLEX

❅❅❅

The restaurant at Solarlex presents a bit of a challenge to downhill skiers. It is, really, only readily accessible to energetic walkers or to cross country skiers. One inspector, inspired by premature spring weather, walked there in two and a half hours from Villars. The reassurance factor is that he claimed it was worth it.

In the evenings, the proprietor Bernard Köhli, provides what he calls a luge to drag customers to his restaurant. This device is, fortunately, very different from the aluminium tea trays favoured by Olympic competitors and can comfortably accommodate seven or eight people. When, finally, you arrive, you are surrounded by mountains in

HAUTES CUISINES

what our oxygen starved inspector in an overdose of cliché, but understandably so, called a haven of peace and quiet. The restaurant seats about 70 people with a further 180 provided for on the terrace.

The atmosphere is cosy, warm and traditionally Swiss, and all the better for that. The food reflects this bias. The specialities are cheese, raclette (feu de bois) and fondue. One inspector enthused over the warm welcome from the staff, the delicious viande sèchée and the wide selection of cheeses and cold meats. No plat du jour is available during the week.

The wine list encompasses Swiss wines from the Vaud and Valais regions.

Local residents speak highly of the restaurant, praising it for its lack of crowds, the warmth of its welcome and the quality of its cuisine.

HAUTES CUISINES

WAGRAIN
900m. - Top Station 2015m.
AUSTRIA

Located in the charmingly named Pongau area south of Salzberg, Wagrain is a busy resort offering extensive skiing and links with St Johann and Flachau. It is set quite low at 900 metres so late holidays have to be thought about carefully although Austria's snow record in recent seasons has been good. Not yet widely known in Britain, Wagrain is an attractive village easy to reach via Salzburg and has good facilities for cross country skiers.

EDELWEISS ALM

❅❅❅

The Edelweiss Alm is one of those single storey, cosy traditional huts set in a pine forest that people tend to dream about in the summer and autumn months when thoughts turn to booking the next ski trip. Equipped with an open fire, of course, quick and friendly staff, what else? And a location that is at the confluence of red and blue runs, it exercises a powerful appeal for everyone in the Wagrain area. Throw in a decent menu, which can produce a delicious steak and salad, prices that are a long piste away from outrageous, and you have a recipe for a mountain restaurant that will always be successful. The Sampl family has been running it for many years and the quality of the Edelweiss only serves to prove that breeding will out.

HAUTES CUISINES

WENGEN
1270m. - Top Station 2970m.
SWITZERLAND

Wether it was Wengen or its neighbour Murren (qv) or even the early British visitors to The Bear hotel in Grindelwald (qv), it probably doesn't matter. The Jungfrau region is the cradle of British skiing. It was certainly in Wengen that the British first persuaded the locals to run the mountain railway in winter, so providing the first easy way up the mountain to ski down.

Wengen to-day is a delightful car free village that has resisted change. The mixture of hotels and chalets provide accommodation at accessible prices and is particularly good for families. The short main street is full of shops and bars and the evening promenade is enjoyable.

The outdoor ice rink provides evening exercise and well as good spectator sport. There is also ice hockey and curling. Several of the hotels have swimming pools and saunas and occasionally there is floodlit ski jumping.

The skiing itself is extensive and varied with beginners slopes in the village and the famous Lauberhorn race track for the fliers. The opportunity for ski touring is enhanced by the availability of helicopters to take you up to the Ebenehfluh and other otherwise inaccessible peaks.

Non skiers particularly enjoy the train rides and the walking.

The nearest airports are Berne or Zürich.

HOTEL JUNGFRAU-WENGENALP

❋❋❋

When you arrive at the Wengenalp, remember to use the brush provided outside to clean off your boots, for, once inside, you will feel that even clean boots are a little out of context in these elegant dining rooms. But do not worry, you are welcome, booted or otherwise. The von Allmen family take great pride in their reputation as hosts.

On a cold day, there is great competition to be near one of the fires, either in the small restaurant, or in the larger dining room. Both are constantly fed by the friendly staff and provide the crackle of warmth that is so seductive.

There are four ways to get there. The choice is yours. The train is the easy way, either up from Wengen or down from Kleine Scheidegg. The gentle skiers take the picturesque blue run down from Scheidegg, while the keener take the rambling red from the Lauberhorn, and the intrepid test themselves on the black Lauberhorn race course, but probably sensibly ski around the stomach-churning Hundschopf, to arrive exhilarated at the back of the restaurant.

However you arrive, it is worth bringing a good appetite, for although the menu is not so large, the portions are not so small. Those in search of hot, fast and filling fare will choose the Alp-Topf, a soup full of vegetables, bacon and sausage and served with a chunk of bread for 9.50 Swiss francs. Those looking for a little more substance will choose the Käseschnitte Wengenalp, with egg, tomatoes and ham for 15 francs. Those of a gourmet bent might well choose the steak tartare with calvados, 30 francs.

HAUTES CUISINES

Next door, there is the Alpstübli and here is the place for fondues and raclettes, although you may need to order in advance. This small, woodlined Stübli has only been open for a few years and tends to appeal to the fast feeders who regret every moment they are not skiing.

The wines start at 15 francs for half a litre and are solidly Swiss. In the afternoons, late arrivals are offered a shorter menu but the same welcome. There are some, like the ebullient Ali Ross, who would not eat anywhere else, but even the less enthusiastic come back time and again.

Sunny days spread the crowd out onto the terrace where they can look up to the Jungfrau, the Mönch, the Eiger and across to the Schilthorn and Mürren. More seasoned skiers lie in deck chairs and do their looking with their eyes closed.

EIGERSTÜBLI HOTEL EIGER

❋❋

For those who have skied down to Wengen for lunch there are a number of recommendable choices. To find the best, a good idea is to look for a well-fed local and follow him. If he is not going home, then the odds are he will lead you to the Eiger Stübli. Once inside, he will be greeted by the many other locals who make this their daily meeting place. The conspiratorial group in the corner is probably the Lauberhorn race committee who meet here always to plan the spectacle that flies the racers 100 metres through the air and lands them at 80 mph.

The Eiger Stübli is run by Karl Frictts who took over from his father, who, although retired, is still here adding his smile to that of is son. The restaurant has a cosiness inside that belies the rather dull exterior. It was rebuilt in 1987 following a fire and attention was given to interior comforts rather than exterior pomp.

The menu offers a wide choice at prices considerably cheaper than higher up the mountain. An unusual and warming starter is the Berner Maritsuppe, a thick vegetable soup with chunks of pickled leg of pork in it (17.50 Swiss francs). The röstis start at 10.50 francs and there is a deliciously different Apfelrösti (rösti with grated apples) for 12 francs. Pastas are well represented with a good portion of spaghetti carbonara for 14.50 francs and a dish of noodles with smoked salmon and broccoli for 16.50 francs (Bandnudeln mit Rauchlachsstreifen und Broccoli).

Vegetarians and children are also well looked after, although serious wine addicts will not find anything serious, but can compensate afterwards with a calavados hors d' age or a vieille prune du Perigord.

The Eiger Stübli sits beside the station, so after a good lunch your train awaits to take you back up the mountain. The gentle journey is just the thing for the digestion.

HIRSCHEN HOTEL

❋❋❋

A regular fan of this cosy little restaurant turned up for lunch one day a few years ago and ordered his usual favourite from the short, but adequate, menu. He then turned his

HAUTES CUISINES

attention to the much longer, and more interesting, wine list.

Having treated his palate to Dôle after Dôle, his eye alighted on a Rioja, which he requested the rather new waiter to bring. It arrived at the table dust-caked and dignified. Gran Riserva 1955, read the label. A gulp of disbelief escaped our luncher along with questions like, can it be true? can it be any good? and how much? The questions were answered by a nod to the waiter, who opened the bottle. Our fan was accompanied by three, chatting friends who were paying no attention to his fussing over the wine. The waiter poured a taste into his glass, which he sniffed, tasted, and he then encouraged the waiter to fill it. The waiter, sadly, had been well trained, and so filled the glasses of the others first. The chagrin showed on the host's face, and so he enquired if there might be another bottle. The waiter returned with the sad news that there was not. The 1955 tasted like nothing had before. Old Riojas are rare and good old Riojas rarer still, and very good old Riojas at 27 Swiss francs a bottle are now non-existent.

However, even today, there are fine wines to be found on this list, and for those so inclined, the ski here is worthwhile, just to relieve the palate of another Dôle.

The menu starts at around nine francs for omeletees and rises to about 25 francs for a peppered steak with blackcurrant sauce, vegetables and chips; and, of course, an excuse to return to the wine list. The house speciality is Winzerrösti. The hungry will never forget it. The less hungry will never finish it. The food here is good and they are about to introduce a gourmet menu, which should be even better.

The Hirschen is met as you ski into Wengen, at the junction of the route to the Männlichen cable car and Wengen station. On sunny days, the small terrace outside is quickly filled with those who know. If you are smart, you book, tel:026.55.15.44. After lunch, it is two minutes to Wengen station or five to Männlichen cable.

MARY'S CAFE

❄❄

Nestling at the bottom of the world famous Lauberhorn Run is the best known hut in Wengen. Busy all day, but particularly in the late afternoon when Coffee Mary, a persuasive mixture of local schnapps, coffee and a serious dollop of cream on top, is served, Mary's Café provides the ethereal ending to a day of knee-bending excitement.

A pine cabin, traditional rather than Habitat, blends elegantly with the tree-clad slopes of inner Wengen. At lunchtimes, a period that runs from midday to at least 4.00pm, the afficionados go for the Suppentopf, a soup pot of vegetables, beef and sausage, topped with cheese, in the best tradition of mountain food. The rest of the varied menu offers everything from the slimming Bündnerfleisch and salad to the essential carbohydrates that a body often craves after a day's exercise.

For those who do not want a full lunch, an imaginative range of sandwiches replaces the normal plate of frites. Food, therefore, need not be expensive, and regulars claim it is the best value lunch in Wengen.

Easily reached on the well marked run from 'Bumps', and sitting beside the inner Wengen chair, it provides a wonderful sun trap with an elegiac view of the mountains of the Bernese Oberland.

HAUTES CUISINES

ZERMATT
1620m. - Top Station 3900m.
SWITZERLAND

"Whose yacht is that?"
"The Duke of Westminster's, I expect. It usually is."
So it was in Private Lives and thus it is in Zermatt with the Matterhorn: the mountain is ubiquitous. To find a restaurant or piste which is not dominated by the Matterhorn requires diligent research, an activity greatly encouraged by the proliferation of excellent establishments and some wonderful skiing, which is available all year.

The village is extremely pretty, free of the internal combustion engine (but beware of hectically driven electric cabs; the horses are rather more considerate) and hemmed in by mountains. There are fine five star hotels, good shops and outstanding bars. Good but cheaper accommodation is also available.

There are three main ski areas (Gornergrat-Stockhorn which is a 45 minute train ride; the Sunnegga/Blauherd-Unter Rothorn area where the snow can disappear quite early; and the Furri-Trockener Steg-Schwarzsee-Klein Matterhorn-Cervinia areas, enabling the energetic to ski over into Italy for lunch) providing some 150 kilometres of pistes.

The resort is reached by the Visp-Zermatt railway. Motorists leave their cars in the village of Tasch and complete their journey by train. Horse cabs and electric wagons in hotel livery await the prosperous on arrival.

Zermatt is a place that all skiers should visit at least once; both the skiing and the food demand it.

RESTAURANT ALM

❅❅❅

If you start out from the top of the Gornergrat and ski down the blue run, you will pass any number of tempting restaurants, many of which are listed in this guide. It is, just, conceivable that lack of appetite, the joys of skiing, missed opportunities and blind chance will get you all the way to the bottom without pause for a serious meal. In these unusual circumstances, the Restaurant Alm, equipped without with trout stream and trap, ornamented with a stone barbecue and reached by the lazy, the motorised and the stroller by road, awaits ready to furnish all the refreshment you may require.

It will come as no surprise when, having eagle-eyed, spotted the stream, the menu lists trout as the house speciality. Available for around 20 Swiss francs it makes a light and delicious alternative to the customary röstis and käseschnitten that are also on the menu. Indeed, the Alm lists that well known international gourmet dish the Käseschnitte Hawaii at 14 francs. If you want to stay with fish, start with smoked salmon, 18 francs, continue with trout with almonds (or a fillet of sole if you prefer) and finish with an excellent beignets aux pommes for 5.50 francs.

The wine list is solidly Swiss and averagely priced.

A building of no particular charm, the Alm seats around 40 people in its simple dining room. If weather and the pressure of numbers permit, take a table by the stream and relax in the sun.

HAUTES CUISINES

BLATTEN

❅❅❅

Outside, the M1. Inside, all the charm of the nineteenth century with only electric light to dispel the belief. On a sunny day the terrace is overflowing; on a cold day inside is crammed both upstairs and downstairs with standing room only, and still they come.

The M1 is the piste from Furri back to Zermatt, and from four o'clock onwards, every evening, the mountain pistes channel down to here with skiers arriving from the Kleine Matterhorn area and the Gornergrat. The spectator sport as they funnel through the narrow gap alongside the restaurant is as compulsive as the desire to eat the Buchten, an Austrian speciality of light cake with custard on hot mixed berries. The menu is different enough from higher huts for many to consider skiing down for lunch and then staying for tea, and maybe a quick schnapps before they leave.

It is a hut that is hard to leave and it gets harder still if you are seduced by the delicious and gentle-tasting Vodka Feige, which are served in small brandy snifters and consist of a fat fig on a stick drowned in vodka and topped off with cream. How could anything so pretty be bad for you? A warning: if you are upstairs, do not try to come down forwards, but treat the narrow staircase as a ladder and hang onto the rope.

CHEMIHÜTTA

❅❅

"Next time remember and we'll stop and try it", a remark often made as skiers race past the Chemihütta. It was built about six years ago alongside the piste down from Riffelalp to Furri, a piste the width of a main road, agreeably flat and just the right angle for most skiers to get up a controllable speed and the uncontrollable exhilaration that accompanies it. Skiers are thus so intent on their posture, rhythym and pole planting that it is not until they are past the Chemi that they see it. Last season a banner stretched across the piste advertising some Swiss beer, but it looks so much like the banner at the end of a race that some skiers speed up for it rather than slow down.

You have been warned. Slow down, drop in, for this is a jolly place to stop. The small posters which line the outside walls in an organised random way remind one of a junior school on parents' day. They have a unique tape player that transforms everything played on it into Swiss music.

Outside on the sun seekers' terrace a flag pole flies the Valais flag of stars and stripes above The Stars and Stripes. The Germans and the Japanese are also represented but not the Union Jack. You might mention this to them; I did; they smiled politely and proffered the menu on which there are 63 numbered choices, including five rösti, four Kässeschnitten, two spaghettis and so on and so on. And then you notice that there is no number ten, 16 to 20 are gone, 26 to 30 do not exist, and the same applies to 34 to 40, 46 to 50 and 52 to 60. Ask about these and you get the same reply as you did when you asked about the flag.

Those that remain, however, will do all that you may ask. They will be freshly cooked. They will fill the plate and they will fill you. And if you find that extra bit of space, then

HAUTES CUISINES

try the homemade Apfelstrudel or even the Apfelkuchen. Both are delicious.

CHEZ VRONY
FINDELN

❅❅❅

The first clue is the forest of skis outside. The second is the oddly, but charmingly, painted front door beyond a narrow entrance way usually choked with people - people coming, people going, people trying to decide, either upstairs with its small bar, eclectic lighting and equally eclectic furnishing, or downstairs with its little stüblis, ideal for convivial groups for lunch, or perhaps the entrance floor: duck through the banknote-covered arch and consider a while on one of the sheepskin covered bar stools.

If the sunshine beckons, then one of the terraces is the answer. On the lower floor is a wide deck with sunbathing chairs as well as old cloth covered tables and benches. First come first served is the rule; stake your claim and hang on to it. The ever helpful staff get very busy on a sunny day and yet the service rarely suffers. The main floor terrace is more a verandah which runs around two sides of this wonderful old hut, with just the right space for you, a table and a waitress.

So, with decision one made, music to calm the furrowed brow, a glass in hand, proceed to the menu.

Share a Walliserteller to start, a selection of dried and cured meats, small pickles and cheese and at 19 Swiss francs it splits well for two, as does the carpaccio - wonderful how this Venetian-created dish has become a standard in the mountains. Röstis, of course, offer themselves up in many recognisable varieties.

Our favourite is Rösti Max, served with bacon, covered in tomatoes and cheese and popped under the grill. All for 14 francs. Plan to have late dinner after this.

Max, by the way, is Vrony's brother and Vrony is the lady with the big smile, straw hat and pigtails, who looks as though she has just stepped off one of those old Swiss barometers where the lady swivels out to signify sunshine. Well, it is true: Vrony makes the sun shine inside and out.

The menu continues. Pastas aplenty, fondues aflowing, raclettes, kotelettes and a rather delicious 'wild' salmon with Nüsslisalat and spinach. Something for everyone and just as well for everyone comes here.

To describe the interior would require the services of a cateloguer for an antiques auction house; however, one oddity cannot go without mention and that is the unique, and to our minds precarious, plate lift which serves the upper floor. If you sit near enough to see it you will excitedly anticipate its use, expecting at any moment a crash of plates. You will wait a long time; this skill, as with every other here, has been honed over the years and is as much designed to entertain as to work.

Find Chez Vrony on the Paradis run down from Blauherd, or the easy blue run down from Sunnegga. After lunch, take a delicate ski down to the Findeln chairs.

RESTAURANT ENZIAN
FINDELN

❅❅

Let us assume you want a small hut, with good food, good value and a café Ramba Zamba, then the Enzian

HAUTES CUISINES

gets ticks in all the boxes. Slightly hidden among the cow byres that are its own ancestry, it sits on the edge of the blue run down to the Findeln chairs. Leave your skis on the piste and follow the sign. Clump across the terrace and enter. It is small and rustic and a great smile from Andrea greets you.

The menu delivers the Tagesuppe for five Swiss francs and a good Gulaschsuppe for 8.50 francs. Käseschnitten start at 11.00 francs as do the homemade röstis with the Rösti Ancien at 14.00 francs. Salmon noodles appear here as they do in other restaurants in Findeln. There are crêpes, here called Pfannkuchen, with a variety of fillings.

A chianti Ruffino is the only non-Swiss on the wine list, but at 22 francs a litre it is a welcome one to judge by the empties that line the walls.

The café Ramba Zamba, by the way, is made with apricots and is covered with whipped cream

FARMER HAUS

❄❄

A relatively new member of the Furri restaurant club, this is a real log cabin. Davy Crocket would feel at home here, as do the many skiers who lunch or drink here while struggling with the decision about what to do next - take the cable up to Furg, take the cable up to Trockener Steg, take the path back to Zermatt, go in the bubbles, or perhaps another Jägertee.

If outside, try for one of the leather cinema seats which lean against the little hut next door. Inside, sit anywhere and take notes on how to build a log cabin - a long lunch here with a bottle of wine (try the Chianti) and all you will need are the logs and the garden will never look the same again.

The big charcoal grill delivers steaks and chops; röstis run amok. There are no surprises here and even the prices are ones you have seen before.

A good hut. A pity it is in the wrong place.

ENZOS
FINDELN

For many years, Enzo has delighted palates overloaded with rösti with his homemade pasta. Alas. 1991 was his last season. He has packed his knives, rolled up his tent and headed off to Lugano. Others will take his place. Please let us know what happens. Good luck Enzo.

RESTAURANT FURRI

❄❄

Like the Farmer Haus (qv), the Furri is one of those restaurants that huddle, like animals sheltering from the wind, around the bottom of the Furri lift system. It is easy to see why: runs come down (from Schwarzsee, Furgg, White Pearl, Furri and Riffelalp), lifts go up all over the place and access is easy for walkers. There are more than enough customers for everyone. The Furri is one of the nicest of these competing establishments.

Everything about it is achingly traditional: the architecture is dark wood cosy; the interior pleasingly cramped; the terrace is small, but an overflow is provided by dint of propping benches and tables against contiguous cow byres; and the food

HAUTES CUISINES

has no surprises for anyone who eats occasionally in the mountains.

On offer are soups and bouillon; omelettes and eight varieties of rösti (the house rösti comes with cheese and two eggs and costs 15 Swiss francs); salads, sausage, pork and steak. If you fancy something slightly more adventurous then the Kutteln nach Mailänderart mit Rösti und Salat is definitely for you. This translates as a load of tripe for 17 francs. Oh, yes, and there is spaghetti bolognese as well or pesto, carbonara and the rest of the Italian tribe.

The wines are as Swiss as the rest of Furri: Dôle, Fendant, Johannisberg and Goron and are priced between 32 and 36 francs.

The Furri is attractive, amiable and frequently packed with chattering visitors rubbing ski suits with local guides and instructors. There are few better places from which to consider the agonies of decision making: which lift, which run and when?

GANDEGG HÜTTE

❄❄❄

Although this hut has stood here for over 150 years, it is only in the last four that it has opened in the winter to provide sustenance and shelter for skiers on these relatively uncluttered pistes. In the summer, climbers set out from here to ascend the bald-headed Breithorn or the twins of Castor and Pollux, all three at over 4000 metres.

This is a mountain man's hut and to sit inside provides a sense of certainty and security. The larch lined walls, the oil cloth covered tables, the profusion of radiators, all lend a warmth that is to be sought on those cold winter days when many skiers stay down in the valley and talk about yesterday and tomorrow.

The Perron-Furrer family who brave the often severe conditions up here, provide the sort of menu that they obviously enjoy themselves. This excludes spaghetti bolognese, and even rösti is not to be found, replaced by an excellent homemade potato salad served with the Riesenschüblig (a large Swiss pork sausage) or a serious pork chop. The peasant omelette, made with bacon and potato, is also a recommendation as are the homemade desserts, apple cake and grandmother's chocolate cake.

The wines are Swiss, Swiss and Swiss, but considering they are served at over two miles above the valley where they are produced, they survive extremely well.

Perhaps the experience is summed up by an entry in the visitors' book by members of the Mountaineering Club of Bury who wrote: "after days of cloud and rain we finally got to see the Matterhorn for the first time - what a BEEZER!"

Ski here by taking the Gandegg drag lift up from Trockener Steg and following the marked piste to the left of it. A sign to the hut turns off to your right. Ski through the pylon and over the hill and there you are.

OTHMARS

❄❄

On the run down from the Sunnega area, be you starting from Sunnega itself or from Unterrothorn or Blauherd, there are a number of excellent stops which can be made. Perhaps the most popular is Othmars. Here one can sit in the

HAUTES CUISINES

last rays of the sun, sip coffee or cocktail and watch the sun set behind the Matterhorn. If you miss Othmars, it is just above the Ried, then there is Da Leonardo; if you miss that, there are others. Most are good for lunch, but all are good for that magic last hour of the day.

RESTAURANT PARADIS
FINDELN

❋❋❋❋

Smoked salmon stuffed with salmon mousse, dill sauce and salad, or perhaps the Carpaccio of Venison with a light homemade mayonnaise. The first you will find described as Adam's Schwäche and the second as Eva's Verführung. Names that may not easily roll off the tongue but the dishes themselves will be welcomed by any gourmet's tongue.

Although the concept that Adam and Eve ate this well in the Garden of Eden - the first Paradise - may require the sort of mental leap normally associated with rocket scientists. The fact is that in this paradise on snow you can enjoy the sort of cooking rarely found in the high Alps.

Whether your taste turns to langoustine picatta, to a Ravioli surprise, to a wholesome Ossobucco, or homemade tortellini or spaghetti, The Paradis is as close as you will come to perfection in the Alps.

The hut itself is situated at the end of the Paradis run down from Blauherd and, beyond the fact that it has an agreeable small terrace which allows the view and sun seekers to indulge their passions, the Paradis is a curious mixture of traditional wood work without great atmosphere but with serious food for serious eaters.

Perhaps with such fine food they argue, atmosphere makes itself. Perhaps after a few glasses of wine from their fine list, nobody notices, or perhaps one is being unfair in expecting the interior style of the hut to live up to the cuisine.

Make your own decision as you peruse the menu, and the prices, there are six röstis ranging from 9.50SF up to 16SF and an excellent Tagessuppe at 6.50SF.

A meal here will cost as you choose and the taste experience will remain with you long after the bill has been forgotten.

HOTEL/RESTAURANT RIFFELBERG

❋❋❋

As you ski down from the Gornergrat railway station you will encounter a large self-service restaurant. This you avoid, for just below it lies the Riffelberg, a dignified, stuccoed establishment where it is alleged Winston Churchill used to stay to paint. In the absence of commemorative plaques, memorabilia or even a preserved cigar butt, it is difficult to test this claim especially so because the charming staff look far too young ever to have heard of him. However, if he did, you can see the old boy's point.

Arrive on a warm sunny day; decide to sit outside and before you can say rösti, a red smocked waiter or waitress will have bustled over to drape a rug around your knees. If to ski on a fine day is wonderful and to sit in the sun quite joyful, then to be cosseted by well trained staff is truly divine.

The menu provides everything that fans of mountain food could wish: röstis aplenty, soups, pasta and

HAUTES CUISINES

dried meat. But there is more for those occasions when something a little out of the ordinary (at least by mountain standards) is demanded. Fillets of perch with boiled potatoes and salad seduces at 34.50 Swiss francs; a risotto with boletus mushrooms beckons at 23 francs; prawns in a curry sauce with rice and salad tempt at 38 francs, or, more substantially, a breaded pork chop with chips and vegetables will top up energy levels after a morning's skiing. Puddings are ice cream, crêpes and tarts.

The wine list, too, strays from the norm with a St. Estèphe, a 1978 Château de Marbuzet, at a matching 78 francs; a 1982 L' Ermitage de Chasse Spleen at 69 francs with a variety of chiantis kicking off at 35 francs. Half bottles of champagne, a Moulin à Vent, are a far from extortionate 25 francs.

The only mildly jarring note and an incongrous one, was provided on the day of one visit by the presence on the terrace of a smooth looking chap (slicked, shiny hair, shiny jacket and shiny teeth) who, with the aid of electronic instruments, filled the terrace, and a goodly area beyond, with loud music. His role, apparently, was to entertain the customers. Churchill would have had a word for it.

ROTE NASE HÜTTE

❄

Someone once remarked that staying in Zermatt and skiing on the Stockhorn was akin to living in Brighton and working in London in that the travelling time is the same. However, most would agree that the journey up and out to this steep mogul bashers' dreamland is somewhat more picturesque.

Most who come out here will take the two cable cars out to the Stockhorn, ski the, almost always, beautiful snow down to the Trifti drag lift and get the tow up to the Rote Nase. Those who feel some small, refreshing reward is called for will walk up to the aluminium portakabin that would look more at home on a building site in Docklands. The interior also looks as if it might more commonly be found filled with chaps in yellow hats called Murphy. Somehow the knowledge that this is the best, and only, hut for a long way will cheer you.

The menu is restricted by the size of the kitchen, tiny, the number of cooks, one, and their ambition to get a Michelin star, none. A good warming soup will be six Swiss francs, or a bowl of bouillon 4.50 francs. The Gulaschsuppe comes for 7.50 francs and a reasonable lasagne is 14 francs. Sausage and chips, the best of the Wurst, is 13 francs and a serious door step sandwich is 4.50 francs.

Outside, the terrace has little red tables and chairs and even sun loungers can be rented for 5.50 francs. The view. Well, the view looks up to the Monte Rosa, Switzerland's highest mountain, across to Castor and Pollux and along to yet another view of "that" mountain. On a clear day look down towards the glacier that unfolds from the Monte Rosa and a keen eye can spot those intrepid off pisters skiing down from the top, stopping off at the Monte Rosa hut for a good lunch and some very good wine. Here those skiing down meet those climbing up, both of whom still have thrills in store.

The Rote Nase hut may not offer much of the tradition of good ski

HAUTES CUISINES

huts, but let us be glad that it is there. Those without skis take the cable cars from Gornergrat to Hohtälligrat.

HOTEL SCHWARZSEE

❄❄

Redeemed by a prawn. Rescued from the quotidian and the mundane by a glass of champagne and an umbrella.

It has to be said that the inclusion of the Schwarzsee was a marginal decision. A large, not especially distinguished building fronted by a vast wooden deck, its chief disadvantage from the point of view of the serious luncher and the picky pit stopper, is the presence in the front part of the building of a huge self-service restaurant, which almost distracts one from the smaller and much more attractive proper restaurant behind. But the final vote in its favour was tipped by the siting at the back of its deck on a fine sunny day of a small, umbrella-shaded bar selling grilled sticks of fresh prawns interleaved with cucumber, yours for a very fair nine Swiss francs, lamb kebabs for six francs or lamb cutlets for 12 francs. And while you waited, you could sip a glass of champagne.

This charming note apart, the Schwarzsee's speciality is rösti, ten of them in all. You may wonder quite how one can extract ten varieties from the delicious, but rather limiting, basic ingredient of a grated potato pancake. Well, they have done it. Different cheeses, meats, mushrooms and tomatoes are all brought into play for prices between 15 and 19 francs. Their most remarkable creation, however, is the Mexico, from that well known producer of rösti: strips of pork, a piquant sauce and tortilla chips. The combination of rösti and tortilla chips has to be tried.

For the more conventional and calorie conscious, a salmon salad is only 15.50 francs. The usual range of soups are listed as starters. A dish of the day is competitively priced at 19 francs. Desserts include homemade fruit tarts and fresh strawberries.

The wines on the list are entirely Swiss.

From the deck, that mountain looks awfully close and one has a clear view of the Hörnli Hütte, the summer starting point for climbers aiming for the top.

The Schwarzee is reached by taking the bizarre, but efficient, clustered bubble lifts above Furri.

RESTAURANT SIMI

❄❄❄

It is said that there lived a man in Paris who so hated the Eiffel Tower that every day he took his lunch in the restaurant half way up. His excuse was that it was the only place in Paris from which you could not see the tower itself. Well, if in Zermatt you were fed up with the Matterhorn as well as in need of a great feed, then Simi's is the place.

The speciality here is the grill au feu du bois, and whether you choose a steak, a chop or Bratwurst, it will come with that smoky flavour that transforms the taste. There are daily specials and, although the prices here are not the cheapest in the valley, the place remains very popular.

Inside, it is friendly and one gets the impression that it is much used by locals both during the day and in

HAUTES CUISINES

the evenings - always an encouraging sign. The roof is propped up with great tree logs and the walls boast photographs of ski teams and the trophies they have won. For some reason there are two pianos; perhaps in case one wears out. If you get the table near the grill, then you will be able to watch and hear your lunch being cooked, although this table seems always to be populated by ski instructors and pisteurs. The wines start at 28 Swiss francs a litre for the Fendant and Goron, and for those whose palates long for something else, there are some good but not inexpensive French wines.

Skiers stop here on the way down from Riffelalp to catch the cable at Furri in whose shadow Simi sits. Walkers stroll here from the village and the terminally lazy call for a horse drawn taxi.

RESTAURANT STAFFELALP

❄❄❄

From almost every view the Matterhorn looks the perfect mountain, pyramidic and to the point. Even from the Cervinia side, where they prefer to call it Mont Cervin, it is the definitive mountain. But from outside the Staffelalp, you look up at the north face, dark and intimidating, and you realise that mountains can be mean and those that climb them do so in the knowledge that the three-cornered duel between weather, mountain and man is not to be taken lightly. Like the north face of the Eiger, this route up the Matterhorn has taken its toll.

The Stafelalp is a remote restaurant far from the madding pistes of Trockener Steg and Klein Matterhorn. It is approached by taking the curious bubbles up from Furg to Schwarzsee and setting out along the Weisse Perle run. After about 400 metres a sign to Stafelalp points off to the left. Follow this to the door of the restaurant.

The wooden covered menu, which is available in English, is a designer's nightmare, resembling an invitation to a Halloween party, but what it has to offer makes the ski here, and indeed the ski back, worthwhile.

For those who crave a lunch-like soup, the mountain pot with cheese and sausage is a favourite for nine Swiss francs. One of the eight röstis or five Käseschnitten will fill as much space as you have, particularly the Hawaii (yes, really, the Hawaii) a large slice of bread covered with ham and cheese, grilled and topped with pineapple and cherries; as it says on the menu, "it tastes great", but it is possibly better eaten with your sunglasses on. A special page devoted to small eaters offers good snacks for eight to ten francs. There are tarts with cream and cakes without, and an indulgent jam omelette adds a change of pace and possibly forces a change of diet.

The coffee card offers a confusion of delight, but beware: the ride back to Furri is along a skiable but narrow path and a clear head is surely an advantage. One of our favourite huts.

TONY'S GROTTA

❄❄❄

The wandering, rhythmic blue run that brings you down from Gornergrat and its hotel observa-

HAUTES CUISINES

tory, built in Buck Roger's school of architecture, past the Riffelberg, alongside the railway and down to Riffelalp, is so entrancing that many, enjoying it so much, forget to stop on the way. If this should happen to you, perhaps it is no bad thing, for one of the prettiest huts on this mountain hides here in the snows of Riffelalp.

Tony's Grotta (shame about the name) has been here for ten years, although the hut itself is over 100 years old. It is built in that Swiss tradition of all châlets being the same but being different. The stone-flagged roof and log-locked walls advertise its commitment to stand firm whatever the weather may bring.

The menu here is strongly Italian with homemade lasagne and cannelloni. Vegetarians will enjoy the cannelloni with broccoli and ricotta cheese. There is a forkful of different spaghettis, including a fresh frutta di mare. A choice from one of the crisp salads would make a good starter and lunch for two, including wine, should not be more than 30 Swiss francs a head.

Tony Aufdenblatten keeps a watchful eye and a steadying hand on his charge and is always to be seen strolling around caring for his guests, his white smile flashing beneath his silver hair.

The terrace has much to recommend it on a sunny day, including yet another view of old whatsisname. A big table sits on the terrace, its covering wines and homemade tarts protected from the sun by two big umbrellas.

On a cold day the interior seats about 36 people and the big stove warms them all. Whatever the weather a booking is not a bad idea. Tel: 028.67.44.54.

ZUM SEE

❄❄❄

Max and Gretti Mennig have created one of the most popular huts in Zermatt and from the most unlikely origins. Zum See is a converted farm building. Where cows and sheep once wintered and watered, now weary skiers graze.

Lying just off the sometimes icy red run from Furi to Zermatt village, a wary eye is needed to spot the sign post. A generally easy ski and equally easy walk from the village, it makes an atmospheric meeting place for ski widows and widowers who like to walk up an appetite for lunch.

The hut is small, warm and cosy, with the kitchen opening onto the restaurant. Here Max can be seen cooking fresh food in a traditional way. The menu makes the best of the valley produce, with local cheeses, dried meats, rösti and, although a mountain away from Italy, delicious pasta. The wine list is varied, as is the tempting list of sundowners that set many a skier on his wobbly way back to the village.

No matter how crowded, Gretti always finds space for one more. Misanthropists beware. For everybody else it is a great place to meet friends or make new ones.

There is seating outside the hut with rugs and cushions provided. But do not look to improve your tan early in the season. The hut being low in the valley, the sun goes into hiding mid-afternoon.

HAUTES CUISINES

ZÜRS AM ARLBERG
1720m. - Top Station 2450m.
AUSTRIA

Situated in the narrows of the Flexenpass, Zürs, like its neighbour Lech (qv), tends to be a little exclusive.

The village is made up of about two dozen hotels and a handful of shops. As you would expect in this area, the quality of the hotels is excellent and guests are provided with a special card that allows them to use the ski school entrance at lifts to cut down queuing time. This can be a boon at weekends when people drive in from the surrounding area.

The village is situated in a sunny position but enjoys an excellent snow record. In fact, sometimes too much snow, which closes the pass and cuts off Zürs from the world and even Lech from Zürs.

The skiing here is not exclusively on piste, but a mecca for powder hounds with almost the whole area skiable when conditions are right.

The nearest airport is Zürich.

SCHRÖFLI ALM

❄❄❄

This is the most gemütlich kind of hut, surely one of the prettiest we have encountered, perhaps even a little twee, but try it and see. Inside and out, it is exactly what Hollywood would imagine a mountain hut to be and, sited as it is in Zürs, it has Hollywood people to match. The sunglasses here are of the reflector type. They encourage people to look at each other. After all, that way they can look at themselves at the same time.

The food and wine here are remarkably good value. Excellent soups start bubbling at 45 schillings. Snacks start around 75 schillings, although the wines are a little higher than average, starting at 260 schillings.

Outside, long benches and tables overflow the terrace and lean drunkenly in the snow. After lunch, some customers do the same. Views are average: big mountains, covered in snow, pine trees and blue skies. But who needs scenery when you can see yourself as others see you?

A furry Yeti sits on the roof and a trough full of trout sits on the terrace. Martin Walch, who transformed this old stable three years ago, sits with his customers.

In the evening, there is music and schnapps and in the morning hangovers, but then there is a price for everything.

TRITTALM HUT

❄❄❄

The Zürs-Lech area is known for exclusivity and expensive chic. Style is its middle name. So when one arrives at one of the oldest, and some say chicest, huts, The Trittalm, and reads the long and interesting menu, one is inclined to gasp, how much? The Trittalm Rösti with ham, cheese and a fried egg on top costs only 86 schillings, or perhaps one should try the Holzknechtpalatschinken, a dish of bacon, sausage, egg, onions, garlic and salad, for 95 schillings. It is worth it for the name alone. The menu goes on and on and never manages to rise above 110 schillings and the portions never manage to be mean.

Even if you never get to the main course, the Gulaschsuppe at 57

HAUTES CUISINES

schillings is a meal in itself. The wine list demonstrates a certain point of view: so as not to disappoint anyone, they have both kinds, red and white. A litre of either is 176 schillings.

The decor is agreeably local. A large, green, ceramic-tiled stove inhabits the centre of the room and warms the whole of it. The tables are local marquetry. A collection of pewter-topped steins crowns one wall, while the actual zither upon which the theme of the Third Man was not played, hangs on another. A game rack, with petrified corn cobs, hangs from the dark, raftered ceiling. The clientèle often belongs to that special group who are too smart to be chic, and only wear sunglasses when they are actually skiing.

Outside, the fast set inhabit the spread of tables and collect their own food from a self-service hatch, while their partners lie around, like basking seals in the sun.

The food will, by now, be settling and, while it will not have been a gourmet experience, you will be happy, full and sluggish. Now it is the time to take hold of yourself, shake your head, blink and, realising that you still have some skiing to do, order a Pflümli. It will arrive in a small glass, in which there will be something reminiscent of a pickled item once seen in a doctor's surgery. It will, in fact, be a preserved plum, preserved by the very alcohol you are about to drink. Ask yourself one question: if it can do that to a plum, what can it do to me? Drink it anyway, then take the Hexenboden chair and ski the gentle route back to Zürs.

HAUTES CUISINES

GLOSSARY

ENGLISH: FRENCH/ITALIAN/GERMAN

BILL: L'Addition/Il Conto/Die Rechnung
BOTTLE: La bouteille/La Bottiglia/Die Flasche
A BOTTLE OF BEER: Une Bouteille de Bière/Una Bottiglia di Birra/Eine Flasche Bier
A BOTTLE OF WINE (RED, WHITE):   Une Bouteille de Vin (Rouge, Blanc) / Una Bottiglia di Vino (Rosso, Bianco) / Eine Flasche   Wein (Rot, Weiss)
A BOTTLE OF WATER: Une Bouteille D'Eau/ Una Bottiglia d'Acqua/Eine Flasche Wasser
HALF BOTTLE: Une Demie Bouteille/ Una Mezza Bottiglia/ Eine Halbe Flasche
CHEERS: Santé/Salute/Prost
CUP: La Tasse/La Tazze/Die Tasse
CUP OF COFFEE: Une Tasse de café/Una Tazza di Caffé/Eine Tasse Kaffee
CUP OF TEA: Une Tasse de Thé/Una Tazza de Te/Eine Tasse Tee
FORK: La Fourchette/ La Forchetta/ Die Gabel
GLASS: Un Verre/Un Bicchiere/Ein Glas
GLASS OF BEER: Un Verre de Bière/ Un Bicchiere di Birra Ein Glas Bier
GLASS OF WINE: Un Verre de vin/ Un Bicchiere di Vino/ Ein Glas Wein
GOOD DAY: Bonjour/Buon Giorno/ Guten Tag
GOOD BYE: Au Revoir/ Arrivederci/ Auf Wiedersehen
KNIFE: Le Couteau/ Il Coltello/ Das Messer
LEMONADE: Limonade/ Limonata/ Zitronenlimonade
LOCAL WINE: Vin de Pays/ Vino Locale/ Hiesiger Wein
MEDIUM: À Point/Non Troppo Cotto/ Mittel
MENU: Le Menu/ La Lista/ Die Speisekarte
PEPPER: Le Poivre/Il Pepe/ Der Pfeffer
PLEASE: S'il Vous Plaît/ Prego/ Bitte
RARE, UNDER-DONE: Saignant/ Al Sangue/ Leicht Gebraten
RED WINE: Vin Rouge/ Vino Rosso/ Rot Wein
SALT: Le Sel/ Il Sale/ Das Salz
SPOON: Une Cuillère/ Il Cucchiaio/ Der Löffel
THANKYOU: Merci/ Grazie/ Danke
TOILET: La Toilette/ Il Gabinetto/ Die Toilette
TOOTHPICK: Un cure-dent/ uno Stuzzicadenti/ Zahnstocher
WAITER: Garçon/ Cameriere/ Kellner
WAITRESS: Mademoiselle/Cameriera/Fräulein
WELL-DONE: Bien Cuit/ Ben Cotto/ Gut Durchbraten
WHITE WINE: Vin Blanc/ Vino Bianco/ Weisser Wein
WINE LIST: La Carte des Vins/ La Lista dei Vini/ Die Wein-Karte

HAUTES CUISINES

FRENCH GLOSSARY

ABRICOT - Apricot
AGNEAU - Lamb
AIGUILLETTE - A thin strip of poultry or meat
    Aiguillette De Caneton - Breast of duckling strips
AIL - Garlic
AILE - Wing of poultry or game bird
AILERONS - Wings
    Ailerons De Volaille - Chicken wings
ALSACIENNE - With Sauerkraut, ham and Sausage
ANETH - Dill
ARTICHAUT - Artichoke
    Artichaut à la Vinaigrette - Artichoke with oil and vinegar dressing
    Artichaut Farci - Stuffed Artichoke
ASPERGE - Asparagus
ASSIETTE - Plate
    Assiette de Fromage - Assorted Cheese plate
    Assiette Charcuterie - Plate of dried meats and sausages
AVOCAT - Avocado
AÏOLI - Blend of garlic, egg yolk and olive oil

BANANE - Banana
BAR - Sea Bass
BARBEAU - Carp
BARBUE - Brill - Related to turbot
BASILIC - Basil
BAUDROIE - Monkfish
BÉARNAISE - Sauce of egg yolks, butter, shallots, tarragon, white wine, vinegar and herbs
BÉCHAMEL - White sauce made with butter, flour and milk, sometimes with onion and sometimes with cream added
BELON - Oyster
BIFTECK - Beefsteak, cut from sirloin, the ribs or the rump
    Bifteck à l'Allemande - Hamburger
    Bifteck à l'Hambourgeoise - Hamburger
    Bifteck au Poivre - Peppered steak
BIGARADE - Orange sauce
BISQUE - Shellfish soup
BLANQUETTE - Meat or fish in a white wine sauce
BLANQUETTE D'AGNEAU - Lamb stew with onions and mushrooms
BOEUF - Beef
    Boeuf Bourguignon - Beef stew with red wine, onions and mushrooms
    Boeuf en Daube - Marinated beef stewed in wine and vegetables
BOLET - Wild mushrooms
BOUDIN, BOUDIN NOIR - Pork blood sausage
BOUILLABAISSE - Mediterranean fish soup
BOUILLON - A light soup or broth
BOURGUIGNON - With red wine, onions, mushrooms and bacon
BROCHE, BROCHETTE - Meat or fish and vegetables cooked on a skewer, usually over an open fire

HAUTES CUISINES

CANARD - Duck
CANETON - Duckling
CARRÉ D'AGNEAU - Rack of lamb
   Carré de porc - Rack of porc
   Carré de Veau - Rack of veal
CASSOULET - Casserole of beans, sausages, duck, pork and lamb
CÈPE - large meaty wild mushrooms
CHAMPIGNONS - Mushrooms
CHANTERELLE - Pale curly wild mushrooms
CHARCUTERIE - Cold cooked meats and sausages
CHÂTEAUBRIAND - Thick filet steak
CHÈVRE - A strong goat milk cheese
CHEVREUIL - Venison
CHOU - Cabbage
CHOU-FLEUR - Cauliflour
CHOUCROUTE - Sauerkraut
   Choucroute Garnie - Sauerkraut braised with meats
CHOUX DE BRUXELLES - Brussel sprouts
CITRON - Lemon
   Citron Pressé - Drink of lemon juice water and sugar
CLAFOUTIS - tart of batter, fruit and black cherries
CONFIT - Duck, goose or pork preserved in its own fat
CONFITURE - Jam
CONSOMMÉ - Clear soup
   Consommé a l'oeuf - With an egg
COQUILLES-ST-JACQUES - Scallops
CORNICHON - Gerkins
CÔTE - Chop, rib
CÔTELETTE - Chop
COULIS - Puree of raw or cooked vegetables or fruit
COUPE - Dessert of ice cream and fruit
COUSCOUS - North African dish of semolina served with spicy lamb, chicken and vegetables
CRÈME - Cream
CRÊPE - Thin pancake
CREVETTE - Shrimp
CROQUE MONSIEUR - Toasted cheese and ham sandwich
CROÛTE AU FROMAGE - Toasted cheese
CRU - Raw

DARNE - Slice of fish
   Darne de Saumon Grillée - Grilled salmon steak
DAUBE - Beef stew with red wine
   Daube De Boeuf Provençale - Casserole of beef with wine
DIABLE - Very spicy, peppery sauce
DINDE - Turkey
DORADE - Bream
DUXELLES - Mushrooms and shallots sautéed in butter and cream

EAU - Water
   Eau Gazeuse - Sparkling mineral water

HAUTES CUISINES

Eau Naturelle - Plain Water
ÉCREVISSE - Freshwater crayfish
ÉMINCÉ - Very thin slice of meat
ENDIVES - Chicory
ENTRECÔTE - Beef rib steak
ÉPICE - Spice
ÉPINARDS - Spinach
ESCALOPE - Thin slice of meat
ESCARGOTS - Snails
ESPADON - Swordfish

FAISAN - Pheasant
FARCI - Stuffed
FAUX FILLET - Sirloin steak
FENOUIL - Fennel
FEU DE BOIS - Cooked over a wood fire
FEUILLETE - Pastry leaves
FILET - Boneless cut of meat or fish
    Filets mignon de boeuf - Small cuts of beef
    Filets mignon de porc Normande - Pork with apples in cider
    Filets de Poissons - Fish fillets
FLAGEOLET - Small bean usually cream or green colour
FLAMBÉ - Flamed, usually with brandy
FLORENTINE - With spinach
FOIE - Liver
    Foie de Veau - Calf's liver
    Foie de Volaille - Chicken liver
    Foie gras - Goose liver paté
FONDU - Melted
    Fondu Bourguignonne - Pieces of meat dipped into boiling oil and eaten with various sauces
    Fondue Chinoise - Thin slices of beef dipped into boiling beef broth then eaten with various sauces
    Fondue de fromage - Melted cheese with wine or kirsch into which small pieces of bread are dipped
FRAISE - Strawberry
    Fraise de bois - Small wild strawberries
FRAMBOISES - Raspberries
FRICASSÉE DE VEAU - Veal stew
FROMAGE - Cheese
FUMÉ - Smoked

GARNI - Garnished
GÂTEAU - Cake
    Gâteau au chocolat - Chocolate cake
    Gâteau au fromage - Cheese cake
GIBIER - Game
GIGOT - Leg or haunch
    Gigot d'Agneau - Roast leg of lamb
GINGEMBRE - ginger
GLACE - Ice cream

HAUTES CUISINES

GRATIN - Dish with browned cheese and breadcrumbs topping over a cream sauce
GRILLADE - Grilled meat
    Grillé - Grilled
GRIOTTES - Red, sour cherries

HACHIS, HACHÉ - Chopped
    Viande Haché - Chopped / minced meat
HARICOT - Bean
    Haricots Verts - French green beans
HOLLANDAISE - Beaten egg yolks with lemon and butter
HOMARD - Lobster
HORS-D'OEUVRE - First course
HUITRE - Oyster

JAMBON - Ham
    Jambon cru - Raw, cured ham
    Jambon cuit - Cooked ham
JULIENNE - Vegetables cut into match-size pieces
JUS - juice

LANGOUSTE - Crayfish
    Langoustine - Large prawn
LAPIN - Rabbit
LARD - Bacon
    Lardons - Cubes of fried bacon
LÉGUME - Vegetables
LOTTE - Monkfish
LOUP - Sea Bass
LYONNAISE - Garnished with onions

MAGRET DE CANARD - Breast of duck, grilled rare
MAÏS - Corn
MÉDAILLON - Small circular cut of meat
MÉLANGE - Mixture
MEUNIÈRE - Fish floured and fried in butter
MIEL - Honey
MIREPOIX - Cubes of carrots and onions or mixed vegetables
MOELLE - Beef bone marrow
MORILLE - Wild mushrooms
MORNAY - White sauce with cheese added
MOULES - Mussels
  Moules Marinière - Mussels served in a white wine sauce with shallots and parsley
MOUTARDE - Mustard
MYRTILLE - Blueberry

NAVARIN - Lamb stew with potatoes and onions
    Navarin Printanier - Lamb stew with carrots, onions, potatoes, turnips, green peas and beans
NAVET - Turnip
NIÇOISE, SALADE - Salad of lettuce, tunafish, anchovies, olives and onions

HAUTES CUISINES

NOISETTE - Hazelnut, also refers to small potatoes browned in butter
NOISETTE D'AGNEAU - Lamb cut from the fillet
NOIX - Nuts
NORMANDE - Fish or meat cooked with apples and cream
NOUILLES - Noodles

OEUF - egg
   Oeuf à la Florentine - Egg served with spinach
   Oeuf à la Neige - Egg whites sweetened and poached in a vanilla custard
   Oeuf au Jambon - Egg and ham
   Oeuf au Lard - Egg and bacon
OIE - Goose
OIGNON - Onion
OMBLE - Lake trout

PAILLARDE, VEAU - grilled boneless veal steak or cutlet
PAIN - Bread
PAMPLEMOUSSE - Grapefruit
PAPILLOTE - Cooked in parchment paper or foil envelope
PARMENTIER - Dish with potatoes
PÂTÉ - Minced meat spiced and cooked in a pastry case or mould
PÂTES - Pasta
PETITS POIS - peas
PÉTONCLE - Tiny Scallop
PIED DE COCHON - Pig's foot
PIED DE VEAU - Calf's foot
PLEUROTE - Wild mushrooms
POCHÉ - Poached
PÔELÉ - Fried
POIRE - pear
POIREAU - Leek
POISSON - Fish
POIVRE - Pepper
POIVRON - Green or red pepper
POMME - Apple
POMMES DE TERRE - Potatoes
   Pommes de terre à la Lyonnaise - Sautéed potatoes with onions
   Pommes de terre Dauphinoise - Baked sliced potatoes with Milk/cream and cheese
   Pommes de terre Gratinées - Potatoes browned with cheese
   Pommes de terre purée - Mashed potatoes
   Pommes de terre Vapeur - Boiled potatoes
POMMES FRITES - French fries
PORC - Pork
POTAGE - Soup
   Potage du jour - Soup of the day
POULET, POULARDE - Chicken
PRINTANIÈRE - With vegetable garnish
PRUNE - Plum
PRUNEAUX - Prunes

QUENELLES - Poached featherlight dumplings, usually of veal, fish or poultry

HAUTES CUISINES

QUEUES - Tails
    Queues de Langoustes - Crayfish tails
    Queue de Boeuf - Oxtail

RACLETTE - Melted cheese served with waxy potatoes, gherkins and dried meats
RAGOÛT - Stew
RAIE - Skate
    Raie au beurre noir - Skate with black butter
RATATOUILLE - Mixture of vegetables, aubergines, tomatoes, onion and courgettes
REBLOCHON - Soft cheese
RILLETTE - Spreadable pork or goose paste
RIS D'AGNEAU - Lamb Sweetbreads
RIS DE VEAU - Veal Sweetbreads
RIZ - Rice
ROGNON - Kidney
RÔTI - Roast

SALADE - Salad
    Salade Mêlée - Mixed salad
    Salad Niçoise - Lettuce, tuna fish, anchovies, onions, and olives
    Salade Parmentier - Potato salad
    Salade Verte - Green salad
SAUCISSE - Fresh sausage
SAUCISSON - Salami-like dried sausage
SAUMON - Salmon
    Fumé - Smoked
SAUTÉ - Browned over high heat
SEL - Salt
SERPOLET - Wild thyme
STEAK HACHÉ - Hamburger
STEAK TARTARE - Minced raw steak served with egg yolk, onions, capers, and Worcester sauce.
SUCRE - Sugar

TERRINE - Pâté, either fine or coarse
THON - Tuna fish
TOURNEDOS - Centre of beef fillet, grilled or sautéed
TRUITE - Trout

VARIÉ - Assorted
VEAU - Veal
VENAISON - Venison
VIANDE - Meat
    Viande séchée - Cured/dried meat
    Viande des Grisons - Air dried meat from the Grison area of Switzerland
VIN - Wine
    Vin de Table - Plain table wine, Housewine
    Vin du Pays - Local wine
    Vin Blanc - White wine
    Vin Rouge - Red wine

HAUTES CUISINES

VINAIGRETTE - Olive oil, vinegar and seasoning
VOLAILLE - Chicken

YAOURT - Yogurt

ITALIAN GLOSSARY

ABBACCHIO - Milk fed lamb
ACCIUGHE - Anchovies
ACQUA - Water
   Minerale - Mineral water
AFFETTATO - Sliced cold meat
   Affettati Misti - Mixture of cold meats, hams, and sausages
AFFUMICATO - Smoked
AGLIO - Garlic
AGNELLO - Lamb
AI FERRI - From the grill, grilled
AL ALL', ALLA, ALLE - In the style of
AL FORNO - Oven baked
ALL'AMATRICIANA - Sauce of tomatoes, bacon, onions and garlic
ALLA BOLOGNESE - With tomatoes and meat sauce
ALLA BRACE - Cooked on charcoal
ALLA CAMPAGNOLA - With vegetables
ALLA CARBONARA - pasta with smoked ham or bacon in a creamy white cheese sauce
ALLA CASALINGA - Home made
ALLA GENOVESE - Sauce with basil and other herbs, pine kernels, garlic and oil
ALLA GRATELLA - Grilled
ALLA GRATICOLA - Grilled
ALLA GRIGLIA - Grilled
ALLA MILANESE - Breaded then fried
ALLA NAPOLETANA - Made with cheese, tomatoes, herbs and sometimes anchovies
ALLA PAESANA - Made with bacon, potatoes, carrots, squash and other root vegetables
ANATRA, ANITRA - Duck
ANIMELLE - Sweetbreads
ANTIPASTI, ANTIPASTO - First course, appetizers
ANTIPASTI ASSORTITI - Assorted appetizers of vegetables, cold cuts and olives
ANTIPASTO MISTO - Assorted appetizers
ARISTA - loin of pork
ARROSTO - Roast
   Arrosto di Maiale - Roast pork
   Arrosto di Vitello - Roast veal
ASPARAGI - Asparagus

BEVANDE - Beverages
BIANCHETTE DI VITELLO - Veal stew with herbs and mushrooms in a cream sauce

HAUTES CUISINES

BISI - Peas
BISTECCA - Steak, usually beef
    Bistecca di Agnello - Lamb steak
    Bistecca di manzo - Beef steak
    Bistecca di manzo ai Ferri - Grilled beef steak
    Bistecca di Vitello - Veal steak
BISTECCHINE ALLA GRIGLIA - Hamburgers
BOLOGNESE - Meat sauce for pasta
BONITO - Tuna Fish
BRACIOLE - Rib steak
BRASATO - Braised beef
BRESAOLA AL LIMONE - Salted dried beef with lemon juice
BRODO - Broth, soup, consommé
BUE - Beef
    Bue al Barolo - Beef braised in red wine
BURRO - Butter

CANNELLONI - Tubular pasta filled with meat and covered with a cheesy white sauce
CAPPELLETTI - Small ravioli, filled with either cheese or minced meat
CAPRIOLO ALLA CASALINGA - Home made stew of wild deer
CARNE -Meat
CARPACCIO - Thinly sliced raw beef fillet, usually served with a piquant sauce
CASSATA ALLA SICILIANA - Ice cream made in several different coloured layers with candied fruit and almonds
CAVOLFIORE - Cauliflower
CAVOLO - Cabbage
CERVELLA - Brains, usually veal
CIOCCOLATA - chocolate
CIPOLLE - onions
CONCHIGLIE - Shells of pasta
CONCHIGLIE CON BACON, PISELLE E RICOTTA - pasta shells with bacon, peas, and ricotta cheese
CONDIGLIONE - Mixed salad
COPPA - Smoked raw ham, very finely sliced
COSTA/COSTE/COSTOLETTA/COSTATA - Meat with the bone in
COSTA DI MAIALE - Pork chop
COSTATA ALLA FIORENTINA - Thick cut of beef grilled over coals
COSTATA DI MANZO - Beef rib steak
COSTATA DI MANZO DISOSSATO - Boned rib steak
COSTATA DI VITELLO - Veal chop
COSTOLETTA AL PROSCIUTTO - Steak and ham slices, breaded, fried and topped with melted cheese
COSTOLETTE DI ABBACCHIO ALLA GRIGLIA - Grilled lamb chops
COSTOLETTE DI MAIALE - Pork chop
CREMA - Cream, cream soup or custard
CRESPOLINO - Spinach-filled pancackes in cheese sauce
CROSTATA - Pie or tart
CRUDO - Raw

DELLA CASA - Chef's speciality

HAUTES CUISINES

DIAVOLO - Spicy tomato sauce
DINDO - Turkey
DOLCE - Sweet, soft, mild
DOLCI - Pastries, cakes, sweets, desserts
   Dolci di mele - Apple cakes
   Dolci di Torino - Rich chocolate dessert

ENTRECÔTE - Boneless beef or veal steak
   Entrecôte alla Pizzaiola - Boneless steak fried in oil with garlic and tomato sauce
ERBAZZONE - Spinach pie with onions, ham, cheese, and garlic

FAGIANO - Pheasant
FAGIOLI - Beans
FAGIOLI AL FORNO CON FUNGHI - Baked white beans with tomatoes and mushrooms
FAGIOLINI - Green string beans
FARCITO - Stuffed
FEGATO - Liver
   Fegato di vitello - Calf's liver
FEGATINI DI POLLO - Sautéed chicken livers
FETTUCCINE - Long, thin narrow noodles
FILETTO - Fillet
FINOCCHIO - Fennel
FIORENTINA - Herbs, oil and often spinach
FOIOLO - Tripe
FORMAGGIO - Cheese
   Formaggio Assortiti - Assorted cheeses
FORTE - Hot, spicy, strong
FRAGOLE - Strawberries
FRITTATA - omelette
FRITTO - Fried
FUNGHI - Mushrooms
FUSILLI - Pasta of spiral shapes

GAMBERI - Shrimps, also scampi
GELATO - Ice cream
GELATI MISTI - Assortment of ice creams and sorbets
GIRARROSTO - Roasted on a spit
GNOCCHI - Potato dumplings boiled and served with meat sauce or tomato sauce and grated cheese
GRANITA - Flavoured water ice
GRATINATA - Sprinkled with breadcrumbs and cheese and oven browned
GUANCIALE - Streaky bacon

INSALATA - Salad
   Insalata Condiglione - Mixed Salad
   Insalata di Campo - Lettuce salad
   Insalata di Patate - Potato salad
   Insalata di Verdura - Salad of green vegetables
   Insalata di Mista - Mixed salad

HAUTES CUISINES

INVOLTINI - Stewed rolls of veal, stuffed with mince and spices

LAMPONE - Raspberry
LARDO - Bacon
LASAGNE - Pasta of broad noodles served with tomato and meat sauce
LATTE - Milk
LEGUME/LEGUMI - Vegetables
LENTICCHIA - Lentil
LIMONE - Lemon
LINGUINE - Flat noodles
LOMBATA DI MAIALE - Pork loin
LOMBATA DI VITELLO - Veal loin
LUPO DI MARE - Sea perch

MACCHERONI - Macaroni
MAIALE - Pork
   Maiale alla Pizzaiola - Pork slices braised in tomato, garlic, oil and capers
MANDORLA - Almond
MANDORLATO - Made with almond
MANZO - Beef
   Manzo alla Genovese - Beef braised with vegetables, wine and tomatoes
   Manzo alla Pizzaiola - Grilled steak served with sauce of garlic, oil, tomato and herbs
MARMELLATA - Jam
MARRONE - Chestnut
MAZZAFEGATI - Sausage of pigs liver, seasoned with garlic, pepper and coriander and fried in olive oil
MEDAGLIONE - Round fillet of beef or veal
MELANZANE - Egg plant
MELE - Apples
MELONE - Melon
   Melone con prosciutto - Melon with prosciutto ham
MESSICANI - Rolled stuffed veal slices
MIDOLLO - Bone marrow
MIELE - Honey
MINESTRA/MINESTRINA/ MINESTRONE - Soup
MIRTILLO - Blueberry
MISTO - Mixed
MODINO - Small round fillet slices, usually veal of beef, fried in butter
MORTADELLA - Large pork sausage with garlic pistachio nuts and peppercorns
MOZZARELLA - Cheese made from whey, usually cooked
MUSCOLETTI DI VITELLO CON FUNGHI - Veal shank stewed in wine, tomato and mushroom sauce

NOCE - Walnut
NOCE DI SOTTOFILETTO - Veal top round or roast veal cutlet
NODINO DI MAIALE ALLA GRIGLIA - Small grilled pork steak
NOSTRANO - Local or home grown

OCA - Goose
OLIO D'OLIVA - olive oil

HAUTES CUISINES

OLIVE NERE - Black olives
OLIVE VERDE - Green olives
ORECCHIETTE AL POMODORO - Pasta shells with tomato sauce
OSSIBUCHI ALLA MILANESE - Veal shank braised with tomatoes in wine
OSSO - Bone
OSSO DI PROSCIUTTO CON FAGIOLI - Hambone with white beans
OSSOBUCO - Veal shank braised with tomato, onions, herbs and wine
OSTRICA - Mushroom sauce
OSTRICHE - Oysters

PALLOTTOLINE - Meatballs
PANCETTA - Salted bacon spiced and eaten raw
PANCETTA AFFUMICATA - Bacon and egg
PANE - Bread
PANNA - Cream
PANZEROTTI - Ravioli filled with cheese, anchovies, and egg first fried and then browned in the oven
PAPARDELLE - Noodles
PARMIGIANO - Parmesan cheese, served with pasta dishes
PASTICCINO - Tart, cake, small pastry
PATATE - Potatoes
   Patate Fritte - Chips
   Puré di patate - Mashed potatoes
PEOCI - Mussels
PEPE - Pepper
PEPERONATA - Sauteed sweet peppers onions and tomatoes
PEPERONI - Green or red sweet peppers
PERE - pears
PERLA DI VITELLO - Braised veal with diced ham, flavoured with spices, herbs and onions
PERSICO - Lake perch
PESCA/PESCHE - Peach
PESCE/PESCI - Fish
   Pesce alla Gratella - Grilled fish
PESTO - Sauce of basil leaves, garlic, cheese, pine kernels and marjoram
PETTO DI POLLO - Chicken breast
PIATTI DEL GIORNO - Dish of the day
PICCANTE - Highly seasoned
PICCATA - Thin veal slice
PINOCCHIO - Pine nuts
   Pignoli - Pine kernels
PISELLI/PISELLO - Peas
PIZZA - Flat bread dough base with a variety of toppings
PIZZAIOLA - Tomato sauce with garlic, hot peppers, olive oil and parsley
POLASTRO IN TEGLIA - Chicken casserole with onion, wine, tomato, and mushrooms
POLENTA - Baked, thick cornmeal
POLLO/POLLASTRA/POLLASTRO - Chicken
   Pollo al Rosmarino - Chicken roasted with rosemary
   Pollo alla Cacciatora - Chicken with tomatoes and hot peppers
POLPETTA/POLPETTE - Meatballs
   Polpette in Brodo - Meatballs in soup

HAUTES CUISINES

POMODORO/POMODORI - Tomatoes
PORCINI - Wild mushrooms
PORRI - Leeks
PROSCIUTTO - Salted air cured ham
PRUGNE - Plums

RADICCHIO - Red lettuce with a slight bitter taste
RAGÙ - Meat sauce for pasta also called bolognese
    Ragù alla Napoletana - Meat and tomato sauce
RAVIOLI - Pillow shaped pasta with fillings of meat, cheese vegetables, served in a tomato sauce
RICOTTA - Cottage cheese made from whey, often used as pasta fillings
RIGATONI - Pasta in the shape of tubes
RIPIENE - Stuffed
RISI/RISO/RISOTTTO - Rice
    Risi e bisi - Rice and peas cooked in broth
·   Risotto coi funghi - Rice with mushrooms
ROGNONE - Kidney
    Rognoncini d'agnello saltati con cipolla - Sautéed lamb kidneys with onion
    Rognoni di vitello alla griglia - Pan fried veal kidneys
ROTOLO - Stuffed meat roll

SALE - Salt
SALMONE - Salmon
    Salmone affumicato - Smoked salmon
SALSA - Sauce
    Salsa al burro - Melted butter and herb sauce
    Salsa al Formaggio - Cheese sauce
SALSICCE - Sausages
SALTATE - Sautéed
SALTIMBOCCA - Slices of veal and ham cooked in Marsala wine
SALUMI - Sausages served cold
SARDE/SARDELLE - Sardines
SCALOPPA/SCALOPPINA/SCALOPPINE - Thin veal slices
    Scaloppine al burro - Floured and pan-fried veal slices in butter
    Scaloppine alla cacciatora - Veal slices floured, pan fried in tomato, mushroom and herb sauce
    Scaloppine alla panna e funghi - Veal slices sauteed in a cream and mushroom sauce
SCANELLO - Round steak
SCOTTADITO - Veal cutlet
SECCA - Dried
SELLA DI DAINO - Saddle of venison usually roasted
SELVAGGINA - Game
SENAPE - Mustard
SGUAZZETO - Braised lamb stew
SGUAZZETO ALLA BECHERA - Stew made of various meats
SOFFRITTO - Sautéed
SOGLIOLA - Sole
    Sogliola ai ferri - Grilled sole
    Sogliola dorata - Breaded and fried sole

HAUTES CUISINES

SOPA - Soup
SORBETTO - Sherbet, flavoured water ice
SOTTACETO - Pickled
SOTTOFILETTO - Loin steak
SPEZZATINO/SPEZZATO - Stew
SPIEDI/SPIEDINI/SPIEDINO - Pieces of meat grilled or roasted on a spit
SPINACI - Spinach
SPUMONE/SPUMONI - Ice cream dessert usually with nuts, and or fruit pieces
SQUADRO - Monk fish
STOCCAFISSO - Dried cod
STRACCIATELLA - Thin batter of eggs, flour, grated parmesan cheese, poured into boiling broth
STRACOTTO - Stew
STUFATINO/STUFATO - Stew
SUGO - Sauce or gravy

TACCHINO - Turkey
TAGLIATELLE - Flat noodles
TAVOLA CALDA - Quick-service snack bar
TEGAME - Sautéed in butter or oil in small individual pan
TIMBALLO - Baked pasta casserole with sauce
TONNO - Tuna
TORTA - Pie, tart or cake
TORTELLINI - Small crescents of pasta stuffed with either, pork, turkey, veal steak from tenderloin fillet
TORTINO - Pastrytart filled with cheese and vegetables
TOURNEDOS - Beef or veal steak from tenderloin fillet
TRIPPA - Tripe
TROTA - Trout

UMIDO DI PESCE - Fish stew
UOVA - Eggs
   Uova al lardo - Fried egg with bacon

VERDURE - Green vegetables
VERZA - Green cabbage
VINO - Wine
   Vino Bianco - White wine
   Vino Paese - Local wine
   Vino Rosso - Red wine
VITELLO - Veal

ZABAGLIONE - Dessert of egg yolks, sugar and marsala wine
ZEPPOLA - Deep fried fritter or doughnut
ZEPPOLE DI SAN GIUSEPPE - Dessert fritters with cinnamon and sugar
ZIMINO - Fish stew
ZUCCHERO - Sugar
ZUCCHINE - Squash, courgettes
ZUPPA - Soup
ZUPPA INGLESE - Trifle

HAUTES CUISINES

GERMAN GLOSSARY

ALPKÄSE - Mountain cheese
ALPTOPF - Soup with vegetables, bacon and sausssage
ANANAS - Pineapple
APFEL - Apple
APFELKUCHEN - Apple cake
AUSGEBACKEN - Fried

BACKHÄHNCHEN - Roasted chicken
BACKHENDEL - Roasted chicken
BACKHUHN - Roasted chicken
BARSCH - Perch
BASILIKUM - Basil
BAUERN - Farm style
    Bauernente - Farm grown duck
    Bauernschinken - Ham cured on the fire
BEILAGEN - Garnish
BERGKÄSE - Mountain cheese
BERTHOUD - A dish of melted cheese and white wine into which one dips potatoes
BIRNBROT - Swiss bread made with pears
BLAUBEERE - Blueberry
BLAUKRAUT - Red cabbage
BLUMENKOHL - cauliflower
    Blumenkohl Polnisch - Cooked cauliflower with butter and breadcrumbs
    Blumenkohlsuppe - Cauliflower soup
BLUTWURST - Black pudding, blood sausage
BOHNEN - Beans
BOUILLON - Broth or consommé
    Bouillon mit markklösschen - Broth with marrow dumplings
BRATEN - Roast meats
BRATHUHN - Roast chicken
BRATWURST - Sausage
BRECHBOHNEN - French beans
BROT - Bread
BRÜHE - Broth, consommé
BÜNDNER FLEISCH - Dried meats from the Graubünden area

CHAMPIGNONSOSSE - Mushroom sauce
CHÄSGETSCHADER - Bread soaked in wine, covered in cheese and grilled
CORDON BLEU - Thin slices of veal, ham and cheese covered on breadcrumbs and fried

DEUTSCHES BEEFSTEAK - Hamburger
DÔLE - Swiss wine
DURCHGEBRATEN - Well done

EI - egg
    Spiegelei - Fried egg

HAUTES CUISINES

EIER - Eggs
   Eier mit schinken - Ham and eggs
   Eier und speck - Bacon and eggs
EINTOPF - Meat or vegetable stew
EIS - Ice
ENTE - Duck
ERBSENSUPPE - Pea soup
   Erbsensuppe mit Wiener Würstchen - Pea soup with sausages
ERBSLI/ERBSEN - Peas
ERDBEEREN - Strawberries
ERDÄPFEL - Potatoes
ERDÄPFELKNÖDEL - Potato dumplings

FASAN - Pheasant
FASAN GEBRATENER - Roast pheasant
FELCHEN - Lake trout
FISCH - Fish
FLASCHE - Bottle
FLEISCH - Meat
FLEISCHBRÜHE - Meat soup
FLEISCHEINTOPF - Beef or veal casserole dish
FLEISCHKÄSE - Seasoned meat loaf
FLEISCHKLÖSSE - Meat balls
FLEISCH-SCHNITTE - Steak
FLEISCHSULZE - Meat in aspic
FONDU - Melted cheese, traditionally with schnapps into which small pieces of bread are dipped
FORELLE - Trout
FRISCHE BLATTSALAT SCHÜSSEL - Fresh salad in a bowl
FRITTAKENSUPPE - Soup with tiny meatballs
FRUCHT/FRÜCHTEN - Fruit
FRÜCHTE IN BACKTEIG - Fruit fritters

GANS - Goose
GANZ - Whole, entire
GARNIERT - Garnished
GEBÄCK - Pastry
GEBEIZT - Pickled
GEBRATEN/GEBACKENE - Roasted or fried
GEDÄMPFT - Steamed or sometimes braised
GEFLÜGEL - Fowl
   Geflügelleber Strassburger-Art - Chicken livers in red wine sauce with mushrooms on rice
GEFÜLLTE - Stuffed
GIPFEL - Crescent shaped roll
GEGRILLT - Grilled
GEMISCHTER SALAT - mixed salad
GEMÜSE - Vegetables
   Gemüsesuppe - Vegetable soup
GEMÜTLICHKEIT - Cosy, comfortable
GERÄUCHERTER - Smoked

HAUTES CUISINES

GERMKNÖDEL - Light yeast dumpling with butter, freshly ground poppy seed and powdered sugar, often with a damson filling
GERSTE - Barley
   Gerstensuppe - Barley soup
GESALZEN - Salted
GESELCHTES - Cured and smoked pork
GEWÜRZGURKE - Pickle, gherkin
GETRÄNKEKARTE - Wine list
GESCHMORTE - Stewed or braised
GESCHNETZELTES - Meat cut into small strips
GEWÜRZT - Spice
GLASIERT/GLASIERTEN - Glazed
GLÜHWEIN - Spiced mulled wine
GNAGIWÜRFEL - Salt pork
GRAMMELSCHMALZ - Kidney lard and gristles spread on black or brown bread
GRATINIERT - Oven-browned with breadcrumbs and cheese
GRAUPENSUPPE - Barley soup
GRÖSTL - Fried bread, also grated potatoes with meat pieces
GRÖSTLE - Sausage
   Tiroler Gröstle - Tyrolean sausage
GRÜNE BOHNEN - French beans
GRÜNERSALAT - Green salad
GULASCH - Braised meat with vegetables and seasoned with paprika
   Gulaschsuppe - Goulash soup
GULYASUPPE (Aus) - Goulash soup

HACKBRATEN - Chopped steak or meatloaf of beef and pork
HACKRAHMSTEAK - Hamburger
HAUSGEMACHT - Homemade
HAUSEGEPÖKELT - Home pickled or home cured
HAUSMANNSKOST - House speciality, plain food
HAUPTSPEISEN - Main course
HEIDELBEERSCHMARREN - Blueberry compote
HEIDELBEERSCHNITTEN - Blueberry pie
HEIDELBEERSTRUDEL - Blueberry strudel
HEISS - Hot
HIMBEERE - Raspberry
HIRSCH - Stag, Venison
   Hirschbraten - Roast Venison
   Hirschragout - Venison stew
HOBELKÄSE - Very finely sliced cheese
HOBELKÄSEPLÄTTLI - A platter of thinly sliced cheese
HOBELSPÄNE - Deep fried crisp twists of rum flavoured dough
HUHN - Fowl, including game birds or chicken
HÜHNER - Poultry
   Hühnerbrust - Chicken breast
   Hühnersalat - Chicken salad
   Hühnersuppe - Chicken soup
HUMMER - Lobster
HUMMERKRABBEN - Large crabs

HAUTES CUISINES

INDIANERKRAPFEN - Fritters with whipped cream
INGWER - Ginger

JÄGEREINTOPF - Beef stew with onions, mushrooms and potatoes
JÄGERSCHNITZEL - Veal cutlet with wine, mushrooms and tomato sauce
JÄGERTOPF - Casserole of meat, mushrooms, shallots and tomato sauce
JUNGE ENTE - Duckling
    Gebraten, gedünstet,gefüllt - roast, stewed, stuffed

KAFFEE FERTIG - Coffee and schnapps (Obstler or Batssi)
KAFFEE LUZ - Coffee, hot water and schnapps
KAISERSCHMARREN - Pieces of pancake sprinkled with icing sugar and served with apple or plum sauce
KALB - Veal
KALBSBRATWURST - Veal sausage
KALBSGESCHNETZELTES - Small strips of veal
KALBSKOTELETT - Veal cutlet
KALBSLEBER - Calf's liver
KALBSMILCH - Sweetbreads
KALBSRAHMSCHNITZEL - Veal escalop in cream sauce
KALBSRIPPCHEN - Veal chop
KALTE TELLER - Cold dishes
KARFIOL - Cauliflower
KAROTTEN - Carrots
KARTOFFELN - Potatoes
   Kartoffelbrei - Mashed potatoes
   Kartoffelcroquetten/kartoffelkroketten - Potato croquettes
   Kartoffelknödel - Potato dumpling
   Kartoffelpüree - Mashed potato
   Kartoffelsalat - Potato salad
   Kartoffelschale - Potatoes in their jackets
KÄSE - Cheese
KÄSESCHNITTE - Cheese toast (Welsh rarebit) usually with ham and fried egg but can have tomatoes
KASPRESKNÖDELN IN ZWIEBELSUPPE - Little dumplings in onion soup
KINDERTELLER - Children's menu
KLOSS - Dumpling
KLÖSSCHEN - Small meat and dough dumplings
KNACKIGEN - Crispy, crunchy
KNACKWURST - Garlic flavoured sausage
KNOBLAUCH - Garlic
KNÖDEL - Dumplings
KNUSPRIG - Crispy, crunchy
KOHL - Cabbage
KRAPFEN - Fritter or jelly doughnut
KRAUT - Cabbage
KRAUTSALAT - Coleslaw
KRÄUTER - Herbs
   Kräuterbutter - Herb butter
KRAFTBRÜHE - Clear soup
KREN - Horseradish

HAUTES CUISINES

KUCHEN - Cake
KÜRBIS - Pumpkin

LACHS - Salmon
LACKSFORELLE - Salmon trout
LAMMKOTELETTE - Lamb chop
LAMMSTEAK - Lamb steak
LÄNDLICH - Local
LAUCH - Leek
LEBER - Liver
LEBERKNÖDEL - Chopped liver dumplings
    Leberknödelsuppe - Soup with liver dumplings
LINSEN SUPPE - Lentil soup
LINZER TORTE - Hazelnut or almond cake or tart with raspberry jam

MAÏS - Corn
MAISKÖRNER - Corn on the cob
MAISKOLBEN - Maize
MALUNS - Fried potatoes with cheese and apple sauce
MANDEL - Almond
MARILE - Apricot
    Marillenknödel - Apricot dumplings
MARILLEN ÜBERBACKEN MIT VANILLEEIS - Apricot flambé on vanilla ice
MARK - Bone marrow
    Markknödelsuppe - Soup with bone marrow dumplings
MARMELADEPALATSCHINKEN - Pancakes with jam
MILCHRAHMSTRUDEL - Strudel pastry filled with thick white custard with
    raisins and served with vanilla sauce
MINERAL WASSER - Mineral water
MÖHRE MOHRRÜBE - Carrot

NACHSPEISEN - Desserts
NATUR - Plain
NOCKERL - Small flour dumpling
NUDEL - Noodles
    Nudelsuppe - Noodle soup
NUSSKUCHEN - Nut Cake
NUSSTORTE - Nut Cake

OBST - Fruit
OBSTKNÖDEL - Fruit dumpling
OFENKARTOFFEL MIT SAUERRAHM - Baked potato with sour cream
OMA'S SPÄTZLI-PFANNE - Grandmother's little dumpling saucepan
    (spätzle - ham and mushroom)

PALATSCHINKEN - Pancake filled with jam and curd cheese and served with hot
    chocolate
PANIERTES - Breaded
    Paniert gebacken - Breaded and fried
PARFAIT - Dessert of icecream, fruit or syrup and whipped cream
PASTETE - Pastry or pie

HAUTES CUISINES

Pastetli - Vol au vents
PETERSILIENSOSSE - Parsley sauce
PFANNENGERICHT - Pan fried dishes
PFANNKUCHEN - Pancake
PFEFFER - Pepper
   Pfeffersteak - Steak fried with ground peppercorns
PFERDESTEAK - Steak from horse meat
PFLAUME - Plum
PILZAUFLAUF MIT NUDELN - Baked mushrooms with noodles
PILZE - Mushrooms
POULET - Chicken
   Pouletbrust - Chicken breast
POWIDLTASCHERL - Tartlets filled with plum jam
PREISELBEERE - Cranberry
PUTER - Turkey

RACLETTE - Melted cheese on waxy potatoes served with dried meats and gherkins
RAHM - Cream
   Sauerrahm - Sour cream
RASSIGER - Hot and spicy
RAUCHER - Smoked
   Raucherschinken - Smoked ham
   Raucherspeck - Smoked bacon
   Raucherfleisch - Smoked meat
RAUCHERFISCHSULZE - Smoked fish in aspic
RAUCHERLACHS - Smoked salmon
   Rauchlachsstreifen - Strips of smoked salmon
RAUCHWURST - Smoked pork sausage
REH - Venison
   Rehschnitzel - Venison cutlet
REHRAGOUT - Venison stew
REIS - Rice
RIND/RINDER - Beef
   Rindsfilet - Filet steak
   Rindsuppe - Clear beef broth
RINDERROULADEN - Stewed beef rolls
RINDERSAFTBRATEN - Beef pot roast
RIOJA - Spanish wine
RIPPE - Rib
RIPPENSTÜCK - Rib of beef
ROH - Raw
   Roher schinken - Cured ham
ROHER SCHINKEN - Uncooked ham
ROHSCHINKEN - Cured ham
ROLLSCHINKEN - Rolled ham
ROSTBRATEN - Rump steak
RÖSTI - Shredded waxy potatoes fried in butter
RÖSTIZZA - A marriage of Swiss Rösti and the Italian pizza
   Pizza topping ingredients placed on a bed of Rosti
ROTKOHL - Red cabbage

HAUTES CUISINES

ROTKRAUT - Red cabbage
ROTWURST - Blood sausage
RÜEBLI - Carrots
RÜEBLITORTE - Carrot cake

SACHERTORTE - Chocolate layer cake with jam filling
SAFT - Juice or gravy
SAHNE - Cream
    Sahnekäse - Cream cheese
SAIBLING - Char
SAISONSALAT - Salad in season
SALM - Salmon
SALZ - Salt
SALZKARTOFFELN - Boiled potatoes
SARDELLE - Anchovy
SAUERKRAUT - Hot pickled cabbage with caraway seeds
SAUERRAHM - Sour cream
SCHARFEN - spicy
SCHILL - Pike or perch
SCHINKEN - Ham
    Schinkenstreifen - Ham strips
    Schinkenplatte - Meat, liver sausage and sauerkraut plate
SCHLAGOBERS - Whipped cream
SCHMALZ - Liquid fat
SCHMALZBROT - Lard bread with garlic and onion rings
SCHNITTE - Slice, cut
    Schnitten - Slices, cuts
SCHNITZEL - Cutlet
SCHOKOLADE - Chocolate
SCHOKOLADENCREMETORTE - Chocolate cream cake
SCHOKOLADENMOUSSE - Chocolate mousse
SCHWEIN - Pork
    Schweinsbraten - Roast pork
    Schweinsbratwurstring - Pork sausage
    Schweineschnitzel - Pork escallop
    Schweinekotelette - Pork chop
    Schweinsgeschnetzeltes - Diced pork
    Schweinshaxe - Pork shank
    Schweinerippchen - Pork spare ribs
    Schweinsripperl - Pork spare ribs
SCHÜBLIG - Sausage
SEEZUNGENFILETS - Fillets of sole
SELCHFLEISCH - Smoked pork
SENF - Mustard
SERVIETTENKNÖDEL - Large bread dumpling cooked in a napkin flavoured with onion and parsley
SONNBÜHELSALAT - Sunny hill salad - Baked strips of turkey on a bed of lettuce
SOSSEN - Sauces
SPANFERKEL - Suckling pig
SPARGEL - Asparagus

HAUTES CUISINES

SPÄTZLE - Small boiled flour dumplings
SPECK - Bacon
   Speckeier - Fried eggs with bacon
SPECKMANTEL - Larded with bacon
SPACKTRANCHE - Slices of bacon
SPEISEKARTE - Menu card
SPIEGELEI - Fried egg
SPIESS/SPIESSCHEN - On a skewer
SPINAT - Spinach
SPINÄTZLE - Spinach spätzle
SPITZBUBEN - (Lit. naughty boy) Cookies with almonds, jelly or jam
STEINBUTT - Turbot
STEINPILZE - Wild mushrooms
STELZE - Knuckle of pork
STOLLEN - Loaf cake with raisins, almonds, nuts and candied lemon peel
STREIFEN - Strips
STRUDEL - Thin layers of pastry filled with apple, nuts, and raisins
STÜCK - Piece, slice
SULZE - Aspic jelly
SUPPE/SUPPEN - Soup
SUPPENTOPF - Soup of vegetables, beef and sausage topped with cheese

TAGESGEMÜSE - Vegetables of the day
TAGESUPPE - Soup of the day
TEIGWAREN - Farinaceous food e.g. macaroni, noodles, spaghetti
TELLERGERICHTE - Plate service
TIROLER KNÖDEL - Dumplings made with bacon fat, basil and parsley
TOMATEN - Tomatoes
   Tomatensaft - Tomato juice
   Tomatensalat - Tomato salad
   Tomatenscheiben - Tomato slices
   Tomatensosse - Tomato sauce
   Tomatensuppe - Tomato soup
TOPF - Cooking pot
TÖPFCHEN - Beef or veal casserole dish
TOPFEN - Fresh white cheese
TOPFENKNÖDEL - White cheese dumplings
TOPFENOBERSTORTE - Cheese cake
TOPFENPALATSCHINKEN - Pancakes with curd cheese
TOPFENSTRUDEL - Baked flaky pastry filled with vanilla flavoured white cheese
TROCKENFLEISCH - Dried meats
TRUTHAHN - Turkey
   Truthahnstreifen - Turkey strips

ÜBERBACKEN - Cooked under the grill, can mean flambé
ÜBERKRUSTET - Cooked in hot oven until brown on top

VANILLESAUCE, VANILLESOSSE - Custard made with milk, cream, eggs and
   vanilla essence
VOLLKORN - Whole wheat
VOM FASS - Draught beer

HAUTES CUISINES

VOM GRILL - Grilled dishes
VOM SPIESS - Skewered dishes
VORSPEISEN - Appetizer

WACHTEL - Quail
WAHL - Of your choice
WARMER KARTOFFELSALAT MIT SPECK - Hot potato salad with bacon
WEINKARTE - Wine list
WEISSWURST - Veal sausage
WIENER SCHNITZEL - Slices of veal escallop dipped in egg and breadcrumbs and pan fried
WIENER WÜRSTL - Frankfurter-style sausage
WIENERLI - Frankfurters
WILDBRET - Venison, game
WILDRÜCKENSTEAK - Venison steak
WILDSCHWEIN - Wild boar
WINZERRÖSTI - Rösti with ham, bacon, cheese and a fried egg (Lit. Grape-pickers rösti)
WÜRFEL - Cubed or diced
WURST - Sausage
    Würstchen - Sausages
WÜRSTLI - Small sausages
WÜRZE - Spice, seasoning, pickled

ZANDER - Pike, perch
ZART - Mildly smoked, tender, delicate, soft
ZITRONE - Lemon
ZUCKER - Sugar
ZWETSCHGEN - Plums
ZWETSCHGENKNÖDEL - Sweet plum dumplings
ZWIEBEL - Onions
    Zwiebelringen - Onion ring
    Zwiebelsosse - Onion sauce
    Zwiebelsuppe - Onion soup
ZWISCHENRIPPENSTÜCK - Ribsteak

WHAT IS THE SKI CLUB OF GREAT BRITAIN?

The Ski Club of Great Britain was founded in 1903 by a group of early skiers who met in the Cafe Royale to form an organisation to promote a "most useful sport". Today the Club pursues the original ideas by continuing to promote fun and safe skiing for every type of skier, regardless of their ability, as well as offering many other benefits and social events.

The Club's information Department has been answering questions on all aspects of skiing for many years. Whether you are taking your first tentative steps on snow or you have been pounding the pistes for decades, the Information Department is there to answer any questions you may have.

The Club's Skiing Holidays offer a unique range of specially tailored holidays. Examples include Beginners in Solden, Hotshots in Zermatt and High Level Touring in the Alps. There is something for everyone, young or old, family or single, beginner or expert. Each party is designed with a particular age group of skiing standard in mind and is led by specially trained Ski Club Party Leaders.

Club Representatives can be found in over 30 resorts in Europe and the USA. They are there to ski with members and help them get more enjoyment from their holiday by showing them the best areas to ski and where to find the best snow conditions. Indeed, some of the reports in this guide were supplied by Ski Club Reps.

Ski Survey is Britain's brightest and most informative ski magazine, published by the Ski Club and sent free to all Club members. Articles include equipment, resorts, environmental issues and the latest innovations. Ski Survey is the UK's original skiing magazine.

A large Discount Scheme is available to members on all aspects of skiing. From discounts with shops and tour operators to discounts on car hire, channel crossings and hotels; members can save money and make their skiing more cost effective.

The Holiday Booking Service, run in conjunction with Thomas Cook, offers discounts on all major and smaller ABTA bonded tour operators on both summer and winter holidays. It is just like a high street travel agency on the 'phone, only it's cheaper.

Impartial, accurate snow reports have been a feature of the Club's winter operations over the years and this is still the case. Starting in late October, with Early Snow News, and running through to mid-April, the Club's recorded message 'phone service, Snowline, offers a comprehensive information service to the skier. By dialling 0891 400 150 the most up to date snow and weather information is available seven days a week, 24 hours a day.

If you would like more information about the Ski Club of Great Britain and how to join, please clip the reply coupon from page 199 and return it to the Membership Secretary at 118 Eaton Square, London SW1W 9AF.

Get the best from your skiing, join the Club.

If you would like to receive more information about the Ski Club of Great Britain, please tick this box ( ) and fill in your contact details. By using this coupon to join the Club, you are entitled to a £5 discount on your first year's membership

NAME _____

ADDRESS _____

_____

TOWN _____ COUNTY _____ POST CODE _____

Send to: SKI CLUB OF GREAT BRITAIN, 118 EATON SQUARE, LONDON SW1W 9AF.

Telephone 071 245 1033